Reimagining the Academic Library

Reimagining the Academic Library

David W. Lewis

ROWMAN & LITTLEFIELD
Lanham • Boulder • New York • London

Published by Rowman & Littlefield
A wholly owned subsidiary of The Rowman & Littlefield Publishing Group, Inc.
4501 Forbes Boulevard, Suite 200, Lanham, Maryland 20706
www.rowman.com

Unit A, Whitacre Mews, 26-34 Stannary Street, London SE11 4AB

British Library Cataloguing in Publication Information Available

Library of Congress Cataloging-in-Publication Data Available

ISBN 978-1-4422-3857-2 (cloth : alk. paper)
ISBN 978-1-4422-3858-9 (paper : alk. paper)
ISBN 978-1-4422-6338-3 (ebook)

∞ ™ The paper used in this publication meets the minimum requirements of American National Standard for Information Sciences Permanence of Paper for Printed Library Materials, ANSI/NISO Z39.48-1992.

Printed in the United States of America

Contents

Preface   vii

Acknowledgments   ix

Introduction: There Is a Road   xi

Part One: The Forces We Face

Force One: Disruption   3

Force Two: Digital Documents   13

Force Three: The Book Is Changing   21

Force Four: The New Scholarly Record   31

Force Five: The Economics of Information   45

Force Six: Demographics   61

Interlude: A Conjecture on the Nature of Digital Information   75

Part Two: Steps Down the Road

Step One: Defining the Job   85

Step Two: Creating the Library as Place   93

Step Three: Retiring the Legacy Print Collection   103

Step Four: Preserving Digital Content   113

Step Five: Making the Money Work   125

Step Six: Working with the Smart Machine   141

Conclusion: Ten Things to Do Now   153

Bibliography   159

Index 167

Preface

The aim of *Reimagining the Academic Library* is to examine the nature of the changes academic libraries are confronting and to propose a path forward. My hope is that this reimagining will provide a guide through the sea changes. It will be a reimagining of the academic library in the first phase of the digital era, the time when print becomes used less often and digital technologies become the primary means of access to nearly everything. It will be the period where libraries move from using technology to do old things in new ways to using technology to do new things. It will likely last until about 2025 or 2030. It may be that for some time after this there will be a period of consolidation and institutionalization of the tactics and strategies of managing digital networked information, or maybe not. After 2030, who knows? I have no idea what a library might do or be, assuming Ray Kurzweil is correct in his prediction of the singularity or if Nick Bostrom's predictions of a superintelligent machine come true. [1]

Some have argued that librarians must learn to think like futurists, to practice strategic foresight by using scenario planning and other tools and techniques. This approach is crucial, the argument goes, because too much of what is coming cannot be foreseen. As Brian Mathews, one advocate of this approach, argues, librarians need to develop the skills of "change literacy."[2] I have no objection to this approach as it probably can't hurt, but it isn't the one I will take. Much is uncertain about how libraries will respond to the changes sweeping through their environment, and as the sage Yogi Berra is said to have put it, "It's tough to make predictions, especially about the future." Nonetheless, I think there is much that can be predicted with some confidence. In what follows I will make such predictions. It would be surprising if I get it all right, but I believe the broad trends can be seen and we ignore them at our peril.

The premise of *Reimagining the Academic Library* is that the academic library needs to be reimagined, which assumes two things: first, that significant change is necessary, and second, that a path forward exists and that we can discern it. I believe the first assumption is obvious and the second is true. As we will explore at some length, this path will require a substantial change in the way librarians think about the roles they and their libraries play in universities. We need to find the new things we can do that will add value and be appreciated by our users and the institutions of which we are a part.

We will begin our reimagining by mapping the territory academic libraries now occupy and the forces that are exerting pressure on them—first by considering the work of the business theorist Clayton Christensen on disruptive innovation. We begin here because I firmly believe that libraries and the scholarly ecosystem as a whole is being disrupted, and Christensen's work explains how this is happening and how it will likely unfold going forward.

We will then consider what happens when documents, particularly books, become digital—particularly books—and how this changes scholarly records. We will then look at libraries' two most important resources, the things that they spend the most money on: materials and people. The way money has run and is running through the scholarly communication system needs to be understood if we're going to shape how scholarly communication works in the future. Similarly, it is important to understand the demographics of the academic library profession because we're at the point of a generational change as baby boomers exit the scene over the next decade.

After a brief interlude, where we will consider the nature of digital information and the potential that digital documents have to change the nature of scholarship, we will consider the steps I think we need to take in making a reimagined library real. First we need to define the job that needs doing. We will then look at the library as a place, what we need to do with legacy print collections, and what is required to preserve digital content for the long haul. Finally, we will look at how to make the money work and the challenges librarians will have as they confront a world full of smart machines.

I think the path forward is clear, so we might as well start doing the work.

NOTES

1. Ray Kurzweil, *The Singularity Is Near: When Humans Transcend Biology* (New York: Viking Penguin, 2005); and Nick Bostrom, *Superintelligence: Paths, Dangers, Strategies* (Oxford: Oxford University Press, 2014).

2. Brian Mathews, "Librarian as Futurist: Changing the Way Libraries Think about the Future," *portal: Libraries and the Academy* 14, no. 3 (July 2014): 453–62.

Acknowledgments

I've been an academic librarian for more than 40 years. I've had the opportunity to work with and learn from many exceptional librarians who have shaped my thinking and practice. I will mention a few who were particularly important. I had the opportunity in the early 1980s to spend a year at the Graduate Library School at the University of Chicago and to take one of the last courses taught by Herman Fussler. I learned a great deal from him. Shortly after that I went to Columbia University, where Patricia Battin was director and where she had assembled a remarkable staff. It was a great time to be at Morningside Heights. I am especially grateful for the friendship of Paul Evan Peters, who challenged and stretched my thinking. Since early in my career I have known Maureen Sullivan. I believe I was in the first management training class she offered. We've crossed paths many times since, and I always come away with a better understanding of what it takes to make a library work. In every library I have worked, there have been good librarians. I've spent the last half of my career at the University Library at Indiana University–Purdue University Indianapolis, the past 15 of those as dean. The campus and the library are special places full of innovative colleagues. Barbara Fischler and Philip Tompkins, my predecessors, laid a solid foundation, and I like to think that we've built a good program on it.

I am thankful of Charles Harmon, who talked me into taking this project on and has remained encouraging even as the timeline slipped. I am also thankful to Dan Bowells and Terry Plum, for their comments on early drafts of the book.

Finally, I need to acknowledge my mother, Peg Lewis, who was a librarian before me, and my wife, Ann Bevilacqua, also a librarian, who has been a colleague, coauthor, and collaborator in my work and many other things.

Introduction

There Is a Road

The central purpose of libraries is to provide a service: access to information.—Michael Buckland[1]

The information world has become, decisively and whether we like it or not, a technology industry. . . . Digital networks are the primary means by which information is shared. Books are still *read* in print and likely will be, in varying degrees, for a very long time; but in the developed world a relatively small and shrinking number of people turn to ink on paper in order to *gather information*. Creating, gathering, sorting, storing, organizing, preserving, indexing, and distributing scholarly information are all processes that are, today, inextricably bound up with new and emerging technologies. That simply was not true between 1200 and 1990.—Rick Anderson[2]

Let me start at the core. Libraries have always done three things:

1. They have kept documents for the long haul.
2. They have provided the knowledge and information that the communities and institutions that fund them need.
3. They have assisted individuals in finding and using information.

They have done so to assure that communities and individuals are productive and so that civilizations are long-lasting. The particulars have changed hugely over time, most especially in the transition from paper to the digital world, but the three things remain important and libraries continue to do them.

It is hardly a secret that today academic libraries and their parent institutions are facing challenging circumstances. That change is all around us and that it will affect the operations of academic libraries, and the academy in general, is well understood. How could it be otherwise as we are living through a remarkable time? Erik Brynjolfsson and Andrew McAfee in their book, *The Second Machine Age: Work, Progress, and Prosperity in a Time of Brilliant Technologies*, put it this way, "The exponential, digital, and recombinant powers of the second machine age have made it possible for humanity to create two of the most important one-time events in our history: the emergence of real, useful artificial intelligence (AI) and the connection of most of the people on the planet via a common digital network."[3] Clay Shirky in a 2009 TED Talk framed it this way, "The moment we are living through, the moment our historical generation is living through, is the largest increase in expressive capacity in human history."[4] These are grand and sweeping claims, but Brynjolfsson and McAfee and Shirky make strong cases for them. We are living in a remarkable time, a time in which technology has vastly increased our capacity to create and communicate knowledge. What is simple and mundane today was in many cases unimaginable even a decade or two ago.

The Advisory Board Company in the first sentence of its 2011 report *Redefining the Academic Library: Managing the Migration to Digital Information Services* said, "While predictions of radical change in library and information services are by no means new, a confluence of shifts in technology, changing user demands, and increasing pressures are now forcing academic libraries to either adapt or risk obsolescence."[5] Speaking to the state of education in general, the 2014 OCLC (Online Computer Library Center) report, *At a Tipping Point: Education, Learning and Libraries: A Report to the OCLC Membership,* argues that this is a critical time for the academy:

> This impending education tipping point is not the result of any single event or set of new services. It is not the result of the recent appearance of one online education model, MOOCs. It is not the result of an outcry of parents, looking for alternatives to what many are calling "unfundable college educations." Nor is it because of the rise of easy-to-use self-help videos and tutorials. Education will tip into a new future because of the cumulative weight of all of these factors—new consumer practice, evolving technological capabilities and increasing economic incentives.[6]

The report then goes on to quote Malcolm Gladwell who tells us, "A tipping point is that magic moment when an idea, trend or social behavior crosses a threshold, tips and spreads like wildfire."[7] Goldie Blumenstyk, a senior writer at the *Chronicle of Higher Education*, titled her 2015 book *American Higher Education in Crisis? What Everyone Needs to Know.* After asking the title's question Blumenstyk runs through a list of concerns, including the rapid rise in college costs, the student debt load, the decline in state support, the demand for career-focused training, the promise or threat of new technology, and a "growing insistence that the enterprise spend less, show better results, and become more open to new kinds of education providers." She then answers her question by saying, "So in a word, Yes. Higher education is most assuredly in crisis."[8]

Libraries are the institutions charged with providing access to and preserving artifacts of human expressive capacity, which as Clay Shirky has convincingly argued is exploding. They are also both building new capacities and facing competition from other organizations that are building systems and services around the opportunities provided by useful artificial intelligence and the pervasive digital network. Academic libraries are part of the academy that is according to many observers, "in crisis." So it is no surprise that we are in the middle of the turmoil.

What is far less clear is how to think about and prepare for the changes we know must come. The New Media Consortium's *Horizon Report: 2014 Library Edition* identifies two "wicked" challenges facing academic libraries. The first is embracing the need for radical change. "What makes this challenge a wicked one," the report claims, "is the lack of common language and protocols between libraries for instilling this attitude in library professionals at scale and translating it into realistic action items. . . . While individual libraries and programs are finding successful ways to embrace and instigate transformation, there is still a lack of policies that guide libraries through the sea changes."[9] The second wicked challenge is to maintain ongoing integration, interoperability, and collaborative projects, especially around dissemination and preservation of the outputs of the research enterprise. This is a wicked challenge both because the strategies that will be most effective are unclear and because the structures and the culture required for deep collaboration among institutions do not yet exist. They are in effect arguing that we need to rebuild the airplane while it is in the air and we get to do so without the aid of blueprints.

In a September 2014 *College & Research Libraries* editorial, James G. Neal contends that "the North American library community, feeling the impact of technological progress, economic pressures, and social and political disruption, has spent the last decade thrashing about, seeking a refreshed purpose and new ways to demonstrate and create value and impact." Neal continues, "I would argue that these more recent deliberations are far more robust and substantive. The reasoning is more enlightened, and the enlightenment is more reasoned. We are questioning the authority of tradition with new thinking about what we are, what we do, how we are viewed and understood, and how we do it."[10] I certainly hope he is right. It is certainly the case that librarians are asking provocative questions. Questions are good, but what would be really useful would be provocative answers.

One thing that we need to be clear about from the beginning is that additional money as the means to solve libraries' problems will not be an option. Colleges and universities are facing increasing financial pressures that will not ease in the near term. As Clay Shirky puts is, "The biggest threat those of us working in colleges and universities face . . . [is] the fact that we live in institutions perfectly adapted to an environment that no longer exists."[11] Higher education is stressed with a cost structure that makes increasing efficiency and productivity nearly impossible and this cost structure is baked into the established culture of the academy. Student debt and concerns for affordability are constraining tuition and state and federal support is unlikely to increase in the current political climate.

There are increasing demands to educate more students, many of whom are not the traditional eighteen-year-olds most higher education institutions were built to serve. Many of the new students are first-generation college students and many are not fully prepared to do college-level work. Many others are working adults whose obligations to work and family constrain their ability to fit into established university schedules and structures.

These new students will require new services and additional support, and these will require new expenditures. As Deanna Marcum puts it in the summary of her Ithaka S+R report, commissioned by the Lumina Foundation, on flagship universities, "Most of the chief financial officers reported that they have exhausted or are close to exhausting their initiatives for bringing in additional revenue or cutting costs. There is also talk about the current model being 'broken' and 'unsustainable,' but there is very little evidence of anyone actively working to institute anything significantly different at the university level."[12] All of this means belt tightening for a library's parent institution and little likelihood that libraries will be in position to argue for significant additional resources. So there is not only no new money coming to libraries, but also there is rarely even a plan at the university level to solve higher education's underlying problems. I view this in some strange way as a positive. It will force academic libraries to be assertive in making the changes they will have to make eventually. Librarians can be leaders on their campuses by setting an example of how to use digital technologies and the power of networked information. It is my belief that libraries based on a fully digital, scholarly communications system will be cheaper, more efficient, and offer opportunities for greater productivity than what we have today.

In his book *How We Got to Now: Six Innovations That Made the Modern World*, Steven Johnson talks about the "adjacent possible" as a necessary condition for invention.[13] The "adjacent possible" is the space opened up for new ways of doing things by technological or conceptual developments. For example, refrigeration could not have been invented in the seventeenth century because the building blocks, as Johnson defines them, "the tools and metaphors and concepts and scientific understanding" were not in place. Without understanding that air is a gas and thus the way pressure and heat interact with gases, using energy to create cold is nonsensical. But when these ideas became commonplace, the space for the invention of refrigeration was opened up. In the past several decades, the "adjacent possible" for academic libraries has expanded immensely. Technological developments abound and new ways of thinking about ways of ordering operations, from user-driven acquisitions to open access, make it possible for us to occupy this new space with new ways of thinking about and providing library services. At a conceptual level this is why now is the time to reimagine the academic library.

The academic library as we know it today has its roots in the late-nineteenth century innovations of Melvil Dewey, Charles Cutter, Justin Winsor, William Fredrick Poole, R. R. Bowker, and others who created new tools and techniques to respond to the increase in scholarly materials brought on by the industrialization of printing and the growth of higher education after the Morrill Act. The particular technologies of the late nineteenth century, the card catalog, classification systems, and printed indexes, are of course mostly long gone, but the strategies, values, and culture that were developed at that time have continued to influence library practice. It is my claim that the technological revolution we are living through today requires not only new technologies, but also new strategies, and maybe new values and a new culture. I am not alone in this view. As Lorcan Dempsey puts it in his introduction to the paper commissioned by ACRL (Association of College & Research Libraries) for its 75th anniversary:

> Rules and roles aren't what they used to be. In fact, they change reflexively as education, technology and knowledge creation practices change, and change each other. Academic libraries have to make choices about priorities, investment and disinvestment, in a complex, continually emerging environment. They have to learn how best to position their resources, and more difficult maybe, they have to unlearn some of what has seemed natural to them. [14]

Michael Buckland argues that the primary role of libraries is to provide access to information for the communities and institutions of which they are a part—primarily by providing documents to users. The primary strategy for doing so has long been to keep and provide access to physical documents. That is, to build a collection. Over the past 25 years documents have transformed from being paper objects and have become digital objects on the network. This fundamental change in the nature of documents, I believe, changes everything else.

The reimagining of the academic library I will propose is at its core quite simple. I will propose that the role of the academic library will flip. In the past a university's library has been primarily a means of bringing knowledge from the outside world into the university so that students and faculty can apply the world's knowledge to their studies, scholarship, and research. In the digital world the library will become primarily a means for providing access to and preserving the knowledge created in and by the university so that this knowledge is available to everyone else in the world. Lorcan Dempsey and his colleagues at OCLC talk about moving from an "outside-in" to an "inside-out" model of library collections.[15] I like this terminology. I think it will describe not just library collection, but also will increasingly be a good way to talk about nearly everything academic libraries do.

We tend to compare the digital revolution of our time with the fifteenth-century development of printing and this may be a useful way of indicating significance. Today we are also living through a rare fundamental change in the technologies used to create and communicate knowledge. Printing was the last time there was a fundamental shift of this magnitude. Printing brought about the novel and the scientific journal, which made science as we know it possible, and the use of alphabetical order as a means organizing knowledge and information. Printing was arguably also responsible for the Reformation, the Thirty Years' War, and the rise of the nation-state. Printing made literacy an amateur activity and largely eliminated scribes as a professional class. Institutions that had controlled knowledge, most notably the church, lost much of their control. One might say that the church lost control of its most important asset. When vernacular Bibles became common, the church no longer had a monopoly on the word of God.

Steven Johnson makes an interesting case for the far-flung impact of printing. When printing made reading a widespread activity, many people realized that they were farsighted and need spectacles. To meet this demand there was an increase in spectacle makers whose expertise with lenses led to the invention of the microscope and the telescope. These inventions then allowed people for the first time to see things that were small and far away, and this in turn changed ideas about biology and cosmology.[16]

Printing was a really big deal. It is probably inappropriate to argue that printing was the sole cause of all of this change, but it is fair to say that without printing these changes would not have happened when or as they did. It would be surprising if the development of digital technologies to create and distribute information and knowledge did not create changes of similar magnitude.

But for libraries, printing did not change the fundamentals. Before and after printing libraries collected objects—mostly books. Before printing, the library and the scriptorium were closely linked. After printing, libraries became more clearly focused on providing access to books and their production became a separate activity. The number of books grew hugely with printing and the techniques required to organize these larger collections grew more complex, but the fundamental role of the library did not change. It was primarily the means of bringing knowledge from the outside into an organization or community to enhance the organization's productivity and the community's quality of life. The core strategy for accomplishing this was to collect, organize, and preserve books. Printing profoundly changed the way in which books were produced, but books were, before and after printing, tangible items. Before and after printing, libraries were primarily about collecting and collections.

When documents become digital their very nature changes. Bits are, of course, tangible in their way. They are real physical things of a sort. But documents made from bits, as we will explore in more depth in a later chapter, are in almost every way different from documents made in the ways that came before. If what libraries do is collect, organize, make available, and preserve documents, then at the very least the strategies that we use to do so can be expected to change. I want to go further and argue that it is not just strategies that will need to change, but also roles.

The digitization of the technologies of knowledge will change the whole system of knowledge production, distribution, and preservation. The roles of authors, publishers, libraries, and readers will change and be shifted. As the business theorist Clayton Christensen frames it, the whole value chain will be disrupted. If we look, we can see the beginnings of this change all around us. It has changed the way we act in our day-to-day lives. We all use Wikipedia with the full knowledge that it changes constantly. We all read customer reviews before we buy a washing machine or book a vacation, even though we have no idea who the reviewers are. We rent rooms using Airbnb from and to strangers. We shop online not only because prices might be better but because we can find almost anything we want in minutes and have it delivered to our door in a day or two. We live our lives differently than we did even a decade ago. Not surprisingly though, institutional changes have been slower.

I will propose that libraries have an important role to play in the coming reconfiguration of the knowledge ecosystem. This role will still be at its core about collecting and collections and the skills and capacities libraries and librarians possess will be of great value to colleges and universities. However, what is collected, why it is collected, and the benefits of the collection will change. If libraries fail to take on the new roles, others will step forward to do so. The danger is that, as the resource base to support this work declines, we will not see the need to change and we will continue to maintain what we have always done. As Clay Shirky puts it, "When a profession has been created as a result of some scarcity, as with librarians or television programmers, the professionals are often the last ones to see it when that scarcity goes away. It is easier to understand that you face competition than obsolescence."[17]

It is probably always a good practice to look toward the future and imagine what is coming next, and librarians have been doing so for quite some time, but we are now at a point in library history that is different. In thinking about this I find Michael Buckland's parsing of library history in *Redesign-*

ing Library Services: A Manifesto to be particularly useful as it gives us an understanding of what has changed and why the changes we are now facing are different from those of the past. Buckland divides library history into three eras: the "Paper Library," where both bibliographic tools and documents were in paper; the "Automated Library," where the bibliographic tools were digital, but the documents were still paper, and the "Electronic Library," where both bibliographic tools and documents are digital.

The library innovations of the last quarter of the nineteenth century, the card catalogs, printed indexes, and library architecture based on weight-bearing stacks were responses to the industrialization of printing and growth of the university that brought about a large increase in the volume of scholarship. These innovations made it possible for libraries to keep pace with this growth until the second half of the twentieth century. These innovations and the processes, organizational structures, and culture built on them define Buckland's Paper Library.

But by the end of the 1960s these technologies were no longer sufficient to manage the growing collections that resulted from the post-Sputnik investment in higher education and research. It is hard now to understand the costs that libraries, especially large libraries with specialized collections, then faced in their acquisitions and cataloging departments. For those who have not experienced managing large paper files, it is difficult to comprehend the amount of work they required, but some notion of the complexity can be grasped when you realize that the Library of Congress's last book of rules for filing cards in card catalogs published in 1980 was 118 pages long.[18] In the late 1970s I watched as the cataloging department in the small liberal arts college library in which I worked at the time changed the subject heading "Negros" to "African Americans." Several dozen drawers of cards had the subject headings erased using electric erasers, new subject headings were then typed on the cards and they were refiled. It was a full summer's work for four or five people. We had a party when the drawers were shifted as the final step of the project. The Paper Library was dependent on keeping very large numbers of small pieces of paper—usually 3"x5" cards—in the correct order. This was not all that libraries did of course, but if they did not keep the small pieces of paper in the correct order, nothing else mattered. The processes and organizational structures and culture that this required focused on managing detail and checking work. If a card was out of order, the item it represented might as well not exist.

Buckland published his book in 1992 as libraries were in the midst of the transition from the Paper Library to the Automated Library. This was a massive undertaking. Card catalogs and other files were converted from hundreds or thousands of drawers full of hundreds of thousands—sometimes even millions—of cards to digital files in computer systems. The retrospective conversion of these records took most libraries years to complete.

The MARC standard for a machine-readable format for bibliographic data was created in the 1960s at the Library of Congress and became a national standard in 1971. This created the framework for library automation and allowed the sharing of cataloging records among libraries. The sharing of cataloging data and the general automation of library back-office operations was an escape from crushing personnel costs and it was worth the disruption that came with it. The first cooperatively shared cataloging was done on OCLC, then the Ohio College Library Center, in 1971. The Research Library Group (RLG), a second cataloging cooperative was founded in 1974. By the end of the end of the 1980s most libraries had automated their catalogs, circulation, and acquisitions and cataloging operations. The transition from the Paper Library to the Automated Library made library operations much more efficient. Not everyone was happy with the passing of the venerable nineteenth-century library tools. Nicholson Baker's 1996 lambasting of the San Francisco Public Library in the *New Yorker* might be the most enjoyable rant against the change.[19] But despite these complaints, Melvil Dewey's very clever invention, the card catalog, and many of the related bibliographic technologies and techniques of the Paper Library were now gone.

Parallel developments were taking place with reference tools, particularly journal indexes. The National Library of Medicine launched MEDLARS Online in 1971 and by the end of the decade Lockheed's DIALOG system and BRS made online bibliographic searching a routine library service, though one that, because of its expense, was usually mediated by a librarian and was provided on a cost-recovery basis. In the early 1980s these biblio-graphic databases migrated to CD-ROMs and became available for use by library users without librarian mediation or per use costs. In the early 1990s these databases migrated again, this time to the web and could be made widely available inside the library and beyond. Through the 1990s and 2000s reference tools from outside the library began to have an impact. Web searching developed along with the rapid growth of the web. Google, which was founded in 1998, came to dominate the field with more than a billion searches a day. Wikipedia launched in 2001 and, while it was hardly compre-hensive or authoritative in its early days, within a few years developed into the most widely used reference source on the planet, attracting 470 million unique visitors monthly as of February 2012.[20] By the early 2000s the transi-tion to Buckland's Automated Library was complete.

In the early 1990s the first significant full text collections—LexisNexis and InfoTrac—were in wide use, harbingers of the coming Electronic Li-brary. For the past twenty years libraries have been working through the transition from the Automated Library to the Electronic Library. First there were full-text databases, then full-text journals, then online reference works, and finally electronic books. In some cases this content predated the web and was migrated to it, but more often it was born on the web. The world we currently inhabit has large quantities of digital content that is openly and freely available to everyone connected to the web, and the tools to discover this content are powerful and easy to use. Many of the tasks that had required the professional skills of librarians have become amateur activities. This is the world Buckland imagined as the Electronic Library, though I suspect that he did not then envision the extent to which the digital world would be on the network and thus escape the bounds of the library.

What Buckland recognized was that the significant transition was not from Paper Library to Automated Library, because the change in bibliographic tools, though traumatic, did not fundamentally alter library practice. Readers still had to come to libraries to get and use documents. Buckland recognized that only when both bibliographic tools and documents became digital would fundamental change occur. We are now at, or past, that point. The transition that began with LexisNexis and InfoTrac is now nearly complete. For all practical purposes all documents are now digital and digital documents are different—very different—from the paper documents that preceded them. In 1992, at the end of *Redesigning Library Services,* Buckland says:

> Hitherto library services have been dominated by local catalogs, local collections, and great inequalities in the geographical distribution of services. The constraints on library service are changing right now. . . . All of this requires us to think again about the mission of the library, the role of the library, and the means of providing service. For the first time in one hundred years we face the grand and difficult challenge of redesigning library service.[21]

Today academic libraries are in the midst of a transformation of the basic strategies they use to provide documents and the information they contain. In doing so we are altering centuries-old practice. We are finally getting around to the work Buckland charged us to begin more than twenty years ago.

NOTES

1. Michael Buckland. *Redesigning Library Services: A Manifesto* (Chicago: American Library Association, 1992), 1.

2. Rick Anderson. "My Name Is Ozymandias, King of Kings," *The Scholarly Kitchen* (blog), January 7, 2015, http://scholarlykitchen.sspnet.org/2015/01/07/my-name-is-ozymandias-king-of-kings.

3. Erik Brynjolfsson and Andrew McAfee. *The Second Machine Age: Work, Progress, and Prosperity in a Time of Brilliant Technologies* (New York: W. W. Norton & Company, 2014), 90.

4. Clay Shirky, "How Social Media Can Make History," filmed June 2009, TED video, 15:48, http://www.ted.com/talks/clay_shirky_how_cellphones_twitter_facebook_can_make_history.html.

5. University Leadership Council, *Redefining the Academic Library: Managing the Migration to Digital Information Services* (Washington, DC: Advisory Board Company, 2011), viii, http://www.uab.edu/library/images/documents/redefining-the-academic-library.pdf.

6. OCLC, *At a Tipping Point: Education, Learning and Libraries* (Dublin, OH: OCLC, 2014), 3, http://www.oclc.org/reports/tipping-point.en.html.

7. Ibid.

8. Goldie Blumenstyk. *American Higher Education in Crisis? What Everyone Needs to Know* (New York: Oxford University Press, 2015), 1.

9. L. Johnson, S. Adams Becker, V. Estrada, and A. Freeman, *NMC Horizon Report: 2014 Library Edition* (Austin, TX: The New Media Consortium, 2014), 28, http://www.nmc.org/publications/2014-horizon-report-library.

10. James G. Neal. "A New Age of Reason for Academic Libraries." *College and Research Libraries* 75, no. 5 (2014): 612–15, doi:10.5860/crl.75.5.612, http://crl.acrl.org/content/75/5/612.full.pdf+html.

11. Clay Shirky, "The End of Higher Education's Golden Age," *Clay Shirky* (blog) January 29, 2014, http://www.shirky.com/weblog/2014/01/there-isnt-enough-money-to-keep-educating-adults-the-way-were-doing-it/.

12. Deanna Marcum, "Technology to the Rescue: Can Technology-Enhanced Education Help Public Flagship Universities Meet Their Challenges?" (New York: Ithaka S+R, 2014), 4, http://www.sr.ithaka.org/sites/default/files/files/SR_BriefingPaper_Marcum_20140421.pdf.

13. Steven Johnson. *How We Got to Now: Six Innovations That Made the Modern World* (New York: Penguin Group, 2014). See for example pages 62–64 on the development of refrigeration.

14. Lorcan Dempsey, "Introduction: Rules and Roles," in *New Roles for the Road Ahead: Essays Commissioned for ACRL's 75th Anniversary—Draft for Comments*, by Steven Bell, Lorcan Dempsey, and Barbara Fister, ed. Nancy Allen, 2–5 (Chicago: Association of College & Research Libraries, 2014), http://acrl.ala.org/newroles/wp-content/uploads/2014/11/New-Roles-for-the-Road-Ahead-COMMENT-DRAFT.pdf.

15. Lorcan Dempsey, Constance Malpas and Brian Lavoie, "Collection Directions: The Evolution of Library Collections and Collecting," *portal: Libraries and the Academy* 14, no. 3 (July 2014): 393–423.

16. Johnson, *How We Got to Now*, 20–22.

17. Clay Shirky, *Here Comes Everybody: The Power of Organizing without Organizations* (New York: Penguin Press, 2008), 58–59.

18. Library of Congress, *Library of Congress Filing Rules*, prepared by John C. Rather and Susan C. Biebel (Washington, DC: Library of Congress, 1980).

19. Nicholson Baker, "The Author vs. the Library," *New Yorker* 72, no. 31 (October 14, 1996): 50–62.

20. "Wikipedia: About," Wikipedia, http://en.wikipedia.org/wiki/Wikipedia:About.

21. Buckland, *Redesigning Library Services*, 76.

Part One

The Forces We Face

Force One

Disruption

> I just hate gravity. But gravity doesn't care. It always pulls you down. And that's what you really need to do in order to respond to disruption. You need to say, you know, these guys are coming at me from below and I might hate disruption but disruption doesn't care it will always happen to you.—Clayton Christensen[1]

As we consider the transformations academic libraries can and must make, it is important to begin with an understanding of how disruption works because it is a driving force in the world we live in. It is common to think that disruption is, by its nature, chaotic and unpredictable, and when we think of the word in its everyday usage, this is usually the case. But the work of the business theorist Clayton Christensen, beginning with his now classic book *The Innovator's Dilemma* and continuing through a half dozen other books, has laid out a clear and specific theory of disruption.[2] It is this specific use of the term that we will consider. In this chapter we will explore Christensen's work in some detail. I will summarize the basics so we can apply them to the task of reimagining the academic library. It is also important not to be sloppy with the term. I will use it only in the context of Christensen's theory.

Christensen's work has been favorably, even enthusiastically, received and widely accepted and applied. There has been through some recent push back and it has been pointed out that even some of Christensen's predictions based on the theory were wrong.[3] My view is that Christensen's work can be overused and applied inappropriately. As Christensen himself puts it:

> Unfortunately, disruption theory is in danger of becoming a victim of its own success. Despite broad dissemination, the theory's core concepts have been

widely misunderstood and its basic tenets frequently misapplied. Furthermore, essential refinements in the theory over the past 20 years appear to have been overshadowed by the popularity of the initial formulation. As a result, the theory is sometimes criticized for shortcomings that have already been addressed.[4]

Despite concerns, when the theory is used carefully it provides insights and can be a good guide to action. I think there is much in the world of academic libraries and scholarly communication that it explains and that understanding Christensen's work can inform library leaders in ways that will lead to better decision-making.

Underlying all of Christensen's work is his observation that often products and services get better at a rate that is faster than the consumers of the products and services can absorb the new features and enhancements into their lives. Thus a product that starts out as not being good enough for most users can end up being better than it needs to be for all but the most demanding. When the product is not good enough, the customer is said to be undershot. These customers will seek out and pay more for a better product with more features. This is where firms can make money. The customer for whom the product is better than it needs to be is an overshot customer. These customers have no interest in additional features. They have what Christensen calls "performance oversupply." The product or service has more capacity than these customers can use in their daily lives. It is better than it needs to be. When customers are overshot they begin to look for different attributes of the product or service and make their choices on which firm's products to use based on how well they perform on the new attribute. In most cases the new attributes that come into play are cost, ease of use, and speed. Products that are cheaper, easier to use, or faster gain an advantage. When the basis for competition changes, new products and services can enter markets with new value propositions and over time can come to dominate them. This does not always happen, but the opportunity exists. The power of Christensen's theory is that he explains when this is likely and when it is not.

Christensen argues that there are two kinds of innovations—sustaining and disruptive. Sustaining innovations occur when new technologies or processes are applied to a product or service, but the underlying structure of the product—that is its customers, the market positioning, and its value proposition—remains unchanged. With sustaining innovations, existing providers make a better product for their best customers. They are highly motivated to satisfy these customers and they work hard to do so. In these situations, the established providers almost always maintain their dominance in the marketplace. Interestingly, the technological difficulty or complexity of the innovation is rarely a factor. Some sustaining innovations are incremental, year in and year out, product enhancements; others require a complete reworking of fundamental technological infrastructures. No matter the complexity of the change, the established providers find a way to manage it. For example, the transition from copper to fiber optical wiring in the telecommunications industry meant a nearly complete replacement of the industry's infrastructure with a new one that used different technologies, yet the market leaders were the same at the beginning of the process as they were when it was complete. In the library world the transition from catalogs based on cards to ones run on computer systems was similar. But as we have noted, the transition from the Paper Library to the Automated Library did not fundamentally change the library's service patterns. The OPAC was a sustaining innovation and while the core technology for managing the library operations changed radically from cards to computer files, the fundamentals of the library's relationships with its users was the same after the transition as it was before. The library remained the established information provider on campus.

Disruptive innovations are different. They are often based on new technology, but this is not what makes them disruptive. What matters is that they bring a different value proposition and a new business model to the marketplace. Usually disruptive innovations take a product or service that had been expensive and difficult to use and make it easier to use and more broadly available. Disruptive innovations inevitably start off as being not good enough for established customers. They will sometimes open up the market to new customers who could not afford or did not have the expertise or time to use the established product. In this way the disruptive innovation often begins with little competition. The disruptive innovation cannot compete with established firms for high-end customers because their product rarely has the capacity to serve the needs of these customers. The customers that it can serve are at the bottom of the market, or are new to it, and established firms cannot be bothered to serve them because there is little profit to be had.

There are many easy examples of disruptive innovations in the computer industry. Christensen's PhD dissertation was on the disk drive industry where the process was repeated with alarming regularity. In another example, minicomputers initially could not match the power of the mainframes, but they were relatively cheap and could be more easily deployed. This opened up computing to smaller companies and allowed distributed computing in universities. The personal computer started as a hobbyist's toy, but it was cheap and with a little dedication almost anyone could learn to use it. There are many other examples in other industries. The first hydraulic earthmovers introduced in the 1950s had limited capacity. They did not initially replace the more capable, cable-driven earthmovers, rather they replaced human ditch diggers with shovels. The first transistor radios had awful fidelity, but unlike vacuum tube radios they could be carried around and so they were popular with teenagers who wanted their own music outside of their parent's living rooms.

Over time, as Christensen's theory predicts, personal computers, hydraulic earthmovers, and transistor radios got better and better. Eventually personal computers had enough power to challenge minicomputers. Hydraulics improved and earthmovers using this technology could eventually lift as much earth as their cable-driven competitors. The quality of sound from transistor radios became comparable to that which a tube-based radio could produce. When this happened the basis of competition changed in all of these markets. For personal computers the advantage in price and individual control became the deciding attribute. The safety advantage hydraulics offered over cables became the deciding advantage in the earthmoving market. Transistor radios that were smaller and more reliable made their vacuum tube predecessors seem like dinosaurs. In these cases, as in most others, the disruptive innovation did not capture the market overnight; rather, in the beginning the product could only satisfy customers with limited needs. As the product improved it was able to meet the needs of increasingly sophisticated users and in most cases it was eventually good enough for even the most demanding customers.

We can see this process play out for libraries as quality content moved to the web. There was once a time when students needed to go the library to get the resources needed to complete their assignments. It was the only source of high-quality academic content available to them. Even though it was initially designed as a means to share research results, in the beginning the web did not have enough high-quality academic information to meet anyone's needs. But as is the usual case, the web improved and more high-quality content could be found there. Soon it had enough good academic content for undergraduate students writing short papers. When this happened undergraduates began to prefer the web. It did not matter that the library had much more high-quality academic content than the web because undergraduates did not need this additional content. They became overshot customers and the basis of competition shifted. What mattered now was that the web was easier and more convenient to use and that the web was available at 2:00 a.m. As more academic content moved to the web and it continued to develop, more demanding customers found that they could meet their needs by using the web and they followed the freshman in preferring the web over the library. The library was no match for the web when the basis of competition was ease of use and 24/7 availability and thus the library in many circumstances lost many users to the web. What we see today is not that the library has lost all of its users to the web, rather we are in the midst of a process in which the library is unlikely to prevail as the primary provider of academic content.

Viewed from the perspective of the disrupted organization, disruptive innovation is a negative thing. Often it puts them out of business. But viewed from the perspective of the consumer, disruptive innovation is a positive thing. It is one of the ways products and services get cheaper, faster, and easier. A world in which most academic content is available on the web is a much better world from the perspective of students and scholars, even though it could very well mean the end of libraries, as we have known them, as providers of academic content.

Typically, a disruptive innovation ends up disrupting not only the producer of the established product but also the established product's whole value chain. Not only are the companies that make the established product threatened, but so too are those who sell it, those who service it, and those who provided the materials from which the product is made. One of Christensen's examples is that of transistor televisions. Vacuum tube–based televisions were sold and serviced by appliance shops who made most of their money repairing televisions when tubes burned out. Tube televisions were big and expensive and, because of the nature of the vacuum tube technology, they always needed repair. Transistor televisions were cheaper, smaller, and they didn't break. Appliance stores had little interest in them because they did not fit their repair-based business model. Fortunately for transistor television makers, discount stores like K-Mart appeared on the scene at this time. The discount stores had no capacity to service televisions in the aftermarket, but that did not matter because transistor televisions didn't break. When transistor televisions got to be bigger and better than vacuum tube televisions, not only did all of the vacuum tube television makers go out of business, so did the appliance stores and the makers of vacuum tubes. The whole value chain was replaced. It is tempting to think that you can simply plug a disruptive innovation into an established value chain, but Christensen's work shows us that this is rarely successful.

One of the mysteries of disruptive innovations is why established firms do not see them coming. Christensen spends a great deal of time on this question and provides important insights. To begin with, it is rarely the case that the established firms are blind to the innovation and its potential. When the transistor was developed, all of the established electronics companies whose products were based on vacuum tubes licensed the technology. They understood that it would be important, but they could not integrate it into their products. This was because in the beginning, the transistor, like most new technologies, was not very good. It was not powerful enough to replace vacuum tubes in the televisions or radios these firms produced. The established firms spent millions of dollars trying to make the transistor more powerful so that it would work in their big machines. In Christensen's terminology they tried to "cram" the disruptive technology into their established products and business models. This didn't work because, as we noted above, the disruptive innovation is not simply a new technology; it is a new technology combined with a new business model. Using the new technology with the old business model is inevitably a less compelling proposition for the consumer. Academic libraries need to understand that "cramming" web resources into existing service models is not a winning strategy.

One of Christensen's most powerful insights concerns the extraordinary persistence of business models. They are nearly impossible to change. Christensen argues that business models are fundamental to the success of firms. When innovations are sustaining, it is a good business model that allows firms to accomplish amazing things, but when the innovations are disruptive, the existing successful business model makes deployment of the innovation nearly impossible. Firms, Christensen argues, begin with a value proposition, an idea for a product or service that will meet some need of a customer. To create the product or service the firm brings together resources—people, money, and product inputs. With these resources the firm creates processes that are used to turn the resources into a product or service. The processes define the way the firm does the things it does.

Successful firms cement the process into the life of the firm by creating values. Values are sometimes quite specific, like the structure of fixed costs and profit margins, but they can also include less tangible, but still quite real, things, such as professional values and expectations for career paths. These organizational values in turn define what value propositions the firm can see and pursue. In stable times strong values make processes more consistent and they can be managed with less effort. Everyone understands and has internalized how things should work and they all pull together. Resources are used more efficiently and effectively and more value is delivered to the customer. When confronted with disruption none of this serves the firm well. This is the heart of the innovator's dilemma.

Imagine a business executive who is presented with two proposals for a new investment. The first proposal is for a product using a technology that everyone says is the next great thing. The technology is new and not yet as capable as the technology in the firm's existing product, so the product cannot meet the needs of existing customers; it uses new processes and is sold in a different sales channel, and the margins are lower. The second proposal is for a better version of the existing product with features that the best customers have been asking for, the processes and sales channels are familiar, and the margins are higher. It is nearly impossible for the executive to make the first choice, and even if that choice is made, it has little chance of success, as it will work against the interests of many in the firm. Think about this in the library context. Imagine a library director who comes into a several hundred-thousand-dollar budget increase and has the choice of continuing the library's "big deal" with a commercial journal publisher. Alternatively, the director could take modest cuts in the journal collection and invest in open access publishing ventures and an open access authors fund. The director certainly knows that the success of open access is critical to the library's future, but not continuing the "big deal" in the face of pressure from highly funded science faculty will be nearly impossible.

Christensen goes as far as saying that firms can adapt to disruptive change only by creating new business units that can create a new business model with resources, processes, and values that match the disruptive innovation. Over time the new business unit will cannibalize the older business unit making the established product. Separation, Christensen argues, is the only path forward for firms confronting disruptive innovation. As an example, Christensen cites IBM, the only surviving computer company from the mainframe era. When the minicomputer was developed, IBM did not produce it in the home of its mainframe operations in Armonk, New York. It set up a new, separate operation in Rochester, Minnesota. When the personal computer emerged, IBM's personal computer operation was established in Florida. This separation allowed each unit to develop its own business model with its own processes and values. IBM survived even though the individual business units did not always do so. The "skunk" works that Lockheed used to develop innovative aircraft is a variation on this strategy.

This is an important insight, but one which, if taken to heart, should give librarians pause. Libraries, even large ones, are small organizations and the opportunity to create separate operations outside of the established processes and values of our established organization is limited. Organizations that successfully confront disruptive innovations, like IBM, are prepared to cannibalize their own established business units. It will be difficult for libraries to do so, even when they understand it is necessary.

When confronted with a competitor whose product or service is based on a disruptive innovation, established firms generally cede the bottom of the market and move their focus to the higher end. They use established processes to make better products for their best customers and give up the lower-end customers who are now better served by the disruptive innovation. This often makes the established producer feel good as the lower end of the market is often a commodity market with low margins and more competition and the high end has appreciative customers who will provide higher margins for products with more capacity and features. This strategy can work well for a time, but the bottom of the market will continue to erode and the high end gets smaller and smaller until it eventually disappears.[5] I take away from Christensen's work several lessons that are important for libraries:

- Libraries are squarely confronting the disruptive innovation that is the web, particularly the movement of content of all shapes, sizes, and quality to the web. There was a time not so long ago that libraries had an advantage because of their large stores of content, but that advantage, if it still exists, is quickly disappearing. The web has advantages both to users and creators of content. For users these advantages are clear: web content is easier to find and use and it is cheaper—often free. For creators, the web offers a large audience, though the means for generating income from this audience are not easy or even clear. But for academic content this is often less of a concern as it is recognition, not fortune, which most academic authors are looking for from their publications. I will argue that there will continue to be a role for academic libraries, but it will not primarily be building collections as a means of providing content to the students and faculty on their campuses. As content providers, libraries will be disrupted and the web will win. This is potentially bad for libraries, but likely much better for students and faculty.

- Libraries are encumbered by their legacy infrastructure, practices, and culture. All three will make it hard to compete against the new products and services that the web makes possible. The library is a place and the web is everywhere. The web is open and, despite a long tradition of service to users, libraries are in many ways closed. The culture of libraries grows out of the scarcity of the print-on-paper world and even though libraries tend to be more innovative than many in the academy, they are, by their nature, conservative.

- Creating separate units to drive innovation will be difficult because even the largest libraries are relatively small organizations. It will be very difficult to shield a small innovative unit from the prevailing culture of the library and this will make innovation difficult. Having said this, separation or the creation of separate units to lead innovation is probably the only course that will work and it needs to be pursued even at the risk of organizational dislocation and dissent in the short term.

- When innovating, it will be important to begin with the least demanding customers. For academic libraries this usually means undergraduates. Most libraries tend to create new services for their best customers, the faculty. This is a mistake. Faculty have little need for innovative services. They got to where they are the old-fashioned way using the old services. Initially most innovative services will have limited capacity and faculty will be disappointed. The initial, slow adoption of institutional repositories and open access journal publishing demonstrate this. Remember that services will get better with time and will do so faster than you might expect. Working with graduate students on innovations like new publishing strategies may be a good way to test services that will get better and eventually become attractive to faculty.

- The expectations of our most demanding users will hold us back. Like the executive described above who is facing the innovator's dilemma, library leaders will find it difficult to make investments in innovative products and services even when they know these investments will be best in the long term. The politics of the campus will favor continuing to invest in services valued by faculty—particularly collections. Explaining why this strategy is short sighted will be one of the most important and difficult jobs for library leaders in the next decade.

Christensen's theory of disruptive innovation underlies much of my reimagining of academic libraries. The days of the academic library as the primary information provider on campus are numbered. The web will win. It uses technology more effectively and at scale. It is faster and easier and cheaper. Libraries are burdened with an obligation to preserve print that will continue to have a cost and create less and less value for most of our users. The trick for academic libraries will be to lessen the burden of the print obligations and to find opportunities to be the disrupter who develops new services and products that use the available technologies with new business models.

NOTES

1. Millie Tran, "Revisiting Disruption: 8 Good Questions with Clayton Christensen," *American Press Institute* (blog), January 23, 2014, http://www.americanpressinstitute.org/publications/good-questions/revisiting-disruption-8-good-questions-clayton-christensen/.

2. Clayton M. Christensen has written more than a half dozen books beginning with *The Innovator's Dilemma: When New Technologies Cause Great Firms to Fail* (Boston: Harvard Business School Press, 1997). His two most recent books, Clayton M. Christensen, Michael B. Horn, and Curtis W. Johnson, *Disrupting Class: How Disruptive Innovation Will Change the Way the World Learns* (New York: McGraw-Hill, 2008); and Clayton M. Christensen, Jerome H. Grossman, and Jason Hwang, *The Innovator's Prescription: A Disruptive Solution for Health Care* (New York: McGraw-Hill, 2009), provide good summaries of his theories, as do a number of lectures that can be found on the web—for example, Clayton M. Christensen, *SC10 Keynote with Clayton Christensen* (Portland, OR: Inside HPC, December 4, 2010), video, 1:00:28, accessed September 6, 2011, http://insidehpc.com/2010/12/video-sc10-keynote-with-clayton-christensen/; and Clayton M. Christensen, *The Innovator's Prescription: A Disruptive Solution to the Healthcare Crisis* (Cambridge, MA: MIT video, May 13, 2008), video, 1:27:38, http://video.mit.edu/watch/the-innovators-prescription-a-disruptive-solution-to-the-healthcare-crisis-9380/. I've applied Christensen's work to academic libraries. See David W. Lewis, "*The Innovator's Dilemma*: Disruptive Change and Academic Libraries," *Library Administration & Management* 18, no. 2 (Spring 2004): 68–74, https://scholarworks.iupui.edu/handle/1805/173. I've also used Christensen's theory to explore open access as a disruptive innovation. See David W. Lewis, "The Inevitability of Open Access," *College & Research Libraries* 73 no. 5 (September 2012): 493–506, http://crl.acrl.org/content/73/5/493.full.pdf+html.

3. There have been several journalistic critiques. See Jill Lepore, "The Disruption Machine: What the Gospel of Innovation Gets Wrong," *New Yorker*, June 23, 2015, http://www.newyorker.com/magazine/2014/06/23/the-disruption-machine; and Evan Goldstein, "The Undoing of Disruption," *Chronicle of Higher Education: The Chronicle Review*, September 15, 2015, http://chronicle.com/article/The-Undoing-of-Disruption/233101/. An academic assessment of Christensen's theory was published by Andrew A. King and Baljir Baatartogtokh, "How Useful Is the Theory of Disruptive Innovation?," *MIT Sloan Management Review* 57 no. 1 (Fall 2015):77–90. In response to King and Baatartogtokh, Christensen notes that their assessment was based on a less rigorous methodology than the original research used to establish the theory, "Clay Christensen Explains, Defends 'Disruptive Innovation,'" *Boston Globe*, October 25, 2015, https://www.bostonglobe.com/business/2015/10/24/clay-christensen-explains-defends-disruptive-innovation/fmYOKIJXOSPPMquj8HQM1O/story.html.

4. Clayton M. Christensen, Michael E. Raynor, and Rory McDonald, "What Is Disruptive Innovation?" *Harvard Business Review* 93 (December 2015): 44–53, https://hbr.org/2015/12/what-is-disruptive-innovation.

5. Christensen's classic example, which is worth reviewing, is of integrated steel mills confronting competition from minimills. Christensen tells this story at length in *The Innovator's Prescription: A Disruptive Solution to the Healthcare Crisis* (Cambridge, MA: MIT video, May 13, 2008), video, 1:27:38, http://video.mit.edu/watch/the-innovators-prescription-a-disruptive-solution-to-the-healthcare-crisis-9380/. A concise print version of the story can be found in Clayton M. Christensen, Michael B. Horn, Louis Soares, and Louis Caldera, *Disrupting College: How Disruptive Innovation Can Deliver Quality and Affordability to Postsecondary Education* (Washington, DC: Center for American Progress, February 8, 2011), 16–18, http://www.americanprogress.org/issues/labor/report/2011/02/08/9034/disrupting-college/.

Force Two

Digital Documents

> Different parts of the Ocean contained different sorts of stories, and as all the stories that had ever been told and many that were still in the process of being invented could be found here, the Ocean of the Streams of Story was in fact the biggest library in the universe. And because the stories were held here in fluid form, they retained the ability to change, to become new versions of themselves, to join up with other stories and so become yet other stories; so that unlike a library of books the Ocean of the Streams of Story was much more than a storeroom of yarns. It was not dead but alive.—Salman Rushdie, *Haroun and the Sea of Stories* [1]

Digital documents are fundamentally different from the various forms of tangible documents that preceded them. This is an obvious statement, but we need to make it. Documents are core to what libraries do and if what is core is fundamentally different, then we can expect that everything else will change as well. Until we get our heads around this truth it is easy to try to cram digital documents into the frameworks that libraries have long been using for print documents. As Christensen's theory would tell us, this will not work. Digital documents are a fundamental and revolutionary technology. It is hard to imagine that they will not be the basis for disruption and will alter the business models and everything else for libraries and everyone else who uses or works with information and knowledge.

Written texts from their beginnings have been inscribed on something—first clay tablets then papyrus scrolls and later vellum or paper codex books and their photographic cousins, microforms. In the past half century this has changed. Digital representations of texts began with cards or paper tape and soon migrated to magnetic media. In the beginning, digital media behaved

13

like paper objects to some degree. But with the development of the Internet this changed. Now the experience we have is of a cloud that contains documents of all sorts that are available to everyone from everywhere. The infrastructure behind this experience is of course not really a cloud. It is a complex set of machines, and the bits and the documents made from them have a real physical existence somewhere on these machines. But most of us don't need to care about this as we interact with the web and the documents it contains. This difference in the media will have far ranging effects that we are now only beginning to see and understand.

The change is real and measurable. Two papers by researchers at Google demonstrate this by looking at how scholarly journals are used. It has long been an accepted fact that each discipline has a core of important journals and that publication in these high impact, or elite titles, was a clear indicator of quality work and thus was a fair marker for scholarly excellence. Promotion, tenure, and success in pursuing grants were tied to publication in these elite high-impact journals. Additionally, it was assumed that the most recent literature was the most important, and that with the exception of a few classic articles, as fields advanced quick obsolescing of the literature was a fact of life. But funny things began happening as journals moved from paper copies held in libraries to digital copies available on the web. Both of these long-held assumptions proved to be less about the underlying nature of scholarship and more about the constraints imposed on researchers by the nature of paper documents. Many of these constraints were removed when journals moved to digital formats on the web and things changed.

The existence of a core of elite journals turned out to exist mostly because the full range of the literature was hard to find and retrieve. Based on a study of citations from a large number of journals across the full range of academic disciplines, the Google research team found that, "There are two main conclusions from our study. First, the fraction of highly-cited [*sic*] articles published in non-elite journals increased steadily over 1995–2013. While the elite journals still publish a substantial fraction of high-impact articles, many more authors of well-regarded papers in a diverse array of research fields are choosing other venues."[2] This work confirms earlier studies by Vincent Larivière, George A Lozano, and Yves Gingras who found that throughout most of the twentieth century there was an increase in the strength of the correlation between the journal impact factor and paper citation rates. Beginning in about 1990 with physics, where there was early digitization of papers, and spreading across all disciplines, this relationship weakens.[3] In a later study this research group found that this trend could be found even at the highest level of elite journals, including *Science* and *Nature*.[4]

In a similar study, the same Google research team looked at articles from 1990 to 2013 and the sources that were cited by these articles. They concluded that "the impact of older articles . . . has grown substantially over

1990–2013. Our analysis indicates that, in 2013, 36% of citations were to articles that are at least 10 years old and that this fraction has grown 28% since 1990. The fraction of older citations increased over 1990–2013 for 7 out of 9 broad areas of research and 231 out of 261 subject categories."[5] In addition they found that the trend toward citing older literature accelerated in the second half of the period studied and that the trend was similar when the definition of "older" was extended to more than 15 years old and also when it was extended further to more than 20 years old.

The Google research team concludes that both of the changes in the use of the literature can be ascribed to the change from paper to digital. As they say about older work, "Now that finding and reading relevant older articles is about as easy as finding and reading recently published articles, significant advances aren't getting lost on the shelves and are influencing work world-wide for years after."[6] The explanation for the changes in the use of papers from non-elite journals is exactly the same: "Now that finding and reading relevant articles in non-elite journals is about as easy as finding and reading articles in elite journals, researchers are increasingly building on and citing work published everywhere."[7] George A Lozano, Vincent Larivière, and Yves Gingras reach the same conclusion, "Historically, papers have been physically bound to the journal in which they were published; but in the digital age papers are available individually, no longer tied to their respective journals. Hence, papers now can be read and cited based on their own merits, independently of the journal's physical availability, reputation, or impact factor (IF)."[8] These documented changes in citation patterns are a clear indicator that digital documents can and will be used differently, but the changes documented by the Google research team should be taken as a beginning, not an end point. As we will consider below, other changes can be expected.

I will argue that digital documents favor certain ways of using them and that the institutions we build to manage them need to recognize this and build upon these ways of working. But first we need to look at the ways in which digital documents are different from the paper documents that preceded them.

Local versus universal. Paper documents are local. At any one time they occupy a particular place in the universe and at that time they can only be used in that particular place. The networked digital document is universal; it can be anywhere on the network at any time. The user can be anywhere and the document can come to her.

Designed for one user versus usable by many. Paper documents, at least since the development of printing, have generally been designed to be used by a single individual, most often alone. Children's books, meant to be shared between a child and a parent, may be the most common exception. Many people can use digital documents at the same time. Paper documents are what economists would call "rivalrous"—that is, they can be used by only one person at a time and this use precludes use by others. This makes libraries based on paper documents subject to congestion as they manage a scare resource. Digital documents are nonrivalrous. That is, my use does not preclude the use by others. While not literally true, for all practical purposes everyone can use a digital document everywhere at the same time. This is of course a theoretical perspective. Copyright constrains use and many publishers use copyright and restrictive licensing agreements to constrain digital documents in ways similar to their paper predecessors.

Digital documents can easily incorporate all forms of media. In the pre-digital world different media forms needed different technologies for their production and distribution. Audio and film were separate from print or photographs and all were separate from each other. Digital technology treats all forms of media in similar ways—they are all bits—and one form can be incorporated into another with ease. Beyond the old media forms new ways of representing knowledge, such as simulations and other computer programs, can be easily incorporated as well. What it means to be a document is potentially much more complex in the digital world. Format boundaries are fuzzy and shifting. If it can be represented as bits—and these days nearly everything can—then it can be incorporated into a document.

Immutable versus easily changed. In the print era, documents were unchangeable. This was one of print's great strengths and one of its defining characteristics. That all of the copies of a print edition were the same, along with fast production, was the primary revolutionary aspect of printing. Digital documents are easy to change; they are fungible. This is strength, but also a vulnerability that increases the complexity of managing them. We have standards and practices that are well established and understood for managing print. There are longstanding social structures, and scholarly practices that exist around print are so ingrained that we have trouble seeing them and their existence rarely rises to a conscious level. Standards and practices for digital documents are at best tentative and in flux and the social structures and scholarly practices have not yet been firmly established. The fact that digital documents are easily modified also makes reuse and remixing so easy that it is difficult to resist and this makes intellectual property management with digital documents a challenge both conceptually and in practice.

Understood and manageable preservation versus uncertain preservation strategies. For the most part we know how to preserve print documents. What gets preserved is what libraries decide to collect. In its simplest form, the strategy for preserving these chosen documents is that lots of copies in lots of places will assure survival. The strategies and capabilities required for the preservation of digital documents are only now being thought out and we know that much digital content, especially from the cultural realm, has already been lost.

The marginal cost of producing a digital document is zero. The cost of the first copy of a digital document, as was the case for print documents, can be significant. Digital technologies do make the production of the first copy somewhat cheaper and easier, and the cost of entry has been reduced so that almost anyone can be a publisher. Word processing is a huge advance over writing or typing drafts. Audio and video editing is now much more accessible than it was when these were analog media. Anyone with a computer and inexpensive software can do what until recently required a skilled professional with expensive equipment. But the ease of creating a first copy is not where digital documents are most distinctive. What matters most is that they can be reproduced at essentially no marginal cost. For print there is the cost of paper and printing and moving the physical object from here to there. Making a perfect copy of a digital document essentially costs nothing, as does moving it to anywhere in the world. This makes sharing digital documents easy and makes protecting them from unauthorized copying a costly and difficult proposition.

The marketplace for digital documents is different. Most printed documents, at least those produced for the marketplace, were sold and the proceeds from the sale was the mechanism by which publishers financed both the first copy costs and the incremental cost of each additional copy. A physical item was exchanged for money. The same was largely true for audio with vinyl records and compact discs, though radio presented a different economic model. While digital documents can be and are sold, this is rarely done without some strings attached. The first sale doctrine rarely applies as it does for printed items and there is nearly always a license of some sort as the basis for the transaction. Often purchases are limited to the individual market and libraries cannot participate. This is the usual case with many electronic books and some music. Even in the case where a library can acquire a license, in most of these cases the library does not have possession of the actual bits. Most often they are stored on the vendor's servers and the content is subject to modification and deletions. These differences in the economic models and the changes in ownership and control they bring can be problematic for a number of reasons as they create both impediments to access and concerns for long-term preservation.

Digital documents differ in so many ways from the forms of documents that came before them; they are fundamentally different things. They can be made to behave in ways that are similar to paper documents, but that is only one form of the many that they can take. Importantly, digital documents form the technological basis for the disruption of all of the markets and organizations based on print documents. All that is required is a business model that takes advantage of the technology in a new way with a new value proposition. It is inevitable that this will happen, and happen soon, across the scholarly communications system. One easy example is Wikipedia, which takes advantage of the attributes of digital documents to harness a business model using the social production of thousands of editors and contributors who freely contribute their time, supplemented with modest philanthropic funding, to create an open and freely available product.

I have argued that open access is one such disruptive innovation and that it is on track to follow the path laid out by Christensen's theory.[9] There is considerable skepticism about the "inevitability" of open access, but even if I am wrong and open access turns out not to be the disruption that takes down the established players of the scholarly journal publishing world, someone will come along with another idea that will. The technological opportunity provided by digital documents is too tempting to languish for long.

Digital documents will have some predictable effects on scholarship. We are used to thinking of scholarship and study as solitary activities, at least in the humanities and social sciences. The scholar in her study reading or writing or in a library or archive surrounded with books and notes are the images many of us, at least of my generation, have of how scholarly work is done. On the other hand, it could be argued that scholarship has always been the result of social production. One scholar proposes a theory. Others test and refine it and offer proof or grounds for reassessment. Over time, through the work of many, knowledge is advanced. What is different is that in the world where scholarly communication was conducted with paper-based media the social production took place in slow motion and among a select group of experts. Scholarly conversations took place over years as the response to a book or article would be made in another book or article. An Ithaka S+R study looking at improving the speed of book reviews for the American Anthropological Association noted, "Indeed, in 2013, almost 90% of the book reviews in *American Anthropologist* had copyrights of 2010 or 2011 (two or three years earlier than the publication of the review). The oldest reviewed book had a copyright year of 2008, five years earlier. Not one item from 2013 appeared."[10] What will be different going forward is that the pace of the conversation will quicken. Comments attached to articles appear as soon as the article is published. Comments in blog posts follow the next day and tweets are offered in real time as conference papers are being presented.

The second thing that will change is that going forward everyone who cares from anywhere will have a voice. The conversation will no longer be limited to the established elite. Not everyone, especially those among the established elite, will be happy about this development. Dariusz Jemielniak in his *Chronicle of Higher Education* commentary, "Wikipedia, a Professor's Best Friend" begins by quoting Michael Gorman, who among other accomplishments was the president of the American Library Association, as saying, "a professor who encourages the use of Wikipedia is the intellectual equivalent of a dietitian who recommends a steady diet of Big Macs with everything." Jemielniak then goes on to say:

The real reasons for the general dislike of Wikipedia among scholars reach deeper. For one, academics used to have the monopoly on knowledge production. Now a bunch of digital Maoists create and manage knowledge without any remuneration or even asking for obvious credit. There has to be at least a little aversion to a project that is so effective in providing free what academics are paid to provide. [11]

As if to confirm the truth of this statement the first comment on the post by "couchloc" responded, "Jimmy Wales created the site with the intention of opposing the expertise of the professor. His point was to tear down the authority of the professor by 'democratizing' information. (So you may excuse me if I don't feel like helping him a lot.)"[12] Comments like these indicate that those whose position is established based on their expertise will not concede that the wisdom of the crowd can match them. But in the end, the elites will not be the only voice that is heard.

Scholarship with digital documents will present management challenges. Is the conversation moderated? If so, by whom and who gets to set the ground rules? There will also be significant challenges for libraries in capturing these scholarly conversations, sorting out the rights, deciding what should be kept, and then figuring out how to preserve it. Exactly how this will be done is far from clear. What is perfectly clear is that traditional library practice will not be adequate.

NOTES

1. Salman Rushdie, *Haroun and the Sea of Stories* (London: Granta Books, 1991), 72.

2. Anurag Acharya et al., "Rise of the Rest: The Growing Impact of Non-Elite Journals," *Google Scholar Blog*, October 9, 2014, 1, http://arxiv.org/pdf/1410.2217.pdf.

3. George A. Lozano, Vincent Larivière, and Yves Gingras. "The Weakening Relationship between the Impact Factor and Papers' Citations in the Digital Age," *Journal of the American Society for Information Science and Technology*, 63, no. 11 (November 2012): 2140–45, doi:10.1002/asi.22731.

4. Vincent Larivière, George A.Lozano, and Yves Gingras. "Are Elite Journals Declining?," *Journal of the Association for Information Science and Technology*, 65, no. 4 (2014): 649–55, doi:10.1002/asi.23005.

5. Alex Verstak et al., "On the Shoulders of Giants: The Growing Impact of Older Articles," *The Scholarly Kitchen* (blog), November 4, 2014, 1, http://arxiv.org/pdf/1411.0275v1.pdf

6. Ibid., 10.

7. Anurag Acharya et al., "Rise of the Rest," 11.

8. Lozano, Larivière, and Gingras, "The Weakening Relationship between the Impact Factor and Papers' Citations in the Digital Age," 2140.

9. David W. Lewis, "The Inevitability of Open Access," *College & Research Libraries* 73 no. 5 (September 2012): 493–506, http://crl.acrl.org/content/73/5/493.full.pdf+html; and David W. Lewis, "The Inevitability of Open Access: Update One," *Scholar Works*, August 2013, https://scholarworks.iupui.edu/handle/1805/3471.

10. Oona Schmid, "Faster and Cheaper: Can a Digital Centric Workflow Transform the Book Review?," *Ithaka S+R.: Scholarly Communication* (blog), August 27, 2014): 3, http://

www.sr.ithaka.org/blog/faster-and-cheaper-can-a-digital-centric-workflow-transform-the-book-review/.

11. Dariusz Jemielniak, "Wikipedia, a Professor's Best Friend," *Chronicle of Higher Education : Commentary*, October 13, 2014, http://chronicle.com/article/Wikipedia-a-Professors-Best/149337.

12. Ibid., Comment section (couchloc).

Force Three

The Book Is Changing

We have a particular reverence for books in our society, one that borders on
superstition. If you were making a movie and you want to demonstrate that our
world had been reduced to barbarism, you could just show a gang of angry
townsfolk burning some books. Destroying a book has some of the same
emotional tenor as eating a dog. After all, both books and dogs have been loyal
companions and indispensable servants to the human race for millennia. We
know what the traditional book bargain is. Books can be shelved. Treasured.
Lent. Passed on. Books belong to the people who acquire them, but they are
also a responsibility, something to be curated and looked after.—Cory Doctorow [1]

Cory Doctorow is right. The book, and here we mean the printed, paper
book, is special. It is therefore worth spending a little time reflecting on the
book and what is happening to it, as it is central to the ways that most people
have thought about libraries for a very long time. Libraries are places with
books. As the *Oxford English Dictionary*'s first definition states, a library is
"a place set apart to contain books for reading, study, or reference."

We have a longstanding understanding of what the book is. Technically
the book as we know it is a codex. As Wikipedia defines it, a codex is "a
book made up of a number of sheets of paper, vellum or papyrus . . . usually
stacked and bound by fixing one edge and with covers thicker than the
sheets." [2] Robert Darnton, the historian of the book and director of the Harvard University Library, has called the codex "one of the greatest inventions
of all time." [3] The codex replaced the scroll in Europe between the fourth and
the sixth centuries. It is such a familiar object that for a very long time it was

taken for granted. But as we now know, as we watch the book become digital, the book can no longer be assumed to be what it once was.

It is common to suggest that despite the advent of digital versions and their growing popularity, the printed book will be around for the foreseeable future. Darnton is among many who make this argument. He says, referring to the codex book, "It has served well for two thousand years, and it is not about to become extinct. In fact, it may be that the new technology used in print-on-demand will breathe new life into the codex—and I say this with due respect to the Kindle, the iPad, and all the rest."[4]

There are a number of studies that suggest that reading on paper is superior to reading on a screen. A November 2013 *Scientific American* article summarizes them:

> Despite all the increasingly user-friendly and popular technology, most studies published since the early 1990s confirm earlier conclusions: paper still has advantages over screens as a reading medium. Together laboratory experiments, polls, and consumer reports indicate that digital devices prevent people from efficiently navigating long texts, which may subtly inhibit reading comprehension. Compared with paper, screens may also drain more of our mental resources while we are reading and make it a little harder to remember what we read when we are done. Whether they realize it or not, people often approach computers and tablets with a state of mind less conducive to learning than the one they bring to paper. And e-readers fail to re-create certain tactile experiences of reading on paper, the absence of which some find unsettling.[5]

Naomi S. Baron, who has concerns about the consequences of digital reading, summarizes studies of reading on paper and on digital devices by saying this:

> For over two decades, psychologists and reading specialists have been comparing how we read on screens versus in print. Studies have probed everything from proofreading skills and reading speed to comprehension and eye movement. Nearly all recent investigations are reporting essentially no differences.
>
> But a second finding is also consistent: when asked, the majority—sometimes the vast majority—say they prefer reading in print.[6]

I have no doubt that these reported findings are true, but it is important to remember that in evolutionary terms reading is a skill that is very new to humankind. Writing goes back only several thousand years and literacy became common only after the invention of printing and became a required skill to be productive in society only within the past several hundred years. Reading is taught and taught intensively from very early childhood through college. The particulars of how one learns to read would seem to have a significant impact on one's abilities and preferences throughout life. As David M. Durant and Tony Horava put it,

It is vitally important to note that the ability to read is not innate—that is, we are not born to read. Reading is learned. The human brain is not designed for reading; rather, reading developed as a result of a phenomenon called neuroplasticity. . . . In essence, reading was made possible by the brain's ability to rewire itself. The more one reads, the more deeply the neural pathways that facilitate reading take hold. The converse is true as well.[7]

Durant and Horava go on to express their serious concern about what the growth of digital reading might mean, "Based on what we know about the differences between print and digital reading, the shift in favor of the latter offers potentially profound implications. It is possible that not only a textual format but also an entire way of thought, rooted in the stable, linear, analytical nature of deep print reading, will be greatly reduced in importance if not disappear entirely."[8] I suspect their concern is overstated, but some changes in modes of thought are inevitable. Nor is this concern a new one or one confined to the most recent change in ways of communicating knowledge. Socrates was concerned that writing would weaken memory and that simply reading a text could not convey true knowledge the way the back-and-forth argument of dialogue could.

G. Scott Clemons, the president of the Grolier Club, is quoted in the *New York Times* commenting on an exhibition of the Aldus Manutius, the early sixteenth-century Venetian publisher who developed small, cleanly designed editions of the secular classics that were small portable books he called "libelli portatiles": "It's become a cliché to call them the forerunners of the Penguin Classics. . . . But the concept of personal reading is in some ways directly traceable to the innovations of Aldus's portable library."[9] The technology and form of how we convey information and knowledge changes the way we act and probably think. Dialogue creates different modes of thought than does the individual reading made possible by the publishing innovations of Aldus Manutius. So it seems likely that a generation that becomes literate using different means and different tools will inevitably have different preferences and capacities. Rather than despair, I would argue, what makes for a good and effective book today need not make for a good and effective book in the future.

It is not that the printed book is without its merits. It is a very well-refined technology. It is portable, durable, and as the *Scientific American* article points out, print on paper is easy to read. Battery life is not an issue. You can easily write in the margins. The printed book as a technology has few flaws that can be exploited by technologies wishing to replace it. Nonetheless digital books have their advantages in many instances. My mother in her 80s found printed books too heavy to comfortably hold and appreciated the ability to enlarge font sizes on her Kindle. Her only complaint was that the digital technology made buying books too easy.

I think we need to be prepared to reconsider what the book is and what it will become. We know that the purchase and use of digital versions of books is on the rise and on the rise quickly. In July of 2010, Amazon announced that e-book sales for the Kindle topped hardcover sales. Ten months later, in May 2011, Amazon sold more e-books than print books.[10] The *Economist,* in a special essay on the future of the book estimates that in 2015 the sales in dollars from e-books (including audiobooks) in the United State will be about 75% of the sales of printed books, $9.13 billion for printed books and $6.74 billion for e-books. It is projected that e-book sales in dollars will surpass print books sales in the United States in 2017. Interestingly, Japan, Germany, China, and Italy trail significantly in the adoption of e-books. Only Britain matches the United States in e-book adoption with e-book sales expected to surpass printed book sales in 2018.[11]

One direction that the book is clearly heading is backward toward the time before writing. The prevalence of the spoken story, in its contemporary guise—the audiobook, is growing. Listening to stories goes back in human history much further than reading and as a result may be a much more natural way to absorb information. In our time it seems likely that the audiobook will not just be the reading of printed books, but will likely generate new types of works. In late 2014, Jeffery Deaver released an original work, *The Starling Project*, as an audio book. The work features 29 actors reading more than 80 roles with sound and music. No print version is planned. Podcasts like *Serial*, which have five million downloads per episode, offer a possible direction for long form nonfiction. As James Atlas observes in the *New York Times* after asking whether the next development in books will be a direct implant into our brains:

> Is such an innovation even necessary? When you think about it, that's what audio does now. Listening is more efficient than reading: When we read, we absorb print with our eyes and translate it into "meaning," a cumbersome process that requires us first to see the words, then to make sense of them, and finally to employ our imaginations to conjure up events and sounds and characters that aren't there. Reception by aural means is more direct: All you have to do is listen. Not only that, you can multitask, driving to work or walking the dog.[12]

Or, as the *Economist* essay puts it, "Of the various ways in which technology is expanding what a book can be, one of the most successful so far has been to add to books something that children have enjoyed forever, and that most people required until the 20th century: another person to do the reading."[13] If you doubt the power of oral communications think, about all of the song lyrics that inhabit your head.

Academics might argue that audiobooks are good for stories, for fiction, but scholarship is different. It is true that formal scholarly communication is written. The fixity of scholarly communications in print is one of the things that made modern scholarship possible. It is also true though that the lecture and the conference presentation are how much scholarly information gets conveyed, and the popularity of the TED talk supports the notion that alternative formats and channels can be successful.

Another change that digital technology has made is in the relationship between the author, the publisher, and the reader. When printing became industrialized in the nineteenth century, publishers who had scale and specialized skills were required to produce and distribute books to the growing mass market. Publishers managed the relationship between the author and the reader, and through advertising and promotion had significant influence on what was read. Today the infrastructure required to produce and distribute books is available in nearly every household. The specialized skills of editing and book design can be provided by independent contractors and are available at modest cost. Authors need not be dependent on publishers and self-publishing is on the rise. BookBaby, one of a number of companies that makes self-publishing easy, quotes a price of about $3,200 for 500 copies of a 200-page, soft-cover, perfect-bound book shipped two-day delivery anywhere in the United States—and you get e-book versions, too. [14]

According to the *Economist* in 2014 the value of Amazon sales of self-published books was about $450 million. [15] Novels like E. L. James's *Fifty Shades of Grey* and Hugh Howey's *Wool* have successfully crossed over from self-publishing to the mainstream. Social media allows authors to communicate directly with readers and for readers to communicate among themselves and in many cases create passionate communities of fans. Especially in genre fiction, self-publishing has had an economic impact. Harlequin, the world's largest romance publisher, saw its sales decline by $100 million or about 20% between 2009 and 2013. In 2014 HarperCollins, a division of News Corp, bought Harlequin for only a little more than the annual revenue of the company or what *Forbes* called "a pretty good price." [16]

Another clear indication of the trend is the number of best-selling authors for e-books. In 2013 only three publishers, Hachette, Penguin, and Random House, had more bestselling authors than the 99 who were self-published. [17] Self-publishing is a good deal at least for some authors and it creates additional pressures on some publishers. As Jeremy Greenfield, who covers digital publishing for *Forbes*, puts it,

> Many authors who write romance books veer toward self-publishing because of the popularity of the genre digitally (not having a publisher with print distribution hurts less), the amount of creative control they get, and the royalty, which is typically around 70% for a self-published title, versus anywhere between 15% and 25% for traditionally published e-books.

> A decade ago, publishers like Harlequin only had to compete among them-
> selves to attract and retain authors; now they have to compete with the option
> to self-publish, too. [18]

It is clear that the world of romance novels and other genre fiction is different
now than it was even a decade ago as the result of e-book technology and the
new business models that were enabled. Authors have more choices and
more control, and at least some publishers are having difficulty. So what is
the state of the scholarly monograph? A 2015 report to the Higher Education
Funding Council for England (HEFCE) authored by Geoffrey Crossick asked
whether the talk of a crisis of the monograph was justified. His answer was,

> The picture for the UK that has emerged does not suggest that there has been a
> decline in the position of the monograph in this country. The numbers of
> monographs being published continues to grow. There is evidence that librar-
> ies are feeling more constrained in their ability to purchase monographs, but
> they and academics remain the principal market for the growing number of
> monograph titles that are appearing. The perception that academic books are
> not being read, or even read in depth, does not appear to be sustained by the
> evidence. [19]

In a vigorous rebuttal Janneke Adema argues that Crossick has completely
missed the point. It is true, as Crossick states, that monograph publishing is
up at the four large commercial U.K. publishers, but Adema argues that
smaller, not-for-profit presses are hurting and, most importantly, there are
classes of books that are no longer being published, "specialised [*sic*], alternative, experimental and 'first' monographs."[20] As we will discuss in a later
chapter, a change in library purchasing has disadvantaged the monograph,
especially in the humanities and social sciences and thus the economics have
altered and stressed many university presses.

Despite these stresses, there is very little sense that the scholarly monograph as we have known it for the past century or so needs much reconsidera-
tion. There are economic pressures, but the product itself is just fine. There
are occasionally experiments, mostly with digital augmentations. An interesting example of this is the Gutenberg-e Project. The project was an experiment in creating born digital monographs. Begun in 1999, the Gutenberg-e
Project was a joint project of the American Historical Association and Columbia University Press, funded with a grant from the Mellon Foundation.
The project provided $20,000 to each of 36 scholars whose dissertations
demonstrated outstanding promise and were in areas in which it was becoming difficult to publish specialized books. It also funded production at the
Columbia University Press. In the end, the project produced 36 books that
were by all accounts excellent scholarship and interesting in their use of the
technology. But when the grant funding ran out the project ended; there was

no workable strategy for sustainability, though the books are now available as part of the ACLS Humanities E-Book collection.[21]

There is clearly a sense that some form of digital book that would be advantageous for scholarship is inevitable, but there is also a clear sense in some quarters that this is not really a scholarly book. As Cathy Davidson, who is not a Luddite, says in her commentary on the Gutenberg-e Project, "Big point: Scholarly publishing isn't just about printing and binding. It is also about the whole complex process of scholarly refereeing. It is about careful copyediting, style sheets, professionalism, and standardization of forms. It is about conventions of the page (that one must know even to break them)."[22] Her point is that a book is a book and the Gutenberg-e works were something else.

It is also clear to most observers, despite Crossick's assurances, that the scholarly monograph is in crisis. The usual way of telling the story is that academic libraries once bought enough scholarly monographs to make the publishing of even specialized, experimental, and first books economically possible. But then the prices of science journals went up and up and up, forcing libraries to reallocate their limited funds away from monographs. So where it once was common to sell 1,000 copies of even works in niche fields, now many good mainstream titles sell fewer than 400 copies. Because of the sizeable first copy costs, the economics become difficult. Often authors are required to provide subsidies of several thousand dollars to assure publication.

This is an interesting story and it is largely true, but it fails to ask an important question. Why is it that scientific journals have maintained their pricing power, while the scholarly monograph has been unable to do so? Clayton Christensen might argue that the customers for the scholarly monograph were overshot—that is, the product had exceeded the needs of its customers—libraries and scholars—and they will no longer pay the price premium for the increased quality of the product. Because of this, established academic publishers have attempted to move upmarket by producing higher quality books for smaller and more exclusive markets (soliciting philanthropic support for some projects). Or the presses have moved into other markets like cookbooks or bird books, or books of local or regional interest where they could sell enough copies to cover expenses. At this point both strategies have exhausted themselves and the scholarly monograph, and maybe academic presses, are endangered species. Christensen would argue that in this situation the possibility for a low-end disruption with a new value proposition to create a product serves the overshot users. This is what self-publishing romance novelists have done, but at least for now in the world of the scholarly monograph, no similar low-end disruption has emerged. Though the Lever Press—a collaboration between the Amherst College Press, Michigan Publishing, and the Oberlin Group that plans to publish with a "digitally native production process designed to support innovative projects" and with institutional rather than author subsidies—may be the first.[23]

It seems odd to me that very few people question the fact that an investment of several years of a scholar's life and the work of editors, designers, and marketing people that goes into producing a scholarly monograph that then sells only a couple hundred copies is reasonable. This doesn't even take into account that many of the copies will sit unused on library shelves for decades. There are efforts to become more efficient and concern with finding the money to pay for the system—that is, different ways to get the required subsidy. But little thought seems to have been given to the possibility that maybe the emperor has no clothes. Maybe the decisions librarians have been making about the relative merit of investments in scholarly monographs versus those made for journals, even though forced upon them by exploitive commercial publishers, are a rational assessment of the return on investment. Considering this possibility requires thinking not about how to get the money to continue past practice, but rather about how to alter practice, altering the way the long-form, scholarly argument is presented, so that the cost is commensurate with the value it provides. Put simply, given the limited audience for many scholarly monographs, we need to find a much cheaper way to produce them.

In considering what books might become in the future, let's begin with the assumption that all content will be developed digitally and that printing will be an option at the final stage of delivery to the reader. Now let's consider what happened when this situation occurred with music. There was a time when we all owned our own music. Actually we owned the objects that contained the music. I once had a vinyl record collection. The album was the unit of measure and the collection took up a fair amount of space. Now many people don't so much own music as access it through one or more small personal devices when they want it by way of a variety of mechanisms and business arrangements. Some of these, but not all of them, involve money changing hands, and not all end up with the ownership of anything. It is easy to imagine a future where text and images, the content previously the province of print books, are quite like the current state of music consumption. One can imagine that printing books using paper or the space to store books that had be read only once might be viewed as a wasteful extravagance. I do not dare predict what format the long-form, scholarly argument will take or how it will be paid for, but one does not need to be clairvoyant to predict that the system we have now will not last.

When we think about the future of the book, we need to keep Christensen's theories of disruption in mind. It seems inevitable that there will be innovations in how books are made, distributed, sold, and read. Some of these innovations will be sustaining, as was the paperback. The paperback took advantage of developments in printing and used distribution channels beyond bookstores, but despite some new entrants in publishing, in the end the major publishers remained the major publishers. As we look at the many innovations technology offers with books, the question we now have is whether they can be combined with a new business model to create a value proposition that is different and offers a product that does a job people want done more cheaply, quickly, and easily. If this happens the whole traditional supply chain for books, including libraries, is at risk of disruption. We have already seen this happen with Amazon as the web and innovations in logistics disrupted bookstores. My own view is that there are so many technological opportunities with lots of smart people trying to figure out what will work that disruption is inevitable. What combination of business model and technology will disrupt whom and when it might happen is difficult to predict, but that it will happen seems to me to be a certainty.

NOTES

1. Cory Doctorow, *Information Doesn't Want to Be Free: Laws for the Internet Age* (San Francisco, CA: McSweeney's, 2014), 14–15.

2. Wikipedia, s.v. "Codex," http://en.wikipedia.org/wiki/Codex.

3. Robert Darnton, "The Library: Three Jeremiads," *New York Review of Books*, December 23, 2010, http://www.nybooks.com/articles/archives/2010/dec/23/library-three-jeremiads/.

4. Ibid.

5. Ferris Jabr, "The Reading Brain in the Digital Age: Why the Brain Prefers Paper," *Scientific American* 309, no. 5 (November 2013): 48–53, doi:10.1038/scientificamerican1113-48.

6. Naomi S. Baron, *Words Onscreen: The Fate of Reading in a Digital World* (New York: Oxford University Press, 2015), 12.

7. David M. Durant and Tony Horava, "The Future of Reading and Academic Libraries," *portal: Libraries and the Academy* 15, no. 1 (January 2015), 8, doi:10.1353/pla.2015.0013, http://muse.jhu.edu/journals/portal_libraries_and_the_academy/v015/15.1.durant.pdf.

8. Ibid., 12.

9. Jennifer Schuessler, "A Tribute to the Printer Aldus Manutius, and the Roots of the Paperback," *New York Times*, February 26, 2015, http://www.nytimes.com/2015/02/27/arts/design/a-grolier-club-tribute-to-the-printer-aldus-manutius.html?_r=0.

10. Claire Cain Miller, "E-Books Top Hardcovers at Amazon," *New York Times*, July 19, 2010, http://www.nytimes.com/2010/07/20/technology/20kindle.html; and Claire Cain Miller and Julie Bosman, "E-Books Outsell Print Books at Amazon," *New York Times*, May 19, 2011, http://www.nytimes.com/2011/05/20/technology/20amazon.html?_r=1&scp=1&sq=E-Books%20Top%20paper%20at%20Amazon%20may&st=cse.

11. "From Papyrus to Pixels: The Digital Transformation of the Way Book are Written, Published and Sold Has Only Just Begun," *The Economist Essay* (London: The Economist, 2015), http://www.economist.com/news/essays/21623373-which-something-old-and-powerful-encountered-vault.

12. James Atlas, "Hearing Is Believing," *New York Times*, January 10, 2015, http://www.nytimes.com/2015/01/11/opinion/sunday/hearing-is-believing.html.

13. "From Papyrus to Pixels."

14. See the "BookBaby Pricing" at https://print.bookbaby.com/quoter/default.aspx.

15. "From Papyrus to Pixels."

16. Jeremy Greenfield, "Three Reasons News Corp Bought Harlequin, World's Biggest Romance Book Publisher," *Forbes*, May 2, 2014, http://www.forbes.com/sites/jeremygreen-

field/2014/05/02/news-corp-buys-harlequin-worlds-biggest-romance-book-publisher-three-reasons/#7fe442d21688.

17. Jeremy Greenfield, "Best Ebook Publishers in 2013—Hachette, Penguin, Random House on Top of Publisher Power Rankings," *DBW: Digital Publishing News for the 21st Century,* December 30, 2013, http://www.digitalbookworld.com/2013/best-ebook-publishers-in-2013-hachette-penguin-random-house-on-top-of-publisher-power-rankings/.

18. Jeremy Greenfield, "Love Affair with Digital Over for Romance Publisher Harlequin?," *Forbes,* March 6, 2014, http://www.forbes.com/sites/jeremygreenfield/2014/03/06/love-affair-with-digital-over-for-romance-publisher-harlequin/#125703893d69.

19. Geoffrey Crossick, *Monographs and Open Access: A report to HEFCE* (London: HEFCE, January 2015), 4, http://www.hefce.ac.uk/pubs/rereports/year/2015/monographs/.

20. Janneke Adema, "The Monographs Crisis Revisited," *OPEN REFLECTIONS* (blog), January 29, 2015, https://openreflections.wordpress.com/2015/01/29/the-monograph-crisis-revisited/.

21. Information on the Gutenberg-e Project can be found in Kate Wittenberg, "The Gutenberg-e Project: Opportunities in Publishing Born-Digital Monographs," *Learned Publishing* 22, no. 1 (January 2009): 36–41, doi:10.1087/095315108X378767; and Jennifer Howard, "Landmark Digital History Monograph Project Goes Open Access," *Chronicle of Higher Education* 54, no. 26 (March 7, 2008): A12, http://chronicle.com/article/Landmark-Digital-History/541. An interesting essay on the potential impact of this form of digital publishing is David A. Bell, "The Bookless Future," *New Republic,* May 2, 2005, http://www.newrepublic.com/article/books-and-arts/the-bookless-future. See also Robert Darnton, "The Library: Three Jeremiads."

22. Cathy Davidson, "Gutenberg-E Publishing Goes Open Access: Is It a Success?," *HASTAC: Humanities, Arts, Science and Technology Alliance and Collaboratory* (blog), February 26, 2008, http://www.hastac.org/blogs/cathy-davidson/gutenberg-e-publishing-goes-open-access-it-success.

23. "Collaboration: Michigan Publishing, Amherst U. Press and Oberlin Group Launching New Open Access Imprint," *Library Journal: InfoDocket,* January 7, 2016, http://www.infodocket.com/2016/01/07/collaboration-michigan-publishing-amherst-u-press-and-oberlin-group-launching-new-open-access-imprint/.

Force Four

The New Scholarly Record

> The features of the evolving scholarly record suggest that autonomous, institution-scale stewardship of the scholarly record is becoming less and less feasible: the volume of materials is too high, the cost of building local stewardship infrastructure and expertise is prohibitive, and much of what potentially constitutes the scholarly record . . . is widely scattered across many custodial hands, and cannot in any realistic sense be gathered and physically located or duplicated at a single institution.—Brian Lavoie and Constance Malpas [1]

Ross Atkinson is often quoted when beginning the task of defining the scholarly record. He defined the scholarly record as, "that which has already been written in *all* disciplines . . . that stable body of graphic information, upon which each discipline bases its discussions, and against which each discipline measures its progress." [2] Brian Lavoie and his colleagues respond to Atkinson's definition by saying, "This definition offers an eloquent conceptualization of the scholarly record, but is nevertheless resistant to practical application." [3]

Atkinson's definition may be resistant to practical application, but it does establish something of importance: that the scholarly record is what matters to a discipline—that is to say what matters and what is useful to researchers and scholars. Importantly, it is also a stable body of work against which progress is measured. Though we may, given changing technologies, need to remove "graphic" from the definition. As we have discussed, in a digital world, individual documents are not by their nature stable, so we will need to find ways to assure that this stability is embedded in the system either by fixing digital documents or by other means. Atkinson makes another important point when he says, "The definition of the record—the designation of those publications which should constitute the record—has always been one of the library's primary social and epistemological functions."[4] That is to say that the scholarly record has been to a great extent what librarians say it is, and more importantly, what librarians choose to add to their collections and keep. What scholars think, of course, influences librarians, but at the end of the day it has been what librarians do that has mattered. What librarians have done in the past has been largely driven by local needs and not coordinated— at least not in any meaningful way. As Brian Lavoie and Constance Malpas put it, "Much as Adam Smith described an invisible hand leading private economic interests toward a socially beneficial outcome, the efforts of individual academic libraries to develop and maintain local collections for local use have led to the formation, maintenance, and long-term preservation of a scholarly record available for use both by today's scholars and future generations."[5]

Going forward, the role of the library is not so clear or so certain. It will be interesting to see whether and how libraries will continue Atkinson's social and epistemological function in the digital networked world. Lavoie and Malpas are optimistic. They suggest,

> As a result, *conscious coordination* is likely to replace the invisible hand as the key principle underpinning stewardship models for the scholarly record, with local decisions taken in the context of broader system-wide conditions; more explicit collecting and curation responsibilities within collaborative arrangements; a greater degree of specialization in collecting activities; and deeper, more robust resource-sharing mechanisms. This in turn will lead to more interdependence across higher education institutions and other organizations in regard to gathering, making available, and preserving the scholarly record in its fullest expression.[6]

What Lavoie and Malpas are really saying is that the management of the scholarly record needs to move from local to network scale. This is probably what should happen, but it is far from clear that it will. What the scholarly record encompasses is changing quickly and a significant portion of it is outside of the traditional channels that libraries are comfortable with or even able to manage. Developing the skills required to manage the digital scholarly record while at the same time developing the organizational capacity and institutional incentives that will be required for conscious coordination at a deep level will be difficult.

Until quite recently what constituted the scholarly record seemed clear, or at least we understood that portion that was the library's responsibility. This included scholarly books and journals and the tools needed to use them— indexes, dictionaries, encyclopedias, and other reference tools. Larger collections would include more niche publications and less formally vetted classes of materials such as conference proceedings, theses and dissertations, and gray literature. In addition, some portion of the cultural corpus was the library's responsibility. This included magazines and newspapers that covered news and events, opinion, and facts. Works of fiction were included as well. Most academic libraries had special collections of rare or unique materials. There may have been some gray areas around the edges, but from the academic library perspective what constituted the scholarly record was generally well understood. The only real question was how much a particular library could afford to collect.

That was then, but now it is much less clear. Because the scholarly record is now nearly exclusively made up of digital documents, it is expanding in two dimensions. First, because digital documents are cheap and easy to replicate and, at least in theory, are not particularly expensive to keep and provide access to, the items beyond the final formal publications are now becoming an accepted part of the scholarly record. In some cases this is happening because of formal mandates—for example, the National Science Foundation data management requirements. In other cases, like blogs and twitter feeds, items find their way into the scholarly record because they are a useful means of advancing scholarly conversations.

The second expansion is also the result of the nature of digital documents that now make up the scholarly record; they are fungible and so there are new versions, revisions, and mash-ups. In the print world, once an item was published it stayed reliably the same. The digital documents that now make up the scholarly record behave in the opposite way. Beyond this, because the scholarly record is in digital form, machines can be used to analyze and extend it. As my conjecture in a later chapter argues, digital documents will encourage openness and social productivity. The scholarly record will change in significant ways as the result of all of these factors.

Herbert Van de Sompel nicely delineates the differences between the established paper-based system and the digital system as it will likely exist in the near future. The following table is an adaptation of his work.[7]

The objects that document the research process and its results are now or will soon be openly visible. They will vary in composition and content and will be compound and inclusive of multiple types and forms of explanation and evidence. They will be informal and available in various forms throughout the research process. Finally, as Lavoie and Malpas argue, there is an increasing distribution, beyond the library, of custodial responsibility for the scholarly record. As they say, "many other pieces of the scholarly record reside elsewhere: on publishers' servers, on proprietary social media platforms, in subject-based data repositories, and so on. . . . The scholarly outputs produced today are in many hands, forming a broad network of custodial responsibility that extends far beyond libraries, archives, and the rest of the cultural heritage community."[8] The established organizations, processes, and

Characterizing Research Process and Outputs

Characteristic	Past Practice	Future
Research process	Hidden	Visible
Nature of the object	Fixed	Varying
Atomicity of object	Atomic	Compound
Process of making public	Discrete	Continuous
Speed of communication	Delayed	Instant
Communicated object	Publication plus data proxies	Publication plus linked data plus linked models
Nature of process	Formal	Informal

procedures used in the past will not be adequate to manage the spread and complexity of the scholarly record as it is developing.

We will consider each of these changes and their impact on scholarship in general and academic libraries in turn. As Brian Lavoie and his colleagues put it, "While in the past we might have thought of the scholarly record as consisting primarily of text-based materials like journals and monographs, today the cohort of materials over which the scholarly record can potentially extend has expanded dramatically, to include research data sets, computer models, interactive programs, complex visualizations, lab notebooks, and a host of other materials."[9] It could also include less formal content such as blogs or tweets. Lavoie and his colleagues have created a diagram that is a useful beginning as we explore the scholarly record as it is evolving.[10]

The "Outcome" box in the middle of the figure below is the content that we have traditionally thought of as the scholarly record. The top portion of the figure shows aspects of the research process that are now more easily captured than in the past and are now expected to be reported as part of the scholarly record. For example, evidence includes data sets and similar products that the National Science Foundation, the National Institutes of Health, and other funding agencies now expect to be preserved and made available as a condition of grant funding. In some fields the creation of bodies of evidence constitutes a valued scholarly contribution and may count toward promotion and tenure.

The most important new piece of the scholarly record is data. There are two reasons for this. First, the investment in research is large and to get the best return on this investment the data produced by one research project needs to be shared and reused by others. Second, to advance understanding, many big, difficult, and important questions—like climate change, or enhancing health and wellbeing—require large diverse data from many places.

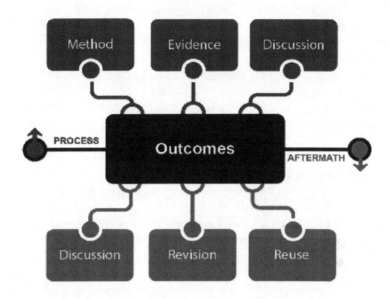

The Scholarly Record. Brian Lavoie, Eric Childress, Ricky Erway, Ixchel Faniel, Constance Malpas, Jennifer Schaffner, and Titia van der Werf, *The Evolving Scholarly Record* **(Dublin, OH: OCLC Research, June 2014), 10. http://oclc.org/ content/dam/research/publications/library/2014/oclcresearch-evolving-scholar-ly-record-2014-5-a4.pdf.**

As an example of evidence entering the scholarly record, Lavoie and his colleagues cite Dryad, a general purpose curated data repository for a "wide diversity of datatypes," whose vision is to "promote a world where research data is openly available, integrated with the scholarly literature, and routinely re-used to create knowledge."[11] Dryad is funded by deposit charges and is dependent on foundation grants for the operation of the repository infrastructure. The use of datasets deposited in Dryad was in some cases substantial. The most downloaded file in 2013, "Parasitic Plants Have Increased Rates of Molecular Evolution across All Three Genomes," deposited in conjunction with a 2013 article in *BMC Evolutionary Biology*, was downloaded nearly 10,000 times.[12]

In 2014 the Nature Group started a similar venture, *Scientific Data*. As they describe it, "*Scientific Data* aims to address the increasing need to make research data more available, citable, discoverable, interpretable, reusable and reproducible. We understand that wider data-sharing requires credit mechanisms that reward scientists for releasing their data, and peer evaluation mechanisms that account for data quality and ensure alignment with community standards."[13] Article processing fees are the mechanism for financial support and the data sets are published under open access licenses.

An interesting aspect is that the Nature Group is clearly marketing *Scientific Data*, as a peer reviewed publication, to researchers as a means of gaining credit that can be cited for the data they have produced.

In some circumstances reports on methods are also considered scholarly contributions. Lavoie and his colleagues cite Elsevier's *MethodsX*, an article-processing, fee-supported, open access journal that was also begun in 2014. Like *Scientific Data* it is clearly marketed to researchers as a way of maximizing the credit they get for their work. As the header on the website puts it, "*Methods X* publishes the small but important customizations you make to methods every day. By releasing the hidden gems from your lab book, you can get credit for the time, effort and money you've put in."[14]

These are interesting examples of what is likely to be the norm, but it may not come easily or quickly. In 2011 Carol Tenopir and her colleagues surveyed scientists about their data-sharing practices and their perceptions of the barriers and incentives for sharing. The issues were clear. As Tenopir and her colleagues put it, "Barriers to effective data sharing and preservation are deeply rooted in the practices and culture of the research process as well as the researchers themselves."[15] As might be expected, scientists cited lack of time and lack of institutional support as impediments to data sharing. Data sharing was not common practice. As the study states, noting that one third of the respondents did not answer the question: "The high percentage of non-respondents to this question most likely indicates that data sharing is even lower than the numbers indicate. Furthermore, the less than 6% of scientists who are making 'All' of their data available via some mechanism, tends to re-enforce the lack of data sharing within the communities surveyed."[16] Tenopir and her colleagues conclude that mandates will certainly increase data sharing, but that incentives, and in some cases disciplinary norms and culture, as well as support structures need to change if data sharing is to be widely adopted.

A number of proposals have been made to encourage data sharing. Most are based on creating incentives that enhance researcher prestige. Vishwas Chavan and Lyubomir Penev propose formalizing data sharing through the development of "data papers" as a means of "fit-for-use" data in biodiversity science.[17] Peter Ingwersen and Vishwas Chavan propose a Data Usage Index as a means of incentivizing data sharing by formalizing recognition.[18] Heather Coates, a practicing data librarian, takes the long view:

> Although preserving valuable research data is a truly important endeavor, I believe success of the data specialist in the next decade will more accurately be reflected by the strength of our relationships with researchers and other campus units than the number of datasets deposited in our IR. Shifting the research practices on our campuses towards more efficient workflows and sustainable infrastructure is a long-term goal requiring deep knowledge of both institutional and disciplinary practices.[19]

The bottom portion of Lavoie's diagram of the expanded scholarly record shows aspects of the scholarly record that come after the traditional content is published. The most important of these is commentary. In the past the traditional scholarly journal included some commentary in the form of letters to the editor and author responses, but these were infrequent and slow. Today commentary comes quickly and from many directions. Altmetric is a company that tracks the impact of academic research on social media. It ranked articles that "caught the public imagination in 2014" and the top article, "Experimental Evidence of Massive-Scale Emotional Contagion through Social Networks" by Adam D. I. Kramer, Jamie E. Guillory, and Jeffrey T. Hancock, was mentioned in 301 news stories, 130 blog posts, 3,801 tweets, and 342 Facebook posts in the six months between its June publication and the release of the Altmetric list in December.[20] This is an exceptional article in that it was reporting on a controversial study of social media and it is unlikely that every tweet or Facebook post is of lasting value, but it is indicative of the mass of content that is now potentially of scholarly concern.

Several things become clear as we begin to think about the scholarly record as it is developing. The first is that there is an increase in the amount of content that needs to be captured, curated, and preserved. And much of this content, particularly in the immediate term will be data sets, something libraries do not have much experience with and in many cases do not have the required expertise or the infrastructure to manage. Second, much of the content that might be captured resides on network scale infrastructure, for example Twitter or Facebook, SlideShare, or YouTube, and in general cannot be managed effectively with institutional scale efforts.

In a 2004 article, Herbert Van der Sompel and his colleagues consider how the scholarly communication system can be rethought.[21] They build on the work of Hans E. Roosendaall and Peter A. Th. M. Geurts and argue that there are five key components to the scholarly communication system:[22]

Registration, which allows claims of precedence for a scholarly finding.

Certification, which establishes the validity of a registered scholarly claim.

Awareness, which allows actors in the scholarly system to remain aware of new claims and findings.

Archiving, which preserves the scholarly record over time.

Rewarding, which rewards actors for their performance in the communication system based on metrics derived from that system.

They argue that reconceptualizing scholarly communication systems requires an explicit recognition of these components outside the established vehicles and processes in which they were embedded in the print world. They note that there are many technical challenges in creating interoperable workflows that take advantage of digital technologies. As they put it,

> We argue that in order for a distributed service approach to be worthy of the
> name scholarly communication "system" (rather than scholarly "chaos"), the
> service hubs need to be interconnected, as if they were part of a global scholar-
> ly communication workflow system. Such a workflow system would allow the
> construction of macro-level workflows for streamlining and concatenating the
> fulfillment of the various implementations of the functions of scholarly com-
> munication. That is, it would allow the chaining of specific implementations of
> the *registration, certification,* etc. functions into a pathway that could be fol-
> lowed by a unit of communication.[23]

It is of course much easier to insist that a system of interconnected hubs
needs to be built than to build it. Van de Sompel and his colleagues presented
this challenge a decade ago and it is not clear that the system has advanced to
far beyond chaos.

In later work Van de Sompel builds the model of the scholarly communication system, shown in the following figure.[24] Van de Sompel's characterization of the process on scholarly communication is interesting for two
reasons. First, it indicates that the process has two stages. The first is when
the reports of research move from the private infrastructure under the control
of the researcher into what Van de Sompel calls the "Recording Infrastructure." These systems are network in scale and libraries generally have little or
nothing to do with them. At a later stage the research object enters the
"Archiving Infrastructure," which aims at making the content persistent. One
would expect libraries to play a significant role here, though it is not clear
that they currently have the capacity to do so.

The second important point that Van de Sompel's model makes is that the
research community interacts with the research objects as soon as they enter
the "Recording Infrastructure." It is here that registration and awareness
components from the earlier model take place and where the certification
component begins. It is an open and interesting question whether or not the
lack of persistence of these aspects of the research process might or might
not be a problem.

Another concern that has been explored by Herbert Van der Sompel is
that it is probably not sufficient to capture only the item documenting the
research itself. Because all current items of scholarly content reference items
are on the web, as with any item on the web, these referenced items are
subject to change or may disappear altogether. If the full scholarly record is
to be preserved, the referenced items need to be captured as they existed
when they were references as well. This is a hard problem. It turns preserving
and curating scholarly content into a problem of large-scale, web archiving.

As an example of the "reference rot" that concerns Van de Sompel, the
Chesapeake Digital Preservation Group, a consortium of law libraries, has
regularly checked the availability of 8,954 legal items that were posted to the
web. The first sample included the URLs for 579 items for content capture in

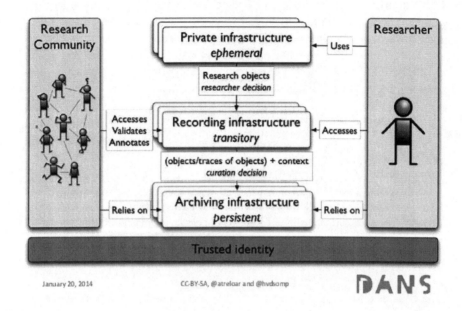

The Scholarly Record. Herbert Van de Sompel and Andrew Treloar, "A Perspective on Archiving the Scholarly Web," in *Proceedings of the 11th International Conference on Preservation of Digital Objects: iPRES 2014*, Melbourne, October 6–10, 2014 (Melbourne: State Library of Victoria, 2014), 194–98, https://www.nla.gov.au/sites/default/files/ipres2014-proceedings-version_1.pdf.

2007–2008. Each year since then the sample was checked to see how many of the URLs were still valid. In 2013, 44.2% of the sample URLs were no longer working and more than 50% of the .gov items were not available.[25] Daniela V. Dimitrova and Michael Bugela conducted a study of the persistence of Internet references in five communications journals and found that for references in articles published between 2000 and 2003, by 2004 39% no longer functioned.[26] In a similar study Dion Hoe-Lian Goh and Peng Kin Ng studied information science journals and found that the half-life of the web citations was five years—that is, half of the references no long functioned after five years.[27]

In what is certainly the largest study to date, Martin Klein and his colleagues, one of whom was Van de Sompel, examined a corpus of articles published between 1997 and 2012 from arXiv, Elsevier, and PubMed Central.[28] The corpus contained 3.5 million articles. The articles in turn had more than a million references to web resources. The study looked at whether the HTTP URI was still responsive and whether a web archive contained a representation of the resources at the time it was referenced. The first check looked at the rate of "link rot" and the second check provided information of "content drift" or the tendency for content on a website to change over time and be different from the content that was referenced. Their first finding was that, unsurprisingly, the rate of the number of references to web content increased significantly over the period. They also found, again maybe unsurprisingly, that link rot and content drift were significant problems. In summarizing their research Klein and his colleagues state,

> Our research shows that, increasingly, articles reference web at large resources. It confirms a general finding of prior link rot studies, in our case derived from significantly vaster corpora, that links to such resources rot over time. As a result, many referenced resources cannot be revisited some time after they were referenced. We also found that a significant amount of links remain operational. However, understanding that web resources are subject to content drift, following those links may eventually lead to content that is different than originally referenced. This consideration begs the question which is worse: following a link to a "404 Not Found" error message or to a page that may no longer be representative of the content that was originally referenced. A least the former is unambiguous, the latter is not. [29]

The conclusion is clear and familiar: "404 Not Found" is a fact of life in the world of contemporary web-based scholarship, or as Jill Lepore put it in a *New Yorker* article discussing the scholarly impact of this phenomenon, "It's like trying to stand on quicksand."[30]

So where does this leave us as we try to define the scholarly record, or more importantly how we, as librarians, try to manage and preserve it? The simple answer is not in a good place. The scholarly record as it exists today, is not well understood; it is shifting and expanding. Because it is made up of digital documents that are malleable and fade quickly if they are not actively managed, and because these documents cite sources that are themselves digital documents with the same tendencies toward impermanence, the task is much more difficult than it was in the world of print on paper. The local institutions that in the past could collectively preserve the scholarly record, even in the absence of close coordination, are now confronted with a web-scale problem without web-scale capacities. The good news is that we are starting to grasp the problem. Now all we need to do is find and implement the solution.

The "conscious coordination" path forward suggested by Lavoie and Malpas has four requirements:

1. Local decisions need to be taken with an awareness of the system-wide requirements for stewardship.
2. Individual institutions need to make explicit commitments to collect, curate, and preserve particular parts of the scholarly record.

3. Formal division of labor arrangements need to be made between institutions.
4. Trusted and reliable networks of reciprocal access need to be established.[31]

After citing examples of how all of these requirements are being developed, they ask the important question, "How can an academic library maintain a clear institutional identity in a stewardship environment where individual libraries function less as autonomous local service hubs, and more like nodes in complex networks of specialization, mutual dependence, and collective responsibility?"[32] As Lavoie and Malpas note, in a consciously coordinated stewardship model the benefits accrue to the system as a whole, to the "common good," not necessarily to the individual institution that is making the investment. The politics of this situation will be exacerbated, as there will inevitably be free riders. Lavoie and Malpas argue that contributions to the global stewardship effort might fit with broader institutional interests in global contributions and that investments in distinctive collections or distinctive skills might bring institutional recognition and enhance institutional "brand."

I wish I could be convinced. The arguments Lavoie and Malpas propose might help, but at the end of the day I think they are insufficient. There needs to be local advantage to justify local investment. In Christensen's terms, there needs to be a job to be done. The only jobs I can see that universities will pay to have done are providing services to researchers that will make them more productive in the face of increasing demands (1) to expand their responsibility for new aspects of the scholarly record, and (2) to collect, curate, and preserve the work done by these researchers—not so much as a contribution to the consciously coordinated effort, but because those jobs enhance the productivity and thus the reputation of local researchers and, through them, the local institution.

At the end of the day, for better or worse, the scholarly record is what libraries, or the network scale institutions they create, decide to keep and what they can successfully preserve. Digital content is, of course, harder to keep than paper because the preservation of digital content, at least for now, needs to be an active rather than a passive process. Untended bits rot. Libraries will develop means to preserve digital content, but resource constraints will inevitably limit their capacities. Content that is harder to keep because it does not match these capacities or fit easily into the systems libraries develop will be harder and more expensive to preserve. As a result, it will be less likely to survive in the long haul. Published works will in nearly all cases meet these requirements. For content beyond the published works—and as we have noted the line between published and not published will blur—scholars, individually and collectively, will need to develop research practices that generate content that fits into library systems easily and that will make library acquisition of the content simple. If they don't, the long-term prospects for the survival of their scholarship in its full richness will not be good.

This seems like it should be simple, but the current practice in many disciplines, driven by the flexibility and ease of customizing made possible by digital technology, make the opposite more likely. This is not unlike the first years of the print era. It will take some time for scholarly practices that reliably support preservation to be developed and institutionalized. Until then, much will be lost. For the next decade or two we can expect, despite the best efforts of librarians and scholars, that while the scholarly record will grow and become richer, much will be lost. Those who look back fifty years from now will likely wonder why we did not do better. The reason for this disappointment will not be technical, rather it will be the result of the delay required for social practices and norms to change and catch up with technology.

NOTES

1. Brian Lavoie and Constance Malpas, *Stewardship of the Evolving Scholarly Record: From the Invisible Hand to Conscious Coordination* (Dublin, Ohio: OCLC Research, 2015), 13, http://www.oclc.org/content/dam/research/publications/2015/oclcresearch-esr-stewardship-2015.pdf.

2. Ross Atkinson, "Text Mutability and Collection Administration," *Library Acquisitions: Practice & Theory* 14 no. 4 (1990): 356, doi:10.1016/0364-6408(90)90006-G.

3. Brian Lavoie et al., *The Evolving Scholarly Record* (Dublin, OH: OCLC Research, June 2014), 7, http://oclc.org/content/dam/research/publications/library/2014/oclcresearch-evolving-scholarly-record-2014-5-a4.pdf.

4. Atkinson, "Text Mutability and Collection Administration."

5. Lavoie and Malpas, *Stewardship of the Evolving Scholarly Record*, 5.

6. Ibid., 6.

7. Adapted from: Inge Angevaare, "On-line Scholarly Communications: vd Sompel and Treloar Sketch the Future Playing Field of Digital Archives," *KB Research* (blog), January 22, 2014, http://blog.kbresearch.nl/2014/01/22/on-line-scholarly-communications-and-the-role-of-digital-archives/.

8. Lavoie and Malpas, *Stewardship of the Evolving Scholarly Record*, 11.

9. Lavoie, et. al., *The Evolving Scholarly Record*, 8.

10. Ibid., 10.

11. "The Organization," Dryad, last revised October 22, 2015, http://datadryad.org/pages/organization.

12. "2013 Organizational and Membership Report," Dryad, 11, http://datadryad.org/themes/Mirage/docs/DryadAnnualReport2013.pdf.

13. "Welcome to *Scientific Data*," *Scientific Data*, http://www.nature.com/sdata/about.

14. "MethodsX," *Elsevier: MethodsX*, http://www.journals.elsevier.com/methodsx.

15. Carol Tenopir et al., "Data Sharing by Scientists: Practices and Perceptions," *PLOS ONE*, 6, no. 6 (June 29, 2011): e21101, doi:10.1371/journal.pone.0021101, http://www.plosone.org/article/info%3Adoi%2F10.1371%2Fjournal.pone.0021101.

16. Ibid.

17. Vishwas Chavan and Lyubomir Penev, "The Data Paper: A Mechanism to Incentivize Data Publishing in Biodiversity Science," *BMC Bioinformatics* 12, no. S15 (2011): S2, doi:10.1186/1471-2105-12-S15-S2, http://www.biomedcentral.com/1471-2105/12/S15/S2.

18. Peter Ingwersen and Vishwas Chavan, "Indicators for the Data Usage Index (DUI): An Incentive for Publishing Primary Biodiversity Data through Global Information Infrastructure," *BMC Bioinformatics* 12 no. S15 (2011): S3 doi:10.1186/1471-2105-12-S15-S3, http://www.biomedcentral.com/1471-2105/12/S15/S3.

19. Heather L. Coates, "Building Data Services from the Ground Up: Strategies and Resources," *Journal of eScience Librarianship* 3 no. 1 (2014): 57, http://escholarship.umassmed.edu/jeslib/vol3/iss1/5/.

20. "Altmetric 2014 Top 100," http://www.altmetric.com/top100/2014/?utm_source=announcement&utm_medium=social&utm_term=2014top100&utm_campaign=top1002014social. The full article citation is, Adam D. I. Kramer, Jamie E. Guillory, and Jeffrey T. Hancock, "Experimental Evidence of Massive-Scale Emotional Contagion through Social Networks," *Proceedings of the National Academy of Sciences* 111 no. 24 (June 17, 2014): 8788–90. doi:10.1073/pnas.1320040111, http://www.pnas.org/content/111/24/8788.

21. Herbert Van de Sompel et al., "Rethinking Scholarly Communication," *D-Lib Magazine* 10 no. 9 (September 2004), http://www.dlib.org/dlib/september04/vandesompel/09vandesompel.html#Roosendaal; and Hans E. Roosendaall and Peter A. Th. M. Geurts, "Forces and Functions in Scientific Communication: An Analysis of Their Interplay" (paper used for The First International Workshop: Cooperative Research Information Systems in Physics, Oldenburg, Germany, August 31–September 4, 1997), http://www.physik.uni-oldenburg.de/conferences/crisp97/roosendaal.html.

22. Van de Sompel et. al., "Rethinking Scholarly Communication."

23. Ibid.

24. Herbert Van de Sompel and Andrew Treloar, "A Perspective on Archiving the Scholarly Web," in *Proceedings of the 11th International Conference on Preservation of Digital Objects: iPRES 2014*, Melbourne, October 6–10, 2014 (Melbourne: State Library of Victoria, 2014), 194–98, https://www.nla.gov.au/sites/default/files/ipres2014-proceedings-version_1.pdf.

25. Chesapeake Digital Preservation Group, "'Link Rot' and Legal Resources on the Web: A 2013 Analysis by the Chesapeake Digital Preservation Group," Chesapeake Digital Preservation Group, accessed January 26, 2016, http://cdm16064.contentdm.oclc.org/cdm/linkrot2013.

26. Daniela V. Dimitrova and Michael Bugela, "The Half-Life of Internet References Cited in Communication Journals," *New Media & Society* 9 no. 5 (October 2007): 811–26, doi:10.1177/1461444807081226.

27. Dion Hoe-Lian Goh and Peng Kin Ng, "Link Decay in Leading Information Science Journals," *Journal of the American Society for Information Science and Technology* 58 no. 1 (January 2007): 15–24, doi:10.1002/asi.20513.

28. Martin Klein et al., "Scholarly Context Not Found: One in Five Articles Suffers from Reference Rot," *PLOS ONE* 9 no. 12 (December 26, 2014): e115253, doi:10.1371/journal.pone.0115253, http://journals.plos.org/plosone/article?id=10.1371/journal.pone.0115253.

29. Ibid.

30. Jill Lepore, "Cobweb: Can the Internet Be Archived?," *New Yorker*, January 26, 2015, http://www.newyorker.com/magazine/2015/01/26/cobweb.

31. Lavoie and Malpas, *Stewardship of the Evolving Scholarly Record*, 16.

32. Ibid., 27.

Force Five

The Economics of Information

Commercial interests have taken over the communication of knowledge, and we academics have to fight back.—Robert Darnton [1]

In looking at how scholarly communication has, does, and will function, we need to take the advice Deep Throat gave Bob Woodward and Carl Bernstein and, "Follow the money." (It is unclear if this phrase was actually used by Deep Throat, but it was what Hal Holbrook, playing the character of Deep Throat, said in the 1976 movie version of *All the President's Men.*) As we follow the money, I want to begin with the generally accepted, but not always fully appreciated, truth that scholarly information, like the research or scholarly work it reports, is a public good. One important implication of this truth is that the market, left to its own devices, will not produce the full amount of scholarly information that would lead to the most efficient result for society. Simply put, people left to their own devices will not pay for as much information as they should to provide the best results for the society as a whole. In this situation the way to achieve the efficient result is to provide a subsidy. How the subsidy is provided so that its benefit is maximized and the most value is produced from it is the critical question.

In the world of print-on-paper scholarship. there was a circle in which the works of scholarship traveled. A researcher or scholar wrote a book or article and it was given to a publisher who edited the work and published it. The publisher did a great deal of work in the review and editorial process, in design and printing, in marketing, in warehousing stock and fulfilling orders. Libraries then purchased the resulting books and journals, cataloged them, and added them to their collections. Some individuals bought scholarly books and some subscribed to scholarly journals, but library collections were the primary means of providing access to the content and to assuring its long-term preservation. Scholars and the general public, at least those who had access to libraries, thus had access to the works of scholarship, which then became the grist for future scholarship, and so the cycle was repeated. This cycle is illustrated in the following figure.

How did the money flow through this system? It flowed in the opposite direction from the content. Money came to the library from the university. The library, after taking out roughly half of the funds that were required for processing, access, and reference services, and the cost of the building, would send the remainder to publishers to purchase as much content as possible. Some money flowed from the university to scholars who purchased their own books and journals, and in some cases, scholarly books would reach an audience beyond the academy that would inject some additional money into the system. It was also often the case that universities provided

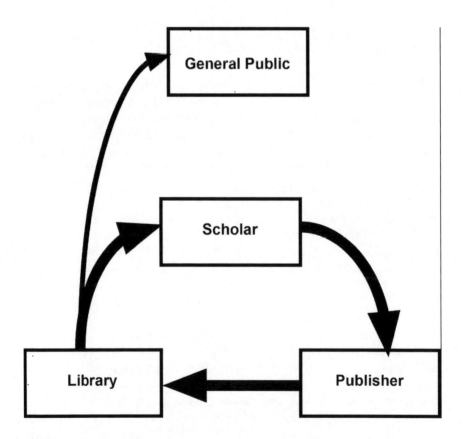

Cycle of Scholarly Communication.

subventions, or direct subsidies, to their university presses. Finally, some money moved from granting agencies to scholars who, especially in the sciences, used it to pay page charges for journal publications. The important thing to understand in all of this is that nearly all of the money that ended up in the hands of the publisher began its journey either with funding agencies or universities. This is the route that the subsidy travelled to make the system function, as illustrated in the next figure.

One of the interesting, or maybe odd, aspects of this arrangement, especially for academic book publishing, is that readers don't really come into play. Jill Lepore put it this way:

> While academic journals and university presses like to have readers who will pay for what they publish, they have been able to do without them; their publications have been subsidized by the universities that house them. University publishing has suited both scholars who need to publish and presses whose mission is to publish them. It has not rewarded clarity or beauty or timeliness, and it has not made a priority of satisfying readers or earning profits because it was not designed to do any of these things: It was designed to advance scholarship.[2]

Lepore's primary concern is with the quality of the writing that this system produces, but as she points out the system is not really a free and open market.

The fact that a subsidy drives the scholarly communications system has some unintended and maybe undesirable outcomes. Her conclusion that the university publishing was "designed to advance scholarship" does not fully unpack what is going on. Faculty authors don't need readers; rather they need the status that comes from publishing with an academic press in the top tier. It is nice to have good reviews in the right disciplinary journals, but whether or not anyone actually reads the work is not the key incentive. You might think that academic publishers need readers, but what they really need is a relatively small number of sales. In many cases a scholarly book can break even with 500 sales, or sometimes fewer, and these sales are mostly to libraries or, for some fortunate titles, to students as required course readings.

In the mythical good old days, publishers used the entire subsidy to create as much quality scholarship as they could. Academic publishers were frugal and wasted little. There was a market for scholarly work and publishers competed to produce the best scholarly works at a good price. This competition in general assured that the quality of the work was high. In the first half of the 20th century this is how things worked. Scholarly publishers often scraped by, but this reflected their attempts to publish as much as possible with the limited amount of subsidy that was available.

The expansion of higher education to accommodate soldiers returning from World War II, the increase in science funding as a response to Sputnik,

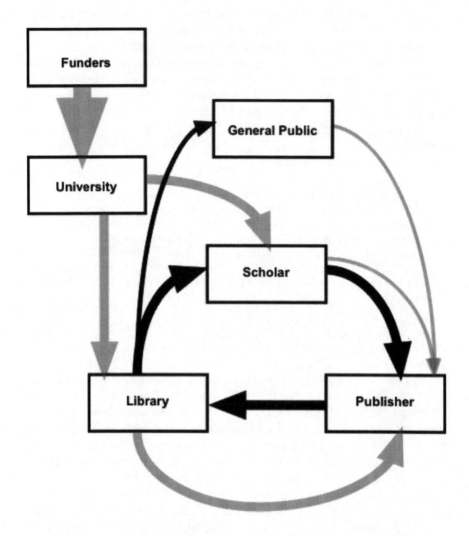

Cycle of Scholarly Communication with Money Flows in the "Good Old Days."

and then the expansion of higher education to accommodate the baby boom generation changed the environment. There was now more money. Importantly, as documented by Jean-Claude Guédon in *In Oldenburg's Long Shadow: Librarians, Research Scientists, Publishers, and the Control of Scientific Publishing*, there were new tools that provided information on which publications, particularly journals, were of the most importance.[3] The groundwork for the new tools was laid in the 1930s with the work of Samuel C. Bradford and his "Law of Scattering." Bradford's law gave librarians a tool to establish which journals provided the most value in particular disciplines, which journals were in the core of that particular discipline.

In the 1960s Eugene Garfield created the *Science Citation Index* (SCI) as a way of tracing the connections in the scientific literature. To do so with the technology of the time he needed to identify an overall core of science journals. To create this core Garfield collapsed the many disciplinary cores identified using Bradford's Law into one core for all of science. It included a few thousand titles. With the growth of the scientific enterprise, institutions were looking for ways to measure impact and rank work.

The SCI soon began publishing impact factors for the journals. Impact factors measured the citations to an average article in a journal over a given period of time. The impact factor became an easy way to measure the apparent quality of a journal and by extension the work of a scientist who published in it. This was, as Guédon calls it, "a lazy approximation," but it took hold nonetheless.[4] One important result was that the pecking order for science journals across all disciplines was established.

In retrospect, what happened next seems unsurprising, but it took several decades for it to become clear and widely recognized. Several astute commercial publishers realized that high-impact-factor journals were valuable properties and began acquiring them. These publishers realized that because of their high-impact factors these journals were monopoly goods that universities could not afford to be without. The demand was inelastic, as faculty would insist that their institutions had to have these high-impact-factor titles or risk their reputations. Publishers found that there were few limits on their ability to raise prices and so they pushed prices up relentlessly. By the mid-1970s the journals in the core were largely owned by commercial publishers and their prices were skyrocketing and libraries had little choice but to pay.

In the next forty years, as Vincent Larivière, Stefanie Haustein, and Philippe Mongeon document, scholarly journal publishing became more concentrated. By 2013 more than 50% of the papers were published by the largest five publishers in both the natural and medical sciences and the social sciences and humanities. In both areas four of the five top publishers were Reed-Elsevier, Wiley-Blackwell, Springer, and Taylor & Francis. In the natural and medical sciences the American Chemical Society was the fifth and in social sciences and humanities it was Sage. As Larivière, Haustein, and Mongeon say, "On the whole, our results show that the top commercial publishers have benefited from the digital era, as it led to a dramatic increase in the share of scientific literature they published. It has also led to a greater dependence by the scientific community on these publishers."[5]

As this happened there was a second interesting shift. Scholars became more dependent on their institution's libraries to fund the literature they read. As Carol Tenopir, Donald W. King, Lisa Christian, and Rachel Volentine document, "The percentage of article readings obtained through personal subscriptions has been decreasing since 1977. Articles obtained from personal subscriptions decreased from 60% in 1977 to 53% in 1984, down to 35.5% by the early 1990s. This decline has continued—only 18% of article readings in 2012 are from personal subscriptions."[6] In the past few years some of this change might be attributed to the increase in open access publications and some might be the result of the ease of sharing that results from digital formats. However, it is likely that the electronic access funded by libraries makes personal subscriptions superfluous. Faculty dependence on institutional support of their access to the literature may explain part of the pressure they exert on libraries to maintain subscriptions.

What is important to understand is that when scholarly journals go from being the province of scholarly societies and similar scientific organizations to being profit centers for large commercial publishers, a large portion of the subsidy designed to produce scientific information is captured and distributed outside the system to the shareholders of the for-profit firms. The amount of the subsidy redistributed in this way is far from trivial. Estimates differ, but the large commercial publishers routinely make a 35% to 45% profit margin on the scientific journal operations. As reported in a *Huffington Post* article, "Academic Journals: The Most Profitable Obsolete Technology in History," in 2013 Elsevier had, at 39% profit, a larger margin than Apple's 37%.[7] Vincent Larivière, Stefanie Haustein, and Philippe Mongeon report on the profits at the largest commercial publishing companies and it is worth quoting them at length:

> As one might expect, the consolidation of the publishing industry led to an increase of the profits of publishers. . . . Between 1991 and 1997, both the profits and the profit margin increased steadily for the company [Reed-Elsevier] as a whole. While profits more than doubled over that period—from 665M USD to 1,451M USD—profit margin also rose from 17% to 26%. Profit margins decreased, however, between 1998 and 2003, although profits remained relatively stable. Absolute profits as well as the profit margin then rose again, with the exception of the 2008–2009 period of economic crisis, resulting in profits reaching an all-time high of more than 2 billion USD in 2012 and 2013. The profit margin of the company's Scientific, Technical & Medical division is even higher. Moreover, its profits increased by a factor of almost 6 throughout the period, and never dropped below 30% from one year to another. The profit margin of this division never decreased below 30% during the period observed, and steadily increased from 30.6% to 38.9% between 2006 and 2013. Similarly high profit margins were obtained in 2012 by Springer Science+Business Media (35.0% . . .), and in 2013 and John Wiley & Sons' Scientific, Technical, Medical and Scholarly division (28.3% . . .) and Taylor and Francis (35.7% . . .), putting them on a comparable level with Pfizer (42%), the Industrial & Commercial Bank of China (29%) and far above Hyundai Motors (10%), which comprise the most profitable drug, bank and

auto companies among the top 10 biggest companies respectively, according to Forbes' Global 2000.[8]

We need to be clear that this profit taking is not some moral failing on the part of the commercial publishers, nor are they evil. They are only doing what they are supposed to do. As for-profit corporations they have a fiduciary responsibility to make as much money as possible and to pass as much of it as they can to their shareholders. This is how capitalism works. Unfortunately, capitalist markets are not always optimal, especially if the product in question is, as is the case for scholarship, a public good.

This system is particularly galling to many because faculty members donate much of the labor that goes into producing a journal article. Richard Darnton describes this nicely:

> Reduced to essentials, it goes like this: we academics devote ourselves to research; we write up the results as articles for journals; we referee the articles in the process of peer reviewing; we serve on the editorial boards of the journals; we also serve as editors (all of this unpaid, of course); and then we buy back our own work at ruinous prices in the form of journal subscriptions—not that we pay for it ourselves, of course; we expect our library to pay for it, and therefore we have no knowledge of our complicity in a disastrous system.[9]

The following figure shows how scholarly communication has operated for the past thirty or forty years. With the green money arrow from the library to the publisher getting bigger each year and the black content arrow from the publisher to the library getting smaller.

By the late 1980s the "serials crisis" was clear to everyone in the field. An *American Libraries* article reporting on an ALA conference session titled "Managing the Crisis in the Library Materials Budget" quoted Richard Dougherty, then the library director at the University of Michigan, as saying that "the latest round of inflation is serious enough to eventually alter the mechanism by which scholarly information is communicated."[10] As *Library Journal* reported in an April 1991 article titled "ARL Reports on Serials Crisis," "That is the latest grim news from the Association of Research Libraries in its ARL Statistics . . . . Due to the dual pressure of increased serials production and increased costs, ARL libraries experienced the largest decrease in serials subscriptions since 1986."[11] Thirty years later, little has changed in the relationship between large commercial publishers and libraries.

As digital technologies developed, journals moved to the web. This was an opportunity, at least potentially, for libraries to alter their relationships with publishers. But the opportunity was short lived and quickly lost. The commercial publishers explored the market and got an early understanding of how it was likely to function. Most notable was Elsevier's TULIP (The

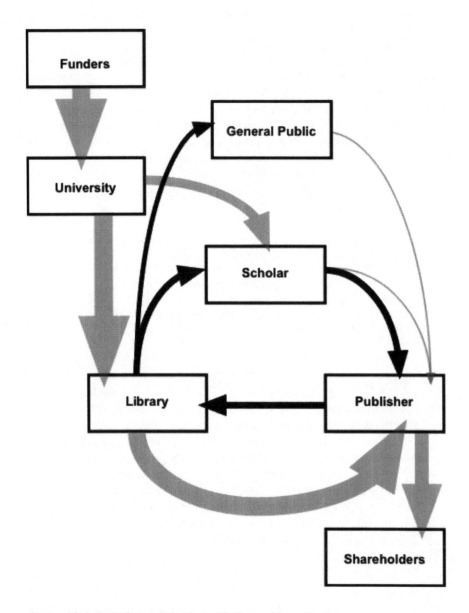

Cycle of Scholarly Communication with Money Flows Today.

University Licensing Project) effort conducted in the early 1990s. The project offered desktop access to bitmapped page images of roughly 45 Elsevier
journals to faculty at a select number of institutions. At the time this was a
significant technical undertaking. The Internet bandwidth at the time was

insufficient for delivery of bitmapped page files and so each participating university built its own distribution system.

The results of the project from a technical perspective were quite impressive and useful. As Clifford A. Lynch put it in his review of the project, "Not only have we gained experience in the development of systems to deliver bitmapped journal articles, but the development of these systems has increased immeasurably our understanding of infrastructure and support requirements for future large-scale production applications."[12] Elsevier's report on the project emphasizes its technical complexity, the difficulty and expense of delivering electronic versions of the journal content, and the need not only to deliver some journals to the desktop but to do so with a critical mass of content. The final conclusion from Elsevier is that "the universities and Elsevier Science have not resolved one critical issue, that of how to make the transition work economically."[13] Lynch wonders about the value of TULIP in assessing economic models, but ends up suggesting that the data might be useful to new journal pricing models and cites article-on-demand purchasing as one possible model.

Ironically, Lynch's suggestion for article-on-demand purchasing as a strategy, which from a library perspective would have been a great improvement, got the final outcome wrong. The opposite happened. One can only assume that through TULIP, Elsevier discovered what anyone familiar with the literature on journal use would have suspected—that the 80/20 rule and Bradford's Law of Scatter still applied in the digital world. A small number of the digital titles provided, as they did in the print world, a large percentage of use and a long tail of other titles provided little value. The publisher's response to this was to bundle their titles together so that the lesser-used titles would still have a market.

This created what has become known as the "Big Deal," where all or most of a publisher's journals were sold together at a "discounted" price. The "Big Deal" had early critics. One was Kenneth Frazier, who in a 2001 article in *D-Lib Magazine* wrote, "Academic library directors should not sign on to the Big Deal or any comprehensive licensing agreements with commercial publishers. . . . The current generation of library directors is engaged in a dangerous 'game' in which short-term institutional benefits are achieved at the long-term expense of the academic community."[14] As it turned out Frazier was right; the "Big Deal" turned out to be, as the publishers had hoped, addictive. Just as Frazier predicted, librarians lost the power to influence the quality of the journal literature through the selection process and the only choice they had was an all-or-nothing one.

"For Elsevier it is very hard to purchase specific journals—either you buy everything or you buy nothing," says Vincent Larivière, a professor at Université de Montréal. Larivière finds that his university uses 20 percent of the journals they subscribe to and 80 percent are never downloaded. He concludes, "The pricing scheme is such that if you subscribe to only 20 percent of the journals individually, it will cost you more money than taking everything. So people are stuck."[15]

The "Big Deal" was one strategy used by serials publishers, but the other was simply to keep pushing up prices. As measured by the *Bowker Annual* and its successor, the *Library and Book Trade Almanac*, the prices for U.S. periodicals, excluding Russian translations, rose 805.3% from an average price of $54.97 in 1984 to an average price of $497.63 in 2010. The average price of chemistry and physics journals rose 1,045.5% from $228.90 in 1984 to an average of $2,622.14 in 2010 and journals in medicine, in psychology, and in zoology increased at nearly the same rate. For a somewhat different group of titles, the average prices across all fields rose 25.2% in four years from $843.46 in 2010 to $1,051.73 in 2014.[16] The Allen Press survey of scholarly society journal prices documents the same trend for a mix of science, medical, and technology society journals. As Kodi Tillery states in reviewing this data, "Since 1989, prices for US society journals have increased 7.3% on average annually. During 2010–2011, average price increases hovered slightly above the historical average. However, the average increase in 2012 dropped, more than a full percentage point below the average, to less than 6%. . . . This was the first time since 1995 that average increases for US journals fell below 6%."[17] The 2013 Allen Press survey showed that the that society journal price increases routinely were at least 4% to 6% above increases in the Consumer Price Index over the past quarter century.[18]

The result of the serials prices increases, especially those of the large for-profit science and medical publishers, but also for journals published by scientific societies, was that library materials budgets were increasingly consumed by the need to purchase these serials and book purchasing suffered. The case for this is often made with the two charts below from the Association of Research Libraries—the first showing expenditure trends and the second showing serial and monograph costs from 1986 to 2012 in the first case and from 1986 to 2011 in the second.[19] In this 26-year period ARL libraries' total expenditures increased 188%. Total salaries increased 134% against an increase of 109% in the Consumer Price Index. Library materials expenditures were up 322% indicating a clear effort to maintain collections. Ongoing resource expenditures (the new name for serials) was up 456%; and one-time resource expenditures (the new name for monographs) was up 100%. From 1986 to 2011 the unit cost of monographs increased 99%. And for the number of monographs purchased, which had dropped by about 25% from the late 1980s to about 2000 and then slowly increased until in 2011, there had been a 10% increase from 1986. It is hard to know what the 456% increase in serials expenditures bought, largely because what was purchased in 1986 was subscriptions to individual titles and what is purchased now is a mix of individual subscriptions, databases of all sorts, and "Big Deal" and other packages.

To put this in context, between 1986 and 2012 the number of students served by ARL libraries increased 47% and the number of faculty increased by 28%. The picture here is a bit murky, but it is clear that ARL libraries worked hard to maintain materials budgets, though they probably lost some ground, especially if the new user base of students and faculty is considered. It is also clear that a significantly larger portion of the budget did go for serials. One final trend from the ARL statistics is worth noting: Per student interlibrary borrowing was up 153% over the 26 years. The bulk of this increase took place from the late 1980s through the early 2000s, when the increase stood at about 200%. Since about 2008 there has been a decline.

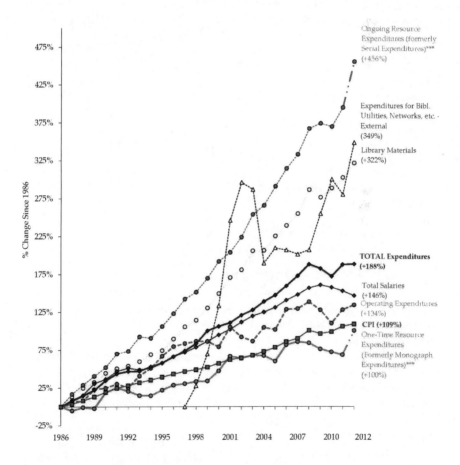

Expenditure Trends in ARL Libraries 1986–2012. Copyright Association of Research Libraries (ARL).

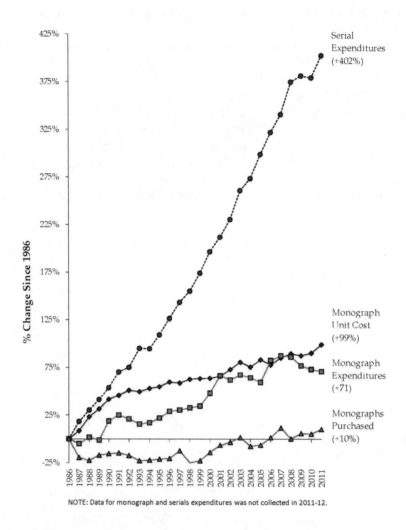

NOTE: Data for monograph and serials expenditures was not collected in 2011-12.

Monograph and Serial Costs in ARL Libraries 1986–2011. Copyright Association of Research Libraries (ARL).

This may suggest that interlibrary loan systems got better and had more capacity, which was likely the case, but it could also indicate that local resources could not be provided to meet many needs because of budget constraints and that interlibrary lending was the only recourse. The recent decline in interlibrary loan might be seen as an indication of increased availability of web-based resources and the growth of open access.

Data from the National Center for Education Statistics (NCES) tells a somewhat clouded, but similar story.[20] NCES has reasonably consistent data from 1992 through 2012. Definitions change over the period and the number of libraries included in the population changes and grows. Despite this variation in the data, several things are clear. Throughout, the period percentage of expenditures devoted to salaries and wages, information resources, and operating expenses (everything else) stay about the same. Salary and wage expenditures are about 50% of the total; information resources are a bit less than 40%, and operating expenses a bit more than 10%. There is a notable change inside information resources expenditures. In 1992, about 35% of information resources expenditures were used for books and similar materials, and about 55% for serials, with the remaining 10% used for a variety of other things such as interlibrary loans and preservation. In 2012, just more than 25% of the information resources expenditures were for books and similar materials and almost 70% was for serials. The 2012 information resources expenditures for the nearly 3,800 libraries surveyed was $2,790,039,494 so the shift in expenditures between books and serials arguably could represent 10% of this, or about $280 million. This is a sizeable change in expenditure patterns. As with the ARL data, there was a noted increase in the use of interlibrary loan. The number of items provided this way nearly doubled between 1992 and 2012 and went from 2.9% to 7.7% of general circulations in the period. As Robert Darnton, the librarian at Harvard, put it in 2010,

> Between 1986 and 2005, the prices for institutional subscriptions to journals rose 302 percent, while the consumer price index went up by 68 percent. Faced with this disparity, libraries have had to adjust the proportions of their acquisitions budgets. As a rule, they used to spend about half of their funds on serials and half on monographs. By 2000 many libraries were spending three quarters of their budget on serials. Some had nearly stopped buying monographs altogether or had eliminated them in certain fields. [21]

The story told above is often used to explain the difficulties encountered by university presses. It is clear that academic library monograph purchasing declined, but it is less clear how this trend impacted university presses. Elisabeth A. Jones and Paul N. Courant argue, I believe convincingly, that the data suggest this is not the reason for the problems that university presses currently face. They show that between 1975 and 2010 purchases of university press books, especially by large academic libraries and despite declines in recent years, actually increased. As they say, "Yes, serials prices have risen astronomically. Yes, overall monographic purchasing has been anemic or in decline over the past few decades. But not all libraries are equal, and neither are all presses. . . . It is equally important to recognize the special status of university press monographs in academia when comparing their treatment by academic libraries." [22]

So in the past 25 to 30 years we have seen scholarly journal prices increase at rates well above the Consumer Price Index, and in excess of nearly everything else as well, including health care. Academic libraries worked hard to keep up with these increases and, given the financial pressures their institutions faced, they did reasonably well. But in the end the relentless price increases compounding year after year were too much. Significant funding was moved from books to journals and journals were cut, although because of the changing nature of what a journal is and how it is packaged and sold, it is hard to determine the extent of the cuts. Interlibrary loan use increased, at least in part as a way to provide users with content that libraries could not afford to provide as part of local collections. The transition from print to digital turned out to be a lost opportunity and was not a means of making content cheaper for libraries and more available for library users.

This is a good story and there is much evidence to support it, but as Paula Gantz writing in the *Professional/Scholarly Publishing Bulletin* argues, the increase in journal pricing that is generally reported misrepresents what is actually happening. She says, "Yet using list prices of print subscriptions to calculate the real increase in serials expenditures is a misleading and inaccurate method for tracking how libraries are spending their serials budgets and fails to recognize the increased value they are receiving from the print-to-digital transition."[23] Gantz reworks the ARL data and asserts that journal prices on average rose only from $138.24 in 1990 to an average of $150.78 in 2010. She says, "Because of both content growth and the expansion in the number of journals included in an average institutional licensing agreement, the effective price of an average journal in 2010 is only 9% higher than in 1990."[24] She goes on to cite a 2010 Association of American Publishers survey that estimated that the cost per article download globally was $2.63 and that across the 5,794 journals in the study there were 1.1 billion downloads in that year.

So what is happening here? Should we take the ARL, *Library and Book Trade Almanac,* and Allen Press data at face value, or does Gantz have a point? Actually, two things happened during the period between 1990 and 2010 as journals moved from print to digital. One was bad for libraries and one was good. The first is what the ARL, *Library and Book Trade Almanac,* and Allen Press data show: journal price increases were extreme. But while the trend carried across all titles and all disciplines to some extent, where it mattered was for commercially published journals in science, medicine, and technology—whether subscribed to individually or as part of a "Big Deal." These increases were real and mattered because they involved very large amounts of money—often in excess of $1 million per "deal" per university. This was only one part of the journal content purchased by libraries, but it consumed a large and growing portion of most libraries' materials budgets.

The other thing that was happening was a huge increase in the number of titles that became available to libraries as the result of the aggregation of journal content by EBSCO, Gale, ProQuest, JSTOR, MUSE, and others.

These aggregations often include thousands of titles. On a per title basis the journals they included were quite inexpensive. As a result, the total number of titles available in most academic libraries increased substantially. In addition, these aggregations were often purchased by consortiums and in some cases were subsidized by states. This meant that large numbers of titles became available at modest prices. This explains how Gantz can come to the conclusion she does. The aggregate databases of articles provide a rich and easy-to-use resource that often is more than adequate for the work of undergraduates in many fields, but the titles in the aggregates do not include the expensive science, medicine, and technology titles that have increased in price so much that they stress nearly all library budgets. The publishers of these titles do not allow them to be included. Why would they?

So, we have two stories and they are both true. The advent of large aggregations of digital content vesting increased the number of journals available in most academic libraries to the benefit primarily of undergraduates. At the same time, the prices of journals that support science, medicine, and technology increased well beyond inflation and stressed library budgets everywhere. It was the best of times, and it was the worst of times.

NOTES

1. Robert Darnton, as quoted in Craig Lambert, "The 'Wild West' of Academic Publishing: The Troubled Present and Promising Future of Scholarly Communication," *Harvard Magazine* 117, no. 3 (January–February 2015): 56–60, http://harvardmagazine.com/2015/01/the-wild-west-of-academic-publishing.

2. Jill Lepore, "The New Economy of Letters," *Chronicle of Higher Education: The Chronicle Review*, September 3. 2013, http://chronicle.com/article/The-New-Economy-of-Letters/141291/.

3. See particularly chapter 6, "The Science Citation Index and Some of Its Consequences," in Jean-Claude Guédon, *In Oldenburg's Long Shadow: Librarians, Research Scientists, Publishers, and the Control of Scientific Publishing* (Washington, DC: Association of Research Libraries, 2001), 19–22, http://www.arl.org/storage/documents/publications/in-oldenburgs-long-shadow.pdf.

4. Guédon, *In Oldenburg's Long Shadow*, 21.

5. Vincent Larivière, Stefanie Haustein, and Philippe Mongeon, "The Oligopoly of Academic Publishers in the Digital Era," *PLOS ONE* 10 no. 6 (June 10, 2015) e0127502, doi:10.1371/journal.pone.0127502, http://journals.plos.org/plosone/article?id=10.1371/journal.pone.0127502.

6. Carol Tenopir et al., "Scholarly Article Seeking, Reading, and Use: A Continuing Evolution from Print to Electronic in the Sciences and Social Sciences," *Learned Publishing* 28, no. 2 (April 2015): 98.

7. Jason Schmidt, "Academic Journals: The Most Profitable Obsolete Technology in History," *Huffington Post: HuffPost Education: The Blog*, December 29, 2014, http://www.huffingtonpost.com/jason-schmitt/academic-journals-the-mos_1_b_6368204.html.

8. Larivière, Haustein, and Mongeon, "The Oligopoly of Academic Publishers in the Digital Era."

9. Robert Darnton, "The Library: Three Jeremiads" *New York Review of Books,* December 23, 2010, http://www.nybooks.com/articles/archives/2010/dec/23/library-three-jeremiads/.

10. "Serials 'crisis' Brings Out the Best in Speakers," *American Libraries* 19, no. 8 (September 1988): 701.

11. Judy Quinn and Michael Rogers, "ARL Reports on Serials Crisis," *Library Journal* 116, no. 7 (April 15, 1991): 16.

12. Clifford A. Lynch, "The TULIP Project: Context, History, and Perspective," *Library Hi Tech* 13, no. 4 (1995): 21–22.

13. Marthyn Borghuis, *TULIP Final Report* (New York: Elsevier Science, 1996), 85. Kenneth Frazier, "The Librarians' Dilemma: Contemplating the Costs of the 'Big Deal,'" *D-Lib Magazine* 7, no. 3 (March 2001), http://www.dlib.org/dlib/march01/frazier/03frazier.html.

14. Ibid.

15. Schmidt, "Academic Journals."

16. Dave Bogart, ed., *Library and Book Trade Almanac. Formerly the Bowker Annual*, 56th ed. (Medford, NJ: Information Today, 2011), 263; and Dave Bogart, ed. *Library and Book Trade Almanac. Formerly the Bowker Annual*, 59th ed. (Medford, NJ: Information Today, 2014), 426–27.

17. Kodi Tillery, "2012 Study of Subscription Prices for Scholarly Society Journals: Society Journal Pricing Trends and Industry Overview," *Allen Press*, 2012, http://allenpress.com/system/files/pdfs/library/2012_AP_JPS.pdf.

18. Danielle Jurski, "2013 Study of Subscription Prices for Scholarly Society Journals: Society Journal Pricing Trends and Industry Overview," *Allen Press*, 2013, http://allenpress.com/system/files/pdfs/library/2013_AP_JPS.pdf.

19. See "Statistical Trends," Association of Research Libraries, http://www.arl.org/focusareas/statistics-assessment/statistical-trends.

20. "Library Statistics Program: Academic Libraries," National Center for Education Statistics, accessed May 16, 2015, http://nces.ed.gov/pubsearch/getpubcats.asp?sid=041#050.

21. Darnton, "The Library: Three Jeremiads."

22. Elisabeth A. Jones and Paul N. Courant, "Monographic Purchasing Trends in Academic Libraries: Did the 'Serials Crisis' Really Destroy the University Press?," *Journal of Scholarly Publishing* 46, no. 1 (October 2014): 67–68, doi:10.1353/scp.2014.0033, https://muse.jhu.edu/login?auth=0&type=summary&url=/journals/journal_of_scholarly_publishing/v046/46.1.jones.pdf.

23. Paula Gantz, "Digital Licenses Replace Print Prices as Accurate Reflection of Real Journal Costs," *Professional/Scholarly Publishing Bulletin* 11, no. 3 (Summer/Fall 2012): 1, http://publishers.org/sites/default/files/uploads/PSP/summer-fall_2012.pdf.

24. Ibid., 3.

Force Six

Demographics

> When library deans and directors make public statements, they invariably acknowledge staff as the library's most important asset. It seems that this platitude is becoming increasingly relevant as academic and research libraries make the transition from collections-centered to services-centered organizations. The staff line is the largest budget line in most library budgets, and staff will determine the success of the 21st-century library. Now is the time to consider the ways in which we think about new and better ways of recruiting, training, and retaining staff.—Deanna Marcum[1]

Academic libraries spend most of their money on two things, people and materials. In the last chapter we looked at the materials side. In this chapter we look at the people side. The staffing of academic libraries will be different a decade from now from what it is today, but the changes will not be particularly dramatic and they will likely follow already well-established trends. There will be several challenges, but for those who are paying attention they should be manageable. I wrote about the staffing of academic libraries in a chapter for the 2010 book *The Expert Library*.[2] I believe the trends I identified then can be expected to continue. If anything, it appears that the 2008 recession accelerated what was already under way. There are two critical facts: The first is the changing mix of the academic library workforce. The second is the aging of academic librarians.

To understand the changing mix of the academic library workforce it is best to begin with the data reported by the National Center for Education Statistics (NCES).[3] Prior to 1998 NCES combined the counts of librarians and other professionals, so in this analysis we will start with 1998 as the base year and go through 2012, the latest available data. There are a number of striking, but not surprising, trends. These trends are clear in the following chart.

Over the 14-year period between 1998 and 2012 the total number of people employed in academic libraries in the United States declined by 10,688 positions or 11.1% from 96,439 to 85,751. The number of librarians employed in academic libraries increased 7.2% from 24,815 to 26,606. Other professional staff increased 49.6% from a low base of 5,225 to 7,817. One way to look at these figures is that even though the number of librarians increased, librarians as a percent of all library professionals decreased from 82.6% in 1998 to 77.3% in 2012. The number of other paid staff (NCES's term for clerical staff) declined 19.0% in the period—from 38,026 to 30,819—and the number of FTE (full-time equivalent) student assistants declined 27.7% from 28,373 to 20,509. If we look at the ratio of librarians and other professionals to other paid employees and student assistants, in 1998 it was 1 to 2.2 in 2012 it was 1 to 1.5. The recession of 2008 slowed the increase in librarians and other professionals slightly, but it notably accelerated the decrease of other paid staff and student assistants.

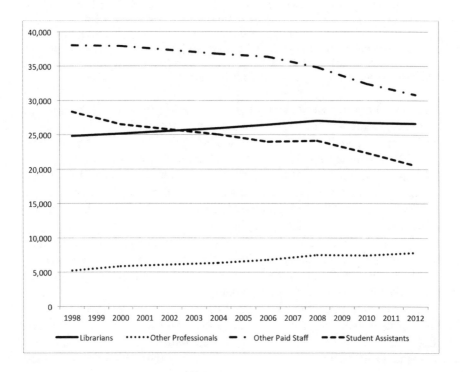

Academic Library Workforce 1998–2012.

There has been an obvious change in the nature of academic library work during this period: paper collections declined and thus much of clerical work to manage them is no longer required. Think about the savings, as the use of paper has declined, from not checking-in and binding periodicals, or the savings from not having to reshelve books, or (more significantly) periodicals. The movement from paper to digital content explains the decline in other paid staff and student assistants. The increase in other professionals probably indicates an increase in the number of technical and computer staff in libraries, but could include other professionals in fields such as development and human resources. It may also reflect an upgrading of some clerical staff as their positions grow to include more complex tasks that were once performed by librarians. If we do simple straight-line extrapolations and carry current trends forward to 2025, we can see the results in the following chart.

Assuming the trends hold, there will be a total of not quite 76,000 academic library positions in the United States in 2025, a decline of 11.6% from the number in 2012. The mix of staff will be quite different. Librarians and other professional staff will make up just more than half of the staff, with a

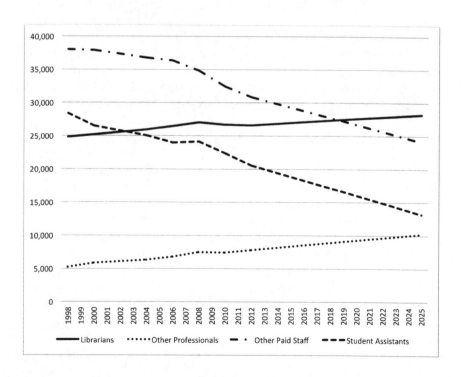

Academic Library Workforce 1998–2025.

ratio of professional to other staff of approximately 1 to 1. The number of librarians will have increased about 6% and the number of other professionals about 30%. This estimate for the increase in the number of academic librarians is consistent with the projections in the *Occupational Outlook Handbook* that projects a 7.4% increase in the number of librarians of all types between 2012 and 2022.[4] Librarians will make up about 73% of professional positions, down from 77.3% in 2012. There will likely be more librarian positions in 2025 than now, but librarians may feel pressured by the easily observable increase in non-librarian professionals. This may especially be the case where librarians have faculty status and the line between librarians and other professional staff is more clearly drawn. Other paid staff and student assistants will continue to decline by about 22% and 36% respectively. The total decline in such positions could be as high as 15,000 over the 13-year period.

The second significant demographic trend is the aging of academic librarians. Stanley J. Wilder has been studying and writing about the demographics of academic librarians for 20 years, though to be precise he is generally looking at librarians working in Association of Research Libraries (ARL) libraries. In his first study in 1995, he noted the aging of the library workforce. As he put it then, "As a group, librarians, including those who work in Association of Research Libraries (ARL) member libraries, are older than members of most comparable professions, and the group is getting older."[5] He documented that at the time the percentage of ARL librarians under 34 were a third of the comparable professions and the percentage over 45 was nearly 75% higher. The ARL population was also aging quickly. Between 1990 and 1994 the ARL librarian population over 45 increased from 48% to 58%.[6]

In Wilder's 2003 study and in a 2012 presentation he continues his analysis.[7] By 2000 63% of librarians were 45 or over, a high percentage compared to comparable professions. This led Wilder to state that "librarianship is indeed unusually old."[8] Basically what Wilder documents is the pig in the python of the Baby Boom generation as it works its way through the academic library workforce. This is a bit more complicated than it might seem on the surface. Not only is there an aging workforce of Baby Boomers working their way from young professionals through to their retirement. As documented in Wilder's 2003 study, MLS graduates are older than they were 20 years earlier.[9] Wilder's 2012 presentation documents a decline in the number of new hires at ARL libraries as a percentage of the librarian population from 14% in 2000 to about 11% in 2010.[10] This is likely the result of hiring constraints during the recession.

Another way to look at the demographics of librarians over the past 25 years is to look at how the generations worked their way through the profession. These are the standard definitions of the generations: the GI Generation (born before 1927), the Silent Generation (born 1927 to 1945), the Baby Boom Generation (born 1946–1964), Generation X (born 1965–1980), and the Millennium Generation (born 1981–2000). If we rework the ARL data presented by Wilder and extrapolate it forward to 2015, we get the next graph.[11]

In 1986 the Silent Generation represented about 50% of the librarians in the workforce. As the Silent Generation retired Baby Boomers grew as a proportion of the workforce and by 1994 they represented more than 60% of the library workforce. The Baby Boomers maintained this dominant portion of the library workforce until 2010 when they began retiring, but even then they were only a bit below 60% of the workforce. By comparison, Gen X librarians had only reached just more than 30% of the library workforce in 2010 when the first Millennium librarians arrived. Even though the Gen X generation has three fewer years than the Baby Boom generation, this is a significant disparity.

There will be several challenges in managing how the Baby Boom generation exits the library workforce. To understand this, it is important to begin with a look at the characteristics of this generation. They began their careers when catalogs had cards and when using them to manage large paper collections and finding information required expert help. Those days are long gone,

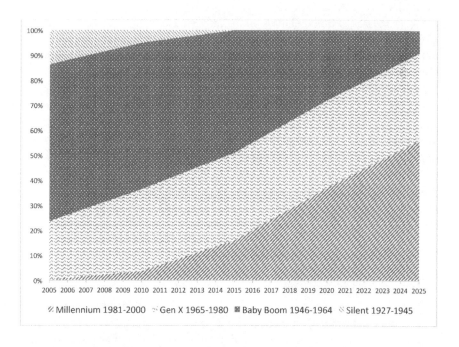

Academic Librarians by Generation (ARL Data).

and while many Baby Boomer librarians have continued to develop the skills and expertise required to keep pace, this gets harder as retirement approaches and they need to learn not simply new techniques, but rather new roles and new functional specialties. This will make it difficult for these librarians to make the same contributions they once did. They are likely to possess a deep understanding of the institutions they serve and are likely to have rich relationships across the campus, but at some point this may not compensate for a lack of the functional expertise that the library requires.

A 2013 Gallup poll looked at when Baby Boomers expected to retire. It found that "nearly half (49%) of boomers still working say they don't expect to retire until they are 66 or older, including one in 10 who predict they will never retire."[12] A part of this is the result of financial insecurity that came with the 2008 recession and the Baby Boomers' general disinclination to save as much for retirement as was prudent. It is also the result of this generation's "live to work" attitude. The analysis in the Gallup article reporting the poll concluded, "Whether by choice or necessity, baby boomers will remain a sizable proportion of the workforce in the years ahead . . . . As they continue to age and work, it is important that their organizations build workplaces with outstanding managers who leverage the experiences of older workers by positioning them to do what they do best—listening to their insights and opinions, and continuing to develop their talents into strengths."[13]

A year later another Gallup study indicated that this concern might be somewhat overstated. As it reported, "Despite some expectations that baby boomers will defy the usual working patterns of aging Americans and stay in the workforce longer than those who came before them, the data do not appear to support that expectation. Boomers aged 65 to 68 are retiring at about the same rate as those who were in that age range a few years ago. By age 68, only about a third of boomers are still in the workforce."[14] In 2015 a TIAA-CREF Institute survey found that only 35% of tenured faculty over 50 expect to retire at the "normal" age. In this survey "normal" was defined as 67. Of those who said they expected to continue working, 16% said they would prefer to retire, but could not, most often for financial reasons. The remaining 49% said they would like and expected to work past the normal retirement age. In this final group 94% said they enjoyed and were fulfilled by their work, and 84% said they remained effective faculty members.[15] For library managers the reluctance of Baby Boomers to retire will be an important challenge and one that will persist, as the youngest Baby Boomers will not reach 65 until 2029.

Maintaining the generational diversity of a library will be important and will take a determined strategy. The easiest strategy is to promote from within and hire new positions at the entry level. This provides leadership opportunities for more experience—most likely for Baby Boomer or Gen X librarians—and provides, with entry-level positions, the opportunity to hire new graduates who will most likely be of the Gen-X or Millennium generations. This strategy requires a clear focus on management and leadership development for existing staff and depends on having staff willing and able to step into leadership positions, but it will provide the opportunity to bring staff with the required new skills and expertise into the organization.

Keeping Baby Boomer librarians engaged and productive as they approach the end of their careers will be one challenge. The second will be building a staff to replace them when they do retire. The first challenge is that, as we can see in the chart above, there are not nearly as many Gen Xers as there are Boomers who will need to be replaced. This will mean that as Boomers retire, Millennials will have to move into those positions. Making sure they are ready will be important.

A recent Deloitte study on Millennials has two clear messages that need to be heeded. The first is that Millennials value organizations that care about them and are going to make an impact in the world. As the report says,

> Millennials believe that an organization's treatment of its employees is the most important consideration when deciding if it is a leader. They then consider its:
>
> - Overall impact on society;
> - Financial performance;
> - Record for creating innovative products or services; and
> - Whether it has a well-defined and meaningful purpose to which it is true. [16]

Those Millennials who were relatively high users of social networking, what Deloitte calls "super-connected Millennials," were even more focused on purpose.

The second message is that many Millennials do not feel the organizations they work in are making "full use" of the skills they currently have to offer. [17] For library administrators looking to get Millennials ready, the Deloitte report makes it clear that you need to care about and develop opportunities for Millennials, but you also need to provide opportunities for them to use their skills to contribute. If a library fails to do so and Millennials are forced to twiddle their thumbs waiting around for the Baby Boomers to finally get out of the way, the good young workers—the ones you are counting on to take over when you go—will move somewhere else. They will have opportunities and your organization had better be one that meets their needs and fulfills their expectations.

In addition, a variety of commentators have expressed skepticism about the ability of library school to produce the required number of graduates with the required skills. A 2004 American Library Association study of when librarians will retire, which reflect the Baby Boomers' exiting the labor force and the replacement rates based on the number of MLS graduates, projects a large deficit beginning in 2015 and extending to at least 2020.[18] James L. Mullins surveyed ARL directors and found that "there was a general consensus among the focus group [members] that the qualifications and preparation of the graduates of the LIS programs were uneven. Additionally, there were some particularly strong negative comments about the quality of several of the distance education programs offered by LIS providers, in particular those that had no residency requirement."[19] Deanna Marcum, once a library school dean herself, puts the problem clearly in a 2015 Ithaka S+R issue brief:

> The enormous changes occurring in research libraries are not matched by the pace of change in library program curricula. Required courses have often failed to keep up with changing practices and needs, but practitioner-led and distance learning courses, both of which can help, too often lack for modern pedagogies. Even though the norm among university libraries is to require applicants for their positions to hold a master's degree in library and information sciences, we have the unenviable logical dilemma of disrespecting the professional schools that produce our colleagues and while also requiring that new professionals must have the same training we received.[20]

In 2011–12 there were 7,441 masters degrees in library science conferred in the United State according to the National Center for Educational Statistics.[21] The *Library Journal* placement data for 2012 library school graduates puts the number of new MLS graduates at 6,184. Of those who responded to the survey and indicated what type of library they were employed at, 34.5% indicated they were employed in a college or university library.[22]

There has been a notable change in the mix of new library positions over the past 20 years as documented by Wilder. The number of catalog positions dropped dramatically beginning in the early 1990s and the number of reference positions dropped beginning in 2000. Throughout the period, the number of functional specialist positions, those involving expertise in web design, digital preservation, data management, assessment, or scholarly communication increased from about 10% in 1990 to more than 35% in 2010.[23]

A final aspect of library demographics that needs to be considered is the difficulty academic librarianship has had in attracting librarians from ethnic minorities. In 2013, the percentage of the United States population that was non-Hispanic white was 62.6%, African Americans represented 13.2%, Asians 5.3%, and Hispanics or Latinos 17.1%.[24] The *Chronicle of Higher Education* documents that the freshmen entering school in 2013 were 68.3% white, 11.9% African American, 11.7% Asian, and 15.0% Hispanic or Latino.[25] The *Chronicle's Almanac of Higher Education 2014* reports the race of faculty for 2011. Across all institutions 73.8% were white, 6.9% were African American, 6.2% were Asian, and 4.3% were Hispanic.[26] In contrast, the percentage of librarians in U.S. ARL libraries were 4.3% African

American, 7.0% Asian, 2.8% Hispanic, and 85.5% white.[27] These numbers are shown in the following chart.

It is quite clear that academic librarians are a significantly less diverse group than the U.S. population as a whole or than students entering colleges and universities, and they are even less diverse than the faculty. The current state, however, is actually an improvement from the past. Wilder reports that in 1980, 88.6% of ARL librarians were white. In 1990 the figure was 89.2%

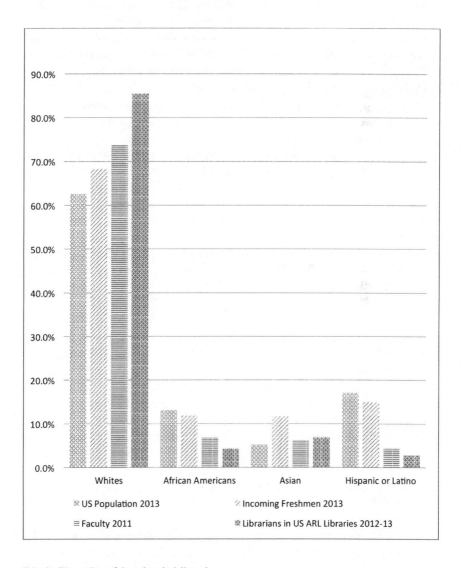

Ethnic Diversity of Academic Librarians.

and in 2000 it was 88.3%, so the current 85.5% is an improvement. [28] However, this disparity between what library users look like and what librarians look like will continue to be a problem. This is especially the case as we can expect the student population to become increasingly diverse.

We can expect these demographic realities to create the following challenges for academic libraries:

- The number of clerical staff will continue to decline: this will especially be the case in technical services and collection management as libraries continue to reduce their paper collections. As a result, collections and collection building in general will become a less significant part of what libraries do. If a library is lucky, it will be able to manage these reductions through attrition rather than reduction in force, but either way it will be a challenge to keep the morale of clerical staff from declining.
- The decline in clerical staff will be matched by a decline in the number of student assistants, which will reduce student employment opportunities through one of the campus's traditionally large student employers. It is generally accepted that on campus, work has a positive impact on student success and so this loss of student employment will be unfortunate. The alternative is to keep the student assistant positions at the cost of clerical positions, but this will lead to worsening clerical staff morale and on many campuses will not be allowable because of campus policy or union contracts.
- The number of librarians will remain about the same or increase slightly. But there will be fewer generalist positions and an increasing need for librarians with specific functional expertise in areas like data management, scholarly communications, digital humanities, visualization, geographic information system, assessment, and instructional design. It is not an accident that all of these areas of expertise have a technology component. Collection development and general reference work will a declining portion of the responsibilities of most librarians. In many cases instruction will be focused on creating digital educational resources—web pages and tutorials. A larger proportion of the work of librarians will be focused on faculty and student research—capturing it, providing access to it, and preserving it. Changing the work patterns of older librarians to meet these needs will require a plan and investments in professional development.

Librarians may perceive the increase in non-librarian professional positions as a threat. This may especially be the case if there is a shortage of qualified librarians. The functional specialist positions that are growing to dominate library hiring can often be filled with capable candidates with credentials other than an MLS. A copyright lawyer might make a good scholarly communications librarian and an instructional technologist could be quite qualified to create information-literacy tutorials. An informatics or computer science degree holder might easily have the credentials to be a user experience librarian. This is what James G. Neal has called the "feral" librarian, meaning that these non-MLS professionals were raised without the standard library training. They were, as Neal puts it "raised by wolves."[29]

While hiring the talent required without regard for whether or not the person has the MLS might be a good, or at least necessary, strategy, it will raise the question of whether the MLS is what defines a librarian. Is a librarian a professional working in a library or is a librarian a person with a library degree? Neal is clear that he believes it is the organizational affiliation that is most important. As he says, after noting the long struggle librarianship has had defining the basis for its professional status, "This ambiguity about the professional characteristics of librarianship suggests that educational preparation for the field does not have an impact on socialization into the field comparable to other professions."[30]

In my view, libraries where librarians have faculty status will probably have a more difficult time managing an influx of non-MLS professionals, especially if they fill positions that were traditionally held by librarians with the MLS credential. The class distinction that is established with faculty status may be hard to understand or justify if non-MLS professionals fill these positions. Librarians will look increasingly like other non-teaching professional staff and less like faculty. To the extent that this makes MLS librarians defensive it may also create problems in developing productive working relationships across the organization. Neal notes that, "if LIS programs don't deliver cultural authority to their graduates, then the various strains of professionals now entering academic libraries may integrate more consistently and effectively."[31] Neal is arguing that the focus for socialization and professional identity should be the organization, the library, not the educational credentials a person brings to the position. I agree, but faculty status can bring important recognition and respect across campus and it will be difficult for many institutions to abandon.

Interestingly, the recently approved "Joint Statement on Faculty Status for College and University Librarians" issued in January 2013 by the Joint Committee on College Library Problems makes no mention of the MLS as a required credential to be a librarian. It argues for faculty status, but states that, as is the case with faculty in other departments, librarians should be responsible for establishing promotion and tenure, and one assumes, appointment requirements.[32] This might provide an out if some positions are defined as "librarian" even if credentials other than the MLS are deemed appropriate. This is already often done with archives positions and candidates with history degrees, and could be expanded to include others with appropriate alternative educational backgrounds. This would allow for an influx of feral librarians while still maintaining faculty status.

While many librarians will have functional expertise, nearly all will have as a primary responsibility a liaison relationship with an academic constituency. In this role subject expertise will be of value, particularly at research-oriented campuses. For larger libraries, creating a mix of positions with functional and subject expertise may not prove that difficult, but for smaller libraries, with fewer librarian positions to work with, building a staff with the full range of skills and expertise they require may prove to be more challenging than it has been in the past.

The changing demographics of academic libraries will create a series of challenges: First, maintaining the morale of clerical staff in the light of a declining number of positions. Second, developing a professional staff, both those with MLS degrees and those without, with the full range of skills and expertise required and with generational and ethnic diversity. These challenges can be managed, but doing so will require focus, commitment, and a clear organizational strategy. Libraries that commit to building and developing a strong workforce will have the human resources they need to tackle the problems they face. Those that do not make the effort to care for this fundamental resource will find themselves, in a world where the competition for talent will be fierce, without the capacities they require and they will thus have little opportunity to be successful.

NOTES

1. Deanna Marcum, *Talent Management for Academic Libraries* (New York: Ithaka S+R, September 1 2015), 2, http://www.sr.ithaka.org/publications/talent-management-for-academic-libraries/.

2. David W. Lewis, "Academic Library Staffing a Decade from Now," in *The Expert Library: Staffing, Sustaining, and Advancing the Academic Library in the 21st Century*, ed. Scott Walter and Karen Williams (Chicago: Association of College and Research Libraries, 2010), 1–29.

3. The National Center for Education Statistics (NCES) reports academic library statistics every two years (though they missed 2002). These reports can be found in the center's Library Statistics Program section at http://nces.ed.gov/surveys/libraries/.

4. "Librarians," Bureau of Labor Statistics: Occupational Outlook Handbook, http://www.bls.gov/ooh/education-training-and-library/librarians.htm#tab-6.

5. Stanley J. Wilder, *The Age Demographics of Academic Librarians: A Profession Apart: A Report Based on Data from the ARL Annual Salary Survey* (Washington, DC: Association of Research Libraries, 1995), viii.

6. Ibid.

7. Stanley J. Wilder, *Demographic Change in Academic Librarianship* (Washington, DC: Association of Research Libraries, 2003); and Stanley J. Wilder, "The Academic Library Workforce in Transition: New Results from the 2010 ARL Demographic Data" (presentation slides, ARL-ACRL Human Resources Symposium, Washington, DC, November 16, 2012), http://www.arl.org/focus-areas/copyright-ip/fair-use/code-of-best-practices/1071-the-academic-library-workforce-in-transition-new-results-from-the-2010-arl-demographic-data#.VAhwNkvj_74.

8. Wilder, *Demographic Change in Academic Librarianship*, xiv.

9. Ibid., 17.

10. Wilder, "The Academic Library Workforce in Transition" slide 7.

11. Data from Wilder, "The Academic Library Workforce in Transition," provided to the author. It should be noted that the conversion of the figures to generations is inexact and while the general conclusions drawn are appropriate, the details should be viewed as approximate.

12. Jim Harter and Sangeeta Agrawal, "Many Baby Boomers Reluctant to Retire," Gallup, January 20, 2014, http://www.gallup.com/poll/166952/baby-boomers-reluctant-retire.aspx.

13. Ibid.

14. Frank Newport, "Only a Third of the Oldest Baby Boomers in U.S. Still Working," Gallup, January 26, 2015, http://www.gallup.com/poll/181292/third-oldest-baby-boomers-working.aspx.

15. Paul J. Yakoboski, "Understanding the Faculty Retirement (Non)Decision: Results from the Faculty Career and Retirement Survey," TIAA-CREF Institute: Trends and Issues, June 2015, https://www.tiaa-crefinstitute.org/public/pdf/understanding-the-faculty-retirement-non-decision.pdf.

16. Deloitte, "Mind the Gaps: The 2015 Deloitte Millennial Survey: Executive Summary," Deloitte, 2015, 4, accessed January 26, 2016, http://www2.deloitte.com/content/dam/Deloitte/global/Documents/About-Deloitte/gx-wef-2015-millennial-survey-executivesummary.pdf.

17. Ibid., 8.

18. Denise M. Davis, "Library Retirements: What We Can Expect," *American Libraries* 36 no. 8 (September 2005): 16, http://www.ala.org/research/sites/ala.org.research/files/content/librarystaffstats/recruitment/lisgradspositionsandretirements_rev1.pdf.

19. James L. Mullins, "Are MLS Graduates Being Prepared for the Changing and Emerging Roles That Librarians Must Now Assume within Research Libraries?," *Journal of Library Administration* 52 no. 1 (2012), doi:10.1080/01930826.2011.629966.

20. Deanna Marcum, *Educating the Research Librarian: Are We Falling Short?* (New York: Ithaka S+R, May 7, 2015), 4–5, http://www.sr.ithaka.org/wp-content/mig/files/SR_Issue_Brief_Educating_the_Research_Librarian050715.pdf.

21. "Table 318.30. Bachelor's, master's, and doctor's degrees conferred by postsecondary institutions, by sex of student and discipline division: 2011–12," National Center for Educational Statistics: *Digest of Educational Statistics*, July 2013, http://nces.ed.gov/programs/digest/d13/tables/dt13_318.30.asp.

22. Stephanie L. Maatta, "Placements & Salaries 2013: Explore All the Data," *Library Journal*, October 17, 2013, http://lj.libraryjournal.com/2013/10/placements-and-salaries/2013-survey/explore-all-the-data-2013/#_.

23. Wilder, "The Academic Library Workforce in Transition," slide 9.

24. "QuickFacts: United States," United States Census Bureau: State & County QuickFacts, http://quickfacts.census.gov/qfd/states/00000.html.

25. "A Profile of Freshmen at 4-Year Colleges, Fall 2013," *Chronicle of Higher Education*, August 18, 2014, http://chronicle.com/article/A-Profile-of-Freshmen-at/147335?cid=megamenu.

26. "Race and Ethnicity of College Administrators, Faculty, and Staff, Fall 2011," *Chronicle of Higher Education: Almanac of Higher Education 2014*, August 18, 2014, http://chronicle.com/article/RaceEthnicity-of-College/148027/.

27. Shaneka Morris and Martha Kyrillidou, "Minority Representation in US ARL University Libraries as of 2012–2013: Taking a Closer Look at the Evidence," Association of Research Libraries: *ARL News*, September 10, 2014, http://libraryassessment.org/bm~doc/24morrisposter.pdf.

28. Wilder, *Demographic Change in Academic Librarianship*, 34.

29. James G. Neal, "Raised by Wolves: Integrating the New Generation of Feral Professionals into the Academic Library," *Library Journal* 131 no. 3 (February 15, 2006): 42–44, http://lj.libraryjournal.com/2006/02/academic-libraries/raised-by-wolves/.

30. Ibid., 42.

31. Ibid., 43.

32. "Joint Statement on Faculty Status of College and University Librarians," American Library Association: Association of College and Research Libraries, January 2013, http://www.ala.org/acrl/standards/jointstatementfaculty. This statement was prepared by the Joint Committee on College Library Problems, a national committee representing the Association of

College and Research Libraries; the Association of American Colleges (now the Association of American Colleges and Universities); and the American Association of University Professors.

Interlude

A Conjecture on the Nature of Digital Information

Doctorow's Third Law: Information Doesn't Want to Be Free, People Do.—
Cory Doctorow [1]

In the past six chapters we have looked at the forces that academic libraries are confronting. We are living in a world of disruption and change to our core technologies and in an economic and demographic environment that is challenging on a good day. It is time for a break. While there are many day-to-day stresses and it is often hard to see that the future is likely to be bright, I want to propose that in the end the forces that are working on us will lead to a better place. My conjecture is that digital information works best in ways that will serve our interests. I take hope from this.

The term "conjecture" is used here to mean an unproven proposition that appears to be correct. Conjectures can be useful in encouraging consideration of problems and in pointing toward possible solutions or ways of understanding.

I want to propose a conjecture on the nature of digital information. My hope is that it advances how we think about digital documents and information. It is my view that the conjecture is generally correct and that it should lead us to think about and develop information products differently than we did when information was based on the scarcity of printing. The medium matters and matters in ways that are not always expected or appreciated. As Clay Shirky puts it, "When we change the way we communicate, we change society."[2]

The Conjecture

1. When information is digital it is non-rival and can be reproduced and distributed at close to zero marginal cost.
2. When information is non-rival and can be reproduced and distributed at close to zero marginal cost, people will want it to be open.
3. When information is open it will encourage social production.

The Argument

Proposition 1: When information is digital it is non-rival and can be reproduced and distributed at close to zero marginal cost.

One of the ways economists think about goods is to categorize them as either rival or non-rival. A rival good can only be used or consumed by a single person at any given time. In contrast, a non-rival good can be used or consumed by one person without preventing the simultaneous use or consumption by others.[3] A tangible good—that is, a good made of atoms—is a rival good, as are many services that take place in the real world such as a visit to the doctor or a trip on an airplane. Some goods like the use of a park or road are non-rival, but only up to the point of the capacity of that good. Information is, on the other hand, a fully non-rival good. One person's having it does not preclude its use by another. As Thomas Jefferson famously said, "He who receives an idea from me, receives instruction himself without lessening mine; as he who lights his taper at mine, receives light without darkening me."[4]

In the past, while information itself was a non-rival good, the means of reproducing and distributing that information—printed items such as books and newspapers—were not. Books and newspapers are rival goods. More recent information channels like the telegraph or radio are more like the use of a park or a road in that they are non-rival up to the capacity of the information channel. Libraries are similar. In the digital world the constraint on the non-rival nature of information is largely removed. There are some limits to the capacity of the network, but in most cases this does not come into play and we can think of information on the network as non-rival.

This is true because of the second important characteristic of digital information: It can be reproduced and distributed at close to zero marginal cost. We need to be very clear that this does not mean that information is free. Information is often very expensive to produce, but the expense is in the first copy. In the digital world, as Carl Shapiro and Hal Varian put it, "Information is costly to produce but cheap to reproduce."[5]

The combination of being non-rival and of being able to be reproduced and distributed at zero marginal cost means that digital information is significantly different from what came before. These differences encourage different desires and behaviors.

Proposition 2: When information is non-rival and can be reproduced and distributed at close to zero marginal cost, people will want it to be open.

"Open" can be tricky to define, but let's start with Peter Suber's definition of "open access." As he defines it, "Open access (OA) literature is digital, online, free of charge, and free of most copyright and licensing restrictions."[6] Many people think of open access as a movement, but it is really a business model. In the open access business model, the first-copy and infrastructure costs are covered in some way that does not involved charging readers or their libraries. There are a variety of ways these costs can be covered—from charging authors to philanthropy or institutional subsidies. The declining cost of technology is driving down the first-copy costs. But what is most important is that once the content is created, it can be distributed over the network and given away freely to readers. Individuals sometimes need to pay for network access, though they often have free alternatives like Starbucks or their local library. Either way the incidental cost of a document can be essentially free. Importantly, open access is cheaper because it does away with most of the costs associated with having paying customers, such as marketing, sales, billing, and the costs of restricting access to only to those who have paid, such as paywalls and lawyers.

I have argued that open access is inevitable, but the case I made was that the business model of open access was a disruptive innovation, as defined by the business theorist Clayton Christensen. And, because of the above-cited cost advantages and others, the open access model will inevitably come to supplant the subscription business model for the scholarly journal literature.[7] The argument here is different.

When information is non-rival and can be reproduced and distributed at close to zero marginal cost, people will want it to be open because they will want to share it. People want to share because that is what people do. We are social beings and sharing is central to how we live our lives. People share goods even when the result is that they are giving up something they would otherwise have had for themselves. Even when there is a cost to the act of sharing, people do it all of the time. But when sharing has close to no cost and when I can keep what I share with you, then sharing will become the default behavior. That this sharing behavior can be used to create value should be obvious as it is the basis for Facebook, YouTube, Twitter, Instagram, Pinterest, Tumblr, and other companies that have a market values of billions of dollars.

Owners of information will try to constrain information sharing in order to maintain their ability to sell it, and under copyright law they have the power to do so in many situations because copyright creates a monopoly for the owner of the information. Owners who wish to extract monetary value from their ownership of information charge for its use and assert their rights through licensing agreements. But in doing so they are working against human nature. They may be successful when they are not overly greedy, but even a law-abiding individual will share in some circumstances, even when this sharing violates the letter of the law. We all want to be generous when we can and the harm done is perceived as minimal.

We also need to be clear that just because we will want digital information to be open, that won't necessarily make it so. We can expect that much information will be closed and tolls will be charged for access as owners extract monopoly rents. We can though expect that over time, generosity will slowly win out and increasingly large portions of digital information will become open. Creators, especially those whose largest return comes from an increase in status, prestige, or popularity, will choose openness because sharing and generosity are not only good things to do, but also because openness serves their personal and professional interests. As one indication of this trend, 1.1 billion digital objects were released with a Creative Commons license in 2015.[8]

Proposition 3: When information is open it will encourage social production.

Social production or, as it is sometimes called, "commons-based peer production" has been championed by, among others, Yochai Benkler who has said of it:

> Social production is a real fact, not a fad. It is the critical long-term shift caused by the Internet. Social relations and exchange become significantly more important than they ever were as an economic phenomenon. In some contexts, it's even more efficient because of the quality of the information, the ability to find the best person, the lower transaction costs. It's sustainable and growing fast.[9]

Benkler discusses social production at length in his book *The Wealth of Networks*.[10] Social production is, as Wikipedia, itself maybe the most successful and well-known product of social production, puts it, "a new model of socioeconomic production in which the creative energy of large numbers of people is coordinated (usually with the aid of the Internet) into large, meaningful projects mostly without traditional hierarchical organization. These projects are often, but not always, conceived without financial compensation for contributors."[11]

Social production works when the project can be clumped into small pieces and/or modularized so that many people can make small contributions, and when the coordinating mechanisms can be built into the project infrastructure. Dan Bricklin identifies several of the attributes that contribute to the success of social production in his classic blog post, "The Cornucopia of the Commons: How to Get Volunteer Labor."[12] He suggests that when contributions that we make for ourselves add to the common resource they are more likely to be successful. The product gets better through use and no altruistic motive is required. Bricklin also suggests that the best systems are guilt free. As he says, "Instead of making you feel bad for 'only' doing 99%, a well-designed system makes you feel good for doing 1%. People complain about systems that have lots of 'freeloaders.' Systems that do well with lots of 'freeloading' and make the best of periodic participation are good."[13]

My favorite example of social production involves a very hard scientific problem. For a decade biochemists had unsuccessfully attempted to decipher the structure of retroviral protease, an enzyme that is key to the way HIV multiplies. Determining the structure or folding of a protein is a difficult task, as the fact that this important problem remained unsolved for ten years demonstrates. To help solve protein folding problems in 2008 a team at the University of Washington developed Foldit, a game that enlisted players to solve protein folding problems.[14] When retroviral protease was introduced into the game, several gamer teams solved it in ten days.[15] When the scientific article reporting the finding appeared in *Nature Structural & Molecular Biology*, two of the authors were the gamer teams the Foldit Contenders Group and the Foldit Void Crushers Group.[16] When *The Onion* got the news that gamers had done in ten days what scientists had failed to do in ten years, they commented, "It wouldn't kill those scientists to spring for a couple cases of Mountain Dew for this."[17]

Benkler sees social production as a fourth means of getting things done. The first three—markets, firms, and bureaucracies—have been around for a long time and are well understood. Social production is not entirely new: think of Amish barn raisings or quilting bees. However now, with the network connectivity that is currently available, social production is a method that can be used to tackle a wide range of more substantial projects.

The motivation for contributing time and energy to social production projects is not clear from within the confines of traditional economic theory that posits self-interest as the primary driver of human behavior. Through this lens, giving away time and energy without an economic return makes no sense. This view is of course limited and incomplete. People do things for each other all of the time with no expectation of monetary compensation. We do this to build and reinforce social bonds and because as people we enjoy creating and sharing. What has changed is that the digital environment allows the scale of social production to grow from families and local communities, where it has largely been in the past, to global enterprises, like Wikipedia, that are now possible. As Clay Shirky nicely puts it, "We are used to a world where little things happen for love and big things happen for money. Love motivates people to bake a cake and money motivates people to make an encyclopedia. Now, though, we can do big things for love."[18]

When information is open, sharing is easy; so too are commenting, enhancing, and remixing. When commenting, enhancing, and remixing are easy, people will do them because this is what people do. When people have made their comments, enhancements, and remixes, they will share them, and if everything is open they will do so easily. If a little coordination is applied a project is born. If the coordination is built into the system then the project can grow to world scale and we end up with Unix, Apache, Wikipedia, the solution to the folding problem of retroviral protease, or any one of thousands of other small and large projects. All of this begins when information becomes digital, continues if the digital information is open, and concludes with remarkable cooperative collaborative accomplishments.

Mark D. W. Edington argues that social production, rather than firms, should be the basis for scholarly communications going forward. He argues that in the print world, "When university presses arose, the capital and material costs of production for the means of communication—printed books—demanded a certain scale of revenue."[19] This made the choice of the firm the inevitable structure for scholarly publishing. This structure led in turn to a tension between the author, who is in search of recognition rather than riches, and the publisher, who requires revenue. Digital technologies, Edington argues, make a commons-based production process possible. As he concludes:

> Successfully and effectively accomplished, open access publishing in scholarship will organize and give structure to a set of circumstances already crystallizing in some fields of the academy: the translation of our basic mission—that is, communicating ideas between researchers and scholars—into a commons between peers rather than a market between consumers and producers. Rather than a system in which the interests of authors and publishers are structurally misaligned (i.e., scholars are not incentivized by monetary return, but publishers in a firm structure must be), open access publishing can give us a system in which these interests are finally and synergistically harmonized.[20]

Like mine, Edington's argument is a conjecture, but one which I believe is correct.

In ending this chapter we will return to where we began—to Cory Doctorow who says, "I have no predictions for what the future holds. But I have hopes and I have fears, and they're both anchored by the same observation: that computers and networks make it easier for us to work as groups. That sounds trivial, I know, but working effectively in groups is the oldest dream our species has." He goes on, "Working with others makes us superhuman. . . . I mean this literally. . . . Computers and networks have come closer to solving the coordination problem than nearly any technology before them.

They outperform the chalkboard, the org chart, the telephone—everything I can think of except for language, the original coordinating technology."[21]

NOTES

1. Cory Doctorow, *Information Doesn't Want to Be Free: Laws for the Internet Age* (San Francisco: McSweeney's, 2014), 93.

2. Clay Shirky, *Here Comes Everybody: The Power of Organizing without Organizations* (New York: Penguin Press, 2008), 17.

3. See Wikipedia, s.v. "Rivalry (economics)," http://en.wikipedia.org/wiki/Rivalry_(economics).

4. Letter from Thomas Jefferson to Isaac McPherson, August 13, 1813, in *The Writings of Thomas Jefferson*, eds. Andrew A. Lipscomb and Albert Ellery Bergh, 20 vols. (Washington, DC: Thomas Jefferson Memorial Association, 1905), 13:333–35. As quoted in Philip B. Kurland and Ralph Lerner, eds., *University of Chicago Press: The Founders' Constitution*, Volume 3, Article 1, Section 8, Clause 8, Document 12, 1987, http://press-pubs.uchicago.edu/founders/documents/a1_8_8s12.html.

5. Carl Shapiro and Hal R. Varian, *Information Rules: A Strategic Guide to the Network Economy* (Boston: Harvard Business School Press, 1998), 21.

6. Peter Suber, *Open Access* (Cambridge, MA: The MIT Press, 2012), 4, http://cyber.law.harvard.edu/hoap/Open_Access_(the_book)#About_the_book.

7. David W. Lewis, "The Inevitability of Open Access," *College & Research Libraries* 73, no. 5 (September 2012): 493–506, http://crl.acrl.org/content/73/5/493.full.pdf+html and http://hdl.handle.net/1805/2929.

8. *State of the Commons*, Creative Commons, 2015, https://stateof.creativecommons.org/2015/.

9. "Yochai Benkler, *The New Open-Source Economics*," filmed July 2005, TEDGlobal, video 17:52, http://www.ted.com/talks/yochai_benkler_on_the_new_open_source_economics.html.

10. Yochai Benkler, *The Wealth of Nations: How Social Production Transforms Market and Freedom* (New Haven, CT: Yale University Press, 2006), http://cyber.law.harvard.edu/wealth_of_networks/Main_Page.

11. Wikipedia, s.v. "Commons-based peer production," https://en.wikipedia.org/wiki/Commons-based_peer_production.

12. Dan Bricklin, "The Cornucopia of the Commons: How to Get Volunteer Labor," *Dan Bricklin. Writings* (blog), August 7, 2000, with additional comments April 23, 2001 and October 12, 2006, http://www.bricklin.com/cornucopia.htm.

13. Ibid.

14. See the Foldit website at http://fold.it/portal/.

15. See Wouter Stomp, "Foldit Success Story: Monkey Virus Retroviral Protease Structure Solved within Days," medGadget, September 19, 2011, http://www.medgadget.com/2011/09/foldit-success-story-monkey-virus-retroviral-protease-structure-solved-within-days.html; or Elizabeth Armstrong Moore, "Foldit Games Leads to AIDS Research Breakthrough," *CNET*, September 19, 2011, http://www.cnet.com/news/foldit-game-leads-to-aids-research-breakthrough/.

16. Firas Khatib, et al., "Crystal Structure of a Monomeric Retroviral Protease Solved by Protein Folding Game Players," *Nature Structural & Molecular Biology* 18 (September 18, 2011): 1175–77, doi:10.1038/nsmb.2119, http://www.nature.com/nsmb/journal/v18/n10/full/nsmb.2119.html.

17. "Gamers Succeed Where Scientists Couldn't," *The Onion*, September 26, 2011, http://www.theonion.com/articles/gamers-succeed-where-scientists-couldnt,26175/.

18. Shirky, *Here Comes Everybody*, 104.

19. Mark D. W. Edington. "The Commons of Scholarly Communication: Beyond the Firm," *EDUCAUSE Review* 50, no. 1 (January/February 2015): 55, http://www.educause.edu/ero/article/commons-scholarly-communication-beyond-firm.

20. Ibid.

21. Doctorow, *Information Doesn't Want to Be Free*, 158–59.

Part Two

Steps Down the Road

Step One

Defining the Job

> The long period of relative stability from the late nineteenth century up to the 1970s in the means for providing library service is just the kind of situation in which it becomes easy for the distinction between ends and means to become blurred.—Michael Buckland[1]

Clayton Christensen argues that too often when thinking about marketing, companies focus on segmenting the population to find the best means to sell to a particular demographic segment and, he argues, this approach is flawed. Rather, he suggests that the question that should be asked is: what product or service can help a person more effectively, conveniently, and affordably do a job they've been trying to do in their lives?[2] Too often, like the companies Christensen says are taking the wrong approach, we approach library services by developing them and then promoting them to different segments of the university community. How can we best engage freshmen in our information literacy program? How do we teach the literature of the disciplines in senior capstone courses or to graduate students? How do we provide research services to humanities faculty versus scientists? Christensen would suggest this is a mistaken strategy. Rather, he would suggest, we should ask what jobs do students and faculty have that the library can help them accomplish? And, importantly, when can we do these jobs better than other alternatives? Christensen argues that the question we should be asking: is who is hiring us and what jobs are they hiring us to do?

Ronald Coase makes a similar point from a very different direction in his classic article, "The Nature of the Firm."[3] Coarse asks the question: if markets are the most efficient means for the economy to work, why do we have firms? The simple version of his answer is "transaction costs." Often the friction of the marketplace means that the cost of doing a transaction using the market is an inefficient option. That is, there are many cases in which using the market is so difficult and time consuming that there are cheaper and more effective ways to get something done. When this is the case, a firm will bring functions in-house and manage them with the management structure of the firm. When Henry Ford began building automobiles in very large numbers, the market could not provide the high quality steel he needed in the quantities required, so Ford built his own steel mill. Some years later steel makers adapted and the market developed so that it could supply the necessary volume of steel to the required specifications. Ford then closed down the in-house steel mill and bought steel from other providers in the marketplace.

We need to remember that academic libraries provide a function for the university that has been brought in-house because the market in the past has been unable to provide the document provisioning and other library services that the university required. Academic libraries were required because the transaction costs for these services in the marketplace were too high or, in many cases, the market could not provide them at all. In the paper world, the market could not efficiently provide yesterday's newspaper. If you were in Chicago, the market could not efficiently provide a newspaper from Paris, and certainly not one from Nairobi. Most books published a year ago, even if they were still in print, were only available with some difficulty and often only with a considerable investment of time. Out-of-print books were even more difficult and time consuming to acquire. Often answering even simple questions was hard. What was the name of the gambler who allegedly fixed the 1919 World Series that the character Meyer Wolfsheim in the *Great Gatsby* is supposedly based on? Who was the last Federalist to run for President and where is he buried? In my youth I was a reference librarian and it was not unusual to get calls in the evening to settle bar bets.

The difficulty of acquiring publications and in getting the answers to many questions meant that having a library inside the university made good sense. As Lorcan Dempsey and his colleagues put it,

> In the print environment, it was convenient for each university to internalize a collection of locally assembled materials, to organize them, and to interpret them for its users. The alternative, where everybody was individually responsible for all of their own information needs, would be inefficient and expensive: the aggregate transaction costs across the university would be very high and many individuals would not avail themselves of the information required to make them good students and productive scholars and researchers. [4]

Too often the question we ask is: what should libraries do now that the world is digital? Again, this is the wrong question. The more appropriate question is: what job does the university, and its students and faculty, need doing that the market is unable to do? The market can now easily provide yesterday's newspaper and usually last year's. Ten years ago might be a stretch, but newspapers from Paris and Nairobi are not. Amazon can deliver books both in and out of print to your door in a day or two. With Google, Wikipedia, and Siri most questions of fact are easy to answer. Wikipedia gets you "Arnold Rothstein" and "Rufus King" within a minute or two and three or four clicks. For good measure you get a picture of Grace Church, Jamaica, New York in whose cemetery Rufus King is buried and a map with the address and latitude and longitude. Today it is hard to even imagine anyone thinking to call a library to settle a bar bet. As Tyler Cowen puts it, "We're close to the point where the available knowledge at the hands of the individual, for questions that can be posed clearly and articulately, is not so far from the knowledge of the entire world."[5]

When librarians are asked the question, "Why do you need a library when everything is on the Internet?" the usual response is to brush it aside by correctly noting that not everything is on the Internet. This is true, but it misses the important point. The market can now provide many of the documents and answers that matter most to people; it can do many of the jobs people need doing that in the past only a library could do. Everything does not have to be on the Internet to threaten libraries. If the Internet and the market, in the form of Google, Amazon, Siri, or Wikipedia, can provide the most important things that in the past the university's in-house academic library was created to do, the university, from a strictly economic perspective, should now rely on the market for some or all of these things. I think it is important for academic librarians to act on the assumption that sooner or later the university will begin to do so.

Let's take as an example a function that has long been considered central to libraries: discovery. Libraries have long focused on discovery. They created catalogs to make it possible for users to discover the books in their collections and developed reference collections full of indexes, bibliographies, dictionaries, and encyclopedias so that users could discover facts and information in a wide variety of sources. Roger C. Schonfeld explores this in his report, *Does Discovery Still Happen in the Library? Roles and Strategies for a Shifting Reality.*[6] Schonfeld begins with the observation that, "based on a long-standing and little-changed vision for their role in discovery, academic libraries have in recent years invested in a new generation of discovery services."[7] Citing the Ithaka S+R 2010 and 2013 surveys of library directors, Schonfeld notes that while the share declined somewhat from 2010, the vast majority of library directors continued to strongly agree with the statement: "It is strategically important that my library be seen by its users as the first place they go to discover scholarly content." The data Schonfeld cites indicates that the share of directors who hold this view across all types of institutions from baccalaureate to doctoral is well above 70% and, as Schonfeld

notes, many are acting on this view and investing in new discovery tools—
first federated search engines and, when this strategy proved to be ineffec-
tive, index-based discovery tools. This inclination to hold on to a traditional
in-house function when the market can provide it is a common, but nonetheless wasteful, strategic mistake. As Dale Askey provocatively puts it, "Why
bother, really? Google won the discovery wars years ago, and nothing we can
do is going to change that. My radical suggestion here is that we—finally—
acknowledge that our inventory control systems are of little interest to our
users, whether an OPAC or a discovery layer."[8] Dempsey makes the same
point when he says,

> Discovery has scaled to the network level. Although the players may change,
> this trend seems clear. Constraining the discovery process by institutional
> subscription or database boundary does not fit well with how people use the
> network. General discovery happens in Google or Wikipedia. And there is a
> variety of niches. Amazon, Google Books, Hathi Trust or Goodreads for ex-
> ample. arXiv, repec, or SSRN. PubMed Central. And so on. These services
> benefit in various ways from scale, and mobilize the data left by users—
> consciously in the form of recommendations, reviews and ratings or uncon-
> sciously in the form of transaction data—to drive their services.[9]

The lesson we need to take from Coase is that when the market provides a
product that works well, trying to keep that function in-house is a futile
exercise.

Dempsey and his colleagues make another important observation about
how Coase's work applies to libraries. They note that in the past most libraries have internalized many functions because the transaction costs in the
market were high. Increasingly, they argue that as transaction costs fall,
many of the functions where this once made sense can now be outsourced or
done through regional or national consortiums. They cite examples beginning with the success of shared cataloging and moving to shared cloud-based
computer systems and shared digital collections like JSTOR or the Hathi-
Trust.[10]

It is interesting to note that libraries have rarely created significant shared
organizations to outsource services. OCLC is the one obvious exception, but
here the economies of scale were so overwhelming and the costs of operating
independently were so crushing that there really was no alternative. There
might be a few more examples. One could argue that serials and book vendors were similar examples and that approval plans were a way of outsourc-
ing book selection. Few libraries ever did much in-house binding. The Center
for Research Libraries was a way of supporting niche collection areas on a
national basis. Most libraries belong to one or more buyers clubs in an
attempt to create scale in dealing with database and journal vendors. And
there are a few recent examples of shared digital collections—JSTOR, Hathi-

Trust, and most recently the Digital Library of America—as a discovery tool. This may seem like a good track record, but arguably, libraries have at most created a significant shared organization every decade or so and many of these, like the Center for Research Libraries or the HathiTrust, serve only a fraction of the academic library community.

For Michael Buckland the role of the library is "to facilitate access to documents."[11] Buckland notes that while librarians often talk about providing access to "knowledge" or "information," what they really mean is providing access to the representations of knowledge—that is, texts and images. In practice this means providing access to the containers of texts and images— books, journals, and databases. For Buckland, 20 years ago the challenge for libraries was to sort out how to provide access to electronic documents. That the marketplace or other organizations at a different scale of operation would in many cases do this much better than libraries was not something he considered.

Christensen looks at the individual and Coase at the firm, but in the end they agree on the question we need to ask: what job that needs doing does the library do for students, faculty, and the university that cannot be done by the market or some other organization at a larger scale? This was once a simple question with an established answer. These days it is far from simple.

One way of answering the question is to argue that libraries are a public good and as such deserve funding. This is an old argument. In 1731 Benjamin Franklin convinced fifty members of Junto, a discussion club in Philadelphia, to create the Library Company of Philadelphia. Each of the fifty shareholders paid forty shillings and promised to pay ten more each year to create and maintain a library for their common use. The motto of the company was "Communiter Bona profundere Deum est," which translates roughly as, "To pour forth benefits for the common good is divine."[12] The Library Company of Philadelphia continues to operate to this day with a membership share costing $200.[13] In Franklin's Philadelphia, books were rare and expensive. Creating a pooled common resource was the only way Franklin and his colleagues could afford a library.

While private or personal libraries exist, libraries mostly support an institution or a community. They are a knowledge-providing infrastructure. Brett M. Frischmann's book *Infrastructure: The Social Value of Shared Resources* provides an important discussion of the nature of infrastructure and we will consider libraries in light of his work.[14] Infrastructure for Frischmann[15] has three defining characteristics:

1. The resources can be consumed nonrivalrously over a significant range of demand.
2. Social demand for the resource is driven primarily by activities that require the resource as an input for downstream activities.

3. The resource may be used as an input for a wide range of activities that may produce private, public, and social goods.

Libraries clearly meet Frischmann's definition. Beginning with the first characteristic, nonrivalrous consumption means that one person can consume the resource without reducing the ability of that same resource to be consumed by others. As we have discussed, the extent to which libraries are a nonrival resource changes as they become more digital and less paper based, nonetheless over significant ranges of demand even paper library resources can be shared and used without congestion. The use of libraries is almost never an end in itself; rather, library use contributes to other goals. Finally, library use can contribute to many kinds of goals that produce a wide variety of products that in turn produce value in a wide variety. This last characteristic explains in part why assessment of libraries is so difficult.

One response of the academic library community to the current quandary of defining the job in the midst of technological ferment is to attempt to justify the value of academic libraries. In 2009 the Association of College & Research Libraries (ACRL) Board of Directors, noting that there was more research in public libraries than in academic libraries on return on investment (ROI), initiated what has become the "Value of Academic Libraries" or VAL program.[16] In 2010, *The Value of Academic Libraries: A Comprehensive Research Review and Report* aimed to bridge this gap. As the report said, "Librarians are increasingly called upon to document and articulate the value of academic and research libraries and their contribution to institutional mission and goals. ACRL's Value of Academic Libraries Initiative responds to these demands and positions academic librarians as contributors to campus conversations on accountability and impact."[17] Unsurprisingly, it turns out to be very difficult to connect all of the dots. The outcomes on which we hope to demonstrate impact—learning and research productivity—are several steps removed from what can be measured in the library and these steps are uncertain for individual libraries as well as for libraries collectively.

It is easy to understand why a focus on "value of return on investment" is attractive, but it is important to understand why it is likely to be impossible to accomplish. Libraries are commons infrastructure and like all other commons infrastructure, measuring value is difficult at best and often impossible. In this way libraries are like parks or bridges. We all understand that they deliver value, but how much and when it will be delivered is often impossible to measure. This is because of what are known as "spillover effects." Often it is not possible to know who benefits or when the benefit occurs. A student taught by a librarian might post an interesting thing they learned on Facebook or she might tell her roommate and so someone who was not directly taught benefits. The student might not use anything from the instruction until several years after they graduate, long after the library is able to measure the impact.

So in concluding the ACRL report, it is not surprising that Meagan Oakleaf focuses not on proving value, but on making academic library services better. The conclusion of the study is, "When academic librarians learn about their impact on users, they increase their value by proactively delivering improved services and resources—to students completing their academic work; to faculty preparing publications and proposals; to administrators needing evidence to make decisions."[18] I do not want to be misunderstood. I believe it is important to understand the services libraries are offering and to be able to assess whether or not they are better this year than they were last year. We should certainly have a clear sense of how we contribute to the mission of our institutions. Rather, I think it is dangerous to attempt to try to prove our value, especially if this is framed as return on investment.

The first step in reimagining the academic libraries is to determine the jobs we are being hired to do. As we do so we need to recognize that at the end of the day what we should be about is not saving the library. Rather, as Christensen suggests, it should be about providing a product or service that can help students and faculty to more effectively, conveniently, and affordably do a job they've been trying to do in their scholarly lives. If the library is to provide value, it needs to find those jobs it can do that cannot be done more effectively by others. Unless we find those jobs, we have no good reason to exist. As we will explore in in the coming chapters, I believe such jobs exist and that libraries and librarians are uniquely positioned to do them, but most of them are different from what we have done in the past.

NOTES

1. Michael Buckland, *Redesigning Library Service: A Manifesto* (Chicago: American Library Association, 1992), 4, http://digitalassets.lib.berkeley.edu/sunsite/Redesigning%20Library%20Services_%20A%20Manifesto%20(HTML).pdf.

2. Clayton M. Christensen, Scott Cook, and Taddy Hall, "Marketing Malpractice: The Cause and the Cure," *Harvard Business Review* 83 no. 12 (December 2005): 74–83.

3. Ronald Harry Coase, "The Nature of the Firm" *Economica* 4 no. 16 (1937): 386–405.

4. Lorcan Dempsey, Constance Malpas, and Brian Lavoie, "Collection Directions: The Evolution of Library Collections and Collecting," *portal: Libraries and the Academy* 14, no. 3 (July 2014): 395.

5. Tyler Cowen, *Average Is Over: Powering America Beyond the Age of the Great Stagnation* (New York: Dutton, 2013), 7.

6. Roger C. Schonfeld, *Does Discovery Still Happen in the Library? Roles and Strategies for a Shifting Reality* (New York: Ithaka S+R, 2014) accessed April 24, 2015, http://www.sr.ithaka.org/sites/default/files/files/SR_Briefing_Discovery_20140924_0.pdf.

7. Ibid., 3.

8. Dale Askey, "Giving Up on Discovery," *Taiga Forum*, September 17, 2013, http://taiga-forum.org/giving-up-on-discovery/.

9. Lorcan Dempsey, "Thirteen Ways of Looking at Libraries, Discovery, and the Catalog: Scale, Workflow, Attention," *EDUCAUSE Review*, December 10, 2012, http://

www.educause.edu/ero/article/thirteen-ways-looking-libraries-discovery-and-catalog-scale-workflow-attention.

10. Dempsey, Malpas, and Lavoie, "Collection Directions," 395–96.

11. Buckland, *Redesigning Library Service*, 3.

12. Edwin Wolf 2nd, *At the Instance of Benjamin Franklin: A Brief History of The Library Company of Philadelphia, 1731–1976* (Philadelphia: The Library Company of Philadelphia, 1976), 1–2, http://librarycompany.org/about/Instance.pdf.

13. See the membership page on the Library Company of Philadelphia's webpage at https://support.librarycompany.org/.

14. Brett M. Frischmann, *Infrastructure: The Social Value of Shared Resources* (New York: Oxford University Press, 2012).

15. Ibid., 61.

16. A summary of the initiative can be found at http://www.ala.org/acrl/issues/value.

17. Megan Oakleaf, *Value of Academic Libraries: A Comprehensive Research Review and Report* (Chicago: Association of College & Research Libraries, September 2010), 6, http://www.ala.org/acrl/sites/ala.org.acrl/files/content/issues/value/val_report.pdf.

18. Ibid., 140.

Step Two

Creating the Library as Place

The academic library as place holds a unique position on campus. No other building can so symbolically and physically represent the academic heart of an institution.—Geoffrey T. Freeman[1]

Today's academic-library buildings, more than any other campus structures, have to be all things to all people—places where social and intellectual pursuits collide, places that serve the community and the individual simultaneously. Dig into a book. Get a latte. Collaborate on a project. Nap during a study session. College libraries are a destination for those activities and more.—Scott Carlson[2]

Perhaps the easiest part of reimagining the academic library is reimagining space—reimagining the library as place. It is easy because there are really only two questions about which there is much dispute. First, how many books do you remove? Or, if you are building a new library, how many books do you include? Second, where do you put the books you keep? Actually, there is only one sensible answer to the second question—keep a small number in the building and the rest go to a remote storage facility or a bookBot. These questions can be politically difficult as the nostalgic and romanticized view of what the library should be is still powerful on many campuses, but once you answer them, the rest is straightforward.

The library building wants to be the place on campus that is reserved for nonclassroom academic work. It wants to provide a variety of spaces that match the variety of ways students and, one would hope to at least some extent, faculty do their work—quietly and privately, in groups, with their own technology, and with technology supplied by the library. The space wants to create modes to match each, and as we will discuss, it wants to be both sacred and a comfortable "third place." There should be electrical power everywhere so devices can be recharged. Beyond simply being study space, the library also wants to house other functions that support academic work and provide opportunities for faculty and students from different disciplines to mingle and mix. The particulars will differ from campus to campus, but the basic framework will be the same.

One of the things that is most clear about academic libraries is that, as physical places, they are in demand, especially for students. At some level this should not be a surprise. Learning is, at least in part, a social activity and the time spent on a campus is a special social period in most students' lives. That an informal, comfortable, nonclassroom place dedicated to study should be a popular place should not be a surprise. The *Chronicle of Higher Education* reported a study by the research firm Student Monitor that found more students, 64%, reported being satisfied with their libraries than any other spaces on campus. The spaces that had the next highest satisfaction rate were computer labs at 54%—a full 10% lower. [3]

In a September 2014 *Ubiquitous Librarian* blog post, Brian Mathews asks the question, "Why do people who love libraries love libraries?" Mathews is not asking about people who like libraries in the general sense, but rather people who come to libraries and who spend their time in them. In answering the question he quotes a student who says in part, "There's just kind of a library community of library people doing library things." Mathews then goes on to argue for the importance of creating this library community because it makes the library a place that is, as he concludes, "different from anywhere else on campus."[4] Mathews's point is well taken.

We often think about the library as a place where certain services are offered or where certain resources can be found. This is increasingly less the case. As we have noted, resources and services are now no longer place bound. Digital content and digitally conveyed expertise can be had anywhere. Students come to the library because it is the place to do "library things." That means, for the most part, to do academic work either individually or in groups, or individually in the company of their friends and classmates. The range of ways that students do their academic work varies greatly based both on the preferences of the individual and the needs the individual has at a particular time. A well-designed library will have places that match all of these needs and wants.

There is another aspect to the library as place that is significant. Using methods drawn from the psychology of religion, Heather Lea Jackson and Trudi Bellardo Hahn make a case for the library as sacred space. As they put it, "This empirical study affirmed our hypothesis that spaces deemed as 'sacred' or 'sanctified' produce affective benefits for people that extend beyond attitudes and into the realm of behavior (projected library use). Circulation statistics do not measure these benefits; students may not actually use the books on the shelves, but they 'sanctify' the books—being around the books makes them feel more scholarly and connected to the institution's educational mission."[5] This echoes the words of the architect Geoffrey T. Freeman, who has designed many academic libraries, who says, "While students are intensely engaged in using new technologies, they also want to enjoy the library as a contemplative oasis. Interestingly, a significant majority of students still considers the traditional reading room their favorite area of the library—the great, vaulted, light-filled space, whose walls are lined with books they may never pull off the shelf."[6]

Scott Bennett looks at learning and the spaces outside of classrooms that campuses provide to encourage learning and concludes, "When one looks at much of non-classroom campus space, its design is more likely to respond to the concerns of service providers—in residence and dining halls and in computer laboratories—than to the needs of students as learners. This has been demonstrably the case in libraries."[7] Bennett suggests that if space is to be designed to support learning, we need to be clear about what type of learning behaviors we are going to encourage and how the space we design will encourage these behaviors. He uses the term "intentional learning" as a frame for discussing nonclassroom spaces. He argues that when students move beyond the classroom they take responsibility for and control of their own learning. Bennett then develops a set of behaviors, mostly drawn from the National Survey of Student Engagement (NSSE).

In a study that spanned six institutions, Bennett used this framework and asked both students and faculty three questions. First, which of the learning behaviors were personally most important? Second, how well did campus spaces support the important learning behaviors? Finally, respondents were asked to identify, from a list, which spaces these were. His findings show that students and faculty don't always agree, but there is consensus on what behaviors are important. They are collaborative learning, studying alone, and discussing material with other students. At most of the institutions both students and faculty felt that some of the behaviors were supported and the library was the most likely place where this happened. Bennett concludes that campuses could make better investments in space if they were more consciously aware of what learning behaviors they wished to encourage and took advantage of underused spaces across the campus to accommodate them. He also argues that, when librarians design space, they too often start with a services perspective rather than a learning perspective. Barbara Fister suggests that, at least to some extent, this is what librarians have begun to do, especially with the use of ethnographic studies such as those done at the University of Rochester and in the ERIAL Project.[8] She says, "Librarians began to seriously consider the library in the life of the user rather than the user in the life of the library."[9]

One of the advantages libraries tend to have as spaces that support student learning is that they generally have scale. They generally have more study spaces under one roof than anywhere else on campus. This has several implications. First, it will be rare that a student looking for a place to work will not find one. This may not be the case for other campus locations where there are a small number of study spots in a given location. Beyond this, a large number of students working in one place means that you can be seen if you wish and you can easily find friends and classmates. Social connections are easier. This might or might not encourage Bennett's intentional learning behaviors, but it does help build community.

Libraries are what are sometimes called "third places" or "third spaces." This concept comes from the work of Ray Oldenburg and his classic book, *The Great Good Place: Cafés, Coffee Shops, Community Centers, Beauty Parlors, General Stores, Bars, Hangouts, and How They Get You Through the Day*.[10] Oldenburg looked broadly at space in America and argued that in post–World War II America what he called the first two spaces, home and work, had expanded to the exclusion of spaces for informal public life. As he says, "In the absence of an informal public life, people's expectations toward work and family life have escalated beyond the capacity of these institutions to meet them. Domestic and work relationships are pressed to supply all that is wanting and much that is missing in the constricted lifestyles of those without community."[11] Translating this concept to a campus, we note that there are a variety of third places, places that are not the classroom or dorm room. This may be one of the reasons the student experience is often viewed as one of the best times in one's life. As we look at what library space needs to become, it's useful to look at the character of third places that Oldenburg proposed and see how libraries stack up against these criteria:

On Neutral Ground. As Oldenburg puts it, "There must be places where individuals may come and go as they please, in which none are required to play host, and in which all feel at home and comfortable."[12] Libraries are neutral ground. Most of the other space on a campus belongs to a department and is thus part of a silo. The library is unsiloed space. One of its great strengths as a place is that people from all parts of the campus and all disciplines can mix in the library.

Leveler. Third places do not restrict who can use them. They are not restrictive or exclusive and they expand possibilities and invite everyone in. Oldenburg also suggests that the third place is upbeat, cheerful, and a place to enjoy the company of others. This is clearly the case with libraries. Although it is not uncommon for certain groups to lay claim to certain library spaces, at the end of the day almost anyone can use almost any space. It might be a stretch to call the library upbeat and cheerful, but it is at least a place to share the company of others.

Conversation Is the Main Activity. Oldenburg states this clearly: "Nothing more clearly indicates a third place than that the talk there is good; that it is lively, scintillating, colorful, and engaging."[13] He goes on to note, "Conversation's improved quality within the third place is also suggested by its temper. It is more spirited than elsewhere, less inhibited and more eagerly pursued."[14] One might make the case that in a library you are having conversations through books with voices from the past. This though is not what Oldenburg had in mind. Conversation is probably not the main activity in the library, but increasingly group study spaces provide this kind of space. Informal conversation when students take study breaks and a well-designed library accommodates this activity.

Accessibility and Accommodation. Anyone can go to a third place at almost any time of day and find acquaintances. Third places keep long hours. They accommodate activities that are, as Oldenburg puts it, "largely unplanned, unscheduled, unorganized, and unstructured."[15] This is a prime characteristic of libraries.

The Regulars. "What attracts the regular visitor to a third place is not supplied by management but by fellow customers."[16] The regulars set the tone for the space, but are generally welcoming. Becoming a regular requires only showing up on a regular basis and behaving according to the norms of the place. In my experience, libraries have regulars who always study in the same place at regular times, and in many cases, these regulars set the tone of the space they use. How much talking, if any, is acceptable? How much space can any one person claim?

Low Profile. Third places tend to be plain. They do not intend to be flashy, to be places to be seen in. Rather they are modest, easy places to be comfortable in. Most library buildings begin their lives with high ambitions, but in many cases over time they slip into being a bit shabby in a way that is comfortable.

The Mood Is Playful. The third place is a place of play. "The persistent mood of the third place is a playful one. Those who would keep conversations serious for more than a minute are almost certainly doomed to failure."[17] Oldenburg goes on to say, "Here joy and acceptance reign over anxiety and alienation."[18] Maybe not joy, but there is often a sense of playfulness, especially in my experience in the evening when all of the old folks have left campus and the library becomes truly a student space.

Home Away from Home. Oldenburg points out that the third place is not home, but rather it has many of the characteristics that we think of as home, providing in its ideal state what for many is not the reality. The third place roots people in a space where they can feel belonging, ease, and warmth. For many students, the library is the home where they can be comfortable doing their academic work in a way that is not possible in the dorm.

So while the library is hardly the neighborhood tavern, it is clearly, at least in the context of a college campus, the kind of space that Oldenburg would identify as a third place. Oldenburg's third place criteria also provide a useful guide to what we should be striving for as we build and renovate library space.

There is an additional aspect to library space that I think we need to consider. As we reduce the size of print collections, space that was once stacks will become available to be used for other purposes. I do not think it unreasonable to predict that in the next decade most academic libraries will find that a third to a half of the shelf space can be freed up, either as volumes are withdrawn from their collections or as they are transferred to storage facilities. If we think that the withdrawal of twenty volumes frees up one square foot of stack space, then withdrawing 100,000 volumes creates 5,000 square feet. (A single-faced section of shelving holds approximately 200 volumes and takes up about 10 square feet.)

This is not really all that much space, but it is, on most campuses, centrally located, open in excess of 100 hours a week, and in many cases it will be space that is not exceptionally expensive to redevelop. It will be important to convey to campus leadership that while there will be open space in the library going forward, it will not be a large amount of space and it will be exceptionally valuable space. For these reasons, it is space that needs to be coveted and used carefully. As Barbara Fister suggests, "A wise library director will say 'yes' to hosting offices and programs that will benefit from synergy with the library's programs. Saying 'yes' without being defensive also gives a librarian sufficient political capital to say 'no' when the relationship is not a good fit or when the space that was vacated has already been dedicated to planned library programs."[19]

I believe the first priority as print volumes are withdrawn and space is freed up should be to create additional study space if there isn't adequate space for this purpose in the library. Whether the need is for quiet space or collaborative space or group study rooms or rich technology space will depend on the individual library's situation. Once this need is met I think the campus should look at academic functions that cut across a range of disciplines, that are focused on academic success, and that benefit from the library's long service hours. Easy examples are writing centers or other tutoring centers, digital humanities centers, or GIS labs—maybe a "maker space" with 3-D printers and laser cutters.

The most useful way to think about redeveloping library space is probably to think about removing a block of shelving. This space either becomes new student space or, if it's developed, office space for one of the functions mentioned above. Probably the best way to think about this office space is to consider it the equivalent of a strip mall. Over time the particular uses will change, but the infrastructure will remain. Walls may move, but the overall space will remain more or less the same. Designing this way provides flexibility going forward.

The most recognized new library today is undoubtedly the James B. Hunt Jr. Library at North Carolina State University. In winning the Stanford Prize for Innovation in Research Libraries (SPIRL), it earned this citation: "As a building, an integrated technology environment, and a suite of services, the Hunt Library is an innovative model for the research library as a high-technology research platform."[20] In reviewing the building, *Library Journal* quoted Susan Nutter, the library director at North Carolina State, as saying it was intended to "create spaces that encourage collaboration, reflection, creativity, and awe" and "to be a place not of the past but of the future."[21]

Designed by international firm Snøhetta and opened in 2013, the 221,000-sq.-ft., LEED (Leadership in Energy & Environmental Design), Silver-certified building was constructed at a cost of $115.2 million. While the Hunt Library gets the most attention, the model it uses is not unique. The Christopher Center for Library and Information Resources at Valparaiso University that opened in 2004 and the Mary Idema Pew Library Learning and Information Commons at Grand Valley State University that opened in 2013 are similar. Collectively they represent the template for new library construction that can be expected to be dominant for the next decade or two.

All three are built around bookBots, or as they are sometime referred to Automated Storage and Retrieval Systems (ASRS or AS/AS), as the primary mechanism for book storage. Based on technology used in automated warehouses these systems have long high aisles with robotic arms that retrieve metal boxes in which books are stored. In the Hunt Library the aisles are 160 feet long and 50 feet high. A computer inventory system tracks individual books and their locations. These systems can store books in one-ninth the space required by traditional open stacks and the temperature and humidity can be keep at levels conducive to the long-term preservation of paper. This allows for the remaining space in the building to be focused on users.

With book storage in a separate space, the traditional entrance to the library can be reimagined. The circulation desk is gone as a feature. As Meredith Schwartz describes entering the Hunt Library, "From the first floor entrance of the Hunt Library there is not a single book in sight, and there's not a staff member, desk, or chair, either. Instead, the focal points are a staircase and a window, called Robot Alley, through which students and visitors can watch the on-site bookBot machinery in action."[22] When you enter the Mary Idema Pew Library the coffee shop is the first thing you see. Both Hunt and Mary Idema Pew, using very different architectural styles, create a wide variety of student study spaces. Mary Idema Pew, possibly because of its proximity to Grand Rapids, Michigan, the home of furniture makers Steelcase, Haworth, and Herman Miller, boasts more than 25 different kinds of chairs. Both libraries have outdoor reading spaces and many group study spaces. Hunt has more than 100 group study rooms. Both contain other campus units that complement library functions, auditoriums and multipurpose rooms. Mary Idema Pew has 100,000 volumes of its 750,000-volume collection in traditional open library stacks. Hunt uses books on open shelving primarily as decoration in its main reading room, using it to create a more sacred space as Jackson and Hahn suggested. The service space in Hunt looks more like the genius bar at an Apple Store than a traditional reference desk, and, in Mary Idema Pew, while there is a service desk, the focus of user support is the "knowledge market" where peer-student tutors help with research strategies, writing, and presentations.

Hunt, as a library for an engineering campus, has some remarkable technology spaces. There is a small detail of Hunt that I think is telling, or maybe inevitable in new construction: The Maker Space is in what was obviously once a very small office or storage room. What clearly happened is that the Maker Space was a late addition for the program or was added after the building was completed and there was nowhere else to put it. It is very difficult to design general purpose unassigned space into a new building, to leave a few spots open in the strip mall, but, as this example from Hunt shows, it is probably a good idea to try to do so.

I believe that are several lessons we can draw from the examples of Hunt and Mary Idema Pew. First, bookBots can work. I have not seen the calculations, but clearly both institutions have done the math and the cost of the initial installation and ongoing maintenance of the bookBot compares favorably with at least open stacks. It would be interesting to me to see a comparison of bookBots versus a Harvard-style, remote, storage facility—especially if we assume a decline in the volume of book use over the life of the building. The density of storage should be about the same, so the cost of maintaining the environmental systems should be similar. The questions then become these: How does the cost of installation and maintenance of the bookBot compare with the cost of people and forklifts in the Harvard-style storage? And what is the location premium for the bookBot, which will be in prime campus space, versus the remote storage facility, which is likely to be on less valuable real estate.

In may be surprising, but I believe Mary Idema Pew made a better choice by keeping a sizable portion of its book collection in open stacks. I am not convinced that the use of these books will justify this allocation of space, rather I think that five or ten years from now this space will be available to be repurposed for Maker Spaces or whatever else it is that will be wanted, but cannot yet be imagined. Hunt, with no books stacks to cannibalize, will have a harder time adapting.

We will conclude with the quote from Geoffrey T. Freeman with which we began this chapter. He said, "The academic library as place holds a unique position on campus. No other building can so symbolically and physically represent the academic heart of an institution." This is the beginning of the last paragraph of an essay of his. He concludes the paragraph by saying,

> If the library is to remain a dynamic life force, however, it must support the academic community in several new ways. Its space must flexibly accommodate evolving information technologies and their usage as well as become a "laboratory" for new ways of teaching and learning in a wired or wireless environment. At the same time, the library, by its architectural expression and siting, must continue to reflect the unique legacy and traditions of the institution of which it is part. It must include flexible spaces that "learn" as well as traditional reading rooms that inspire scholarship. By embracing these distinct functions, the library as a place can enhance the excitement and adventure of the academic experience, foster a sense of community, and advance the institution into the future. The library of the future remains irreplaceable. [23]

NOTES

1. Geoffrey T. Freeman, "The Library as Place: Changes in Learning Patterns, Collections, Technology, and Use," in *Library as Place: Rethinking Roles, Rethinking Space* (Washington, DC: Council on Library and Information Resources, February 2005), 9, http://www.clir.org/pubs/reports/pub129/pub129.pdf.

2. Scott Carlson, "Is It a Library? A Student Center? The Athenaeum Opens at Goucher College," *Chronicle of Higher Education*, September 14, 2009, https://chronicle.com/article/Is-It-a-Library-A-Student/48360/.

3. Steve Kolowich, "5 Things We Know about College Students in 2014," *Chronicle of Higher Education*, December 17, 2004, http://chronicle.com/blogs/wiredcampus/5-things-we-know-about-college-students-in-2014/55313.

4. Brian Mathews, "Why Do People Who Love Libraries Love Libraries?," *The Chronicle: The Ubiquitous Librarian* (blog), September 19, 2014, http://chronicle.com/blognetwork/theubiquitouslibrarian/2014/09/19/why-do-people-who-love-libraries-love-libraries/.

5. Heather Lea Jackson and Trudi Bellardo Hahn, "Serving Higher Education's Highest Goals: Assessment of the Academic Library as Place," *College & Research Libraries* 72, no. 5 (September 2011): 436, http://crl.acrl.org/content/72/5/428.full.pdf+html.

6. Freeman, "The Library as Place," 6.

7. Scott Bennett, "Learning Behaviors and Learning Spaces," *portal: Libraries and the Academy* 11, no. 3 (July 2011): 3, doi:10.1353/pla.2011.0033, http://muse.jhu.edu/journals/portal_libraries_and_the_academy/v011/11.3.bennett.pdf.

8. Nancy Fried Foster and Susan Gibbons, eds., *Studying Students: The Undergraduate Research Project at the University of Rochester* (Chicago: Association of College & Research Libraries, 2007); and Lynda M. Duke and Andrew D. Asher, eds., *College Libraries and Student Culture: What We Now Know* (Chicago: American Library Association, 2012).

9. Barbara Fister, "Repositioning Library Space," in *New Roles for the Road Ahead: Essays Commissioned for ACRL's 75th Anniversary* (draft), by Steven Bell, Lorcan Dempsey, and Barbara Fister, ed. Nancy Allen (Chicago: Association of College & Research Libraries, December 5, 2014), 50–51, http://acrl.ala.org/newroles/wp-content/uploads/2014/11/New-Roles-for-the-Road-Ahead-COMMENT-DRAFT.pdf.

10. Ray Oldenburg, *The Great Good Place: Cafés, Coffee Shops, Community Centers, Beauty Parlors, General Stores, Bars, Hangouts, and How They Get You through the Day* (New York: Paragon House, 1989).

11. Ibid., 9.

12. Ibid., 22.

13. Ibid., 26.

14. Ibid., 29.
15. Ibid., 33.
16. Ibid.
17. Ibid., 37.
18. Ibid., 38.
19. Fister, "Repositioning Library Space," 52–53.
20. "Stanford Prize for Innovation in Research Libraries (SPIRL)—2014 Prizes," Stanford University: Stanford University Libraries, accessed May 16, 2015, http://library.stanford.edu/projects/stanford-prize-innovation-research-libraries-spirl/2014-prizes.
21. Meredith Schwartz, "Tomorrow, Visualized," *Library Journal: Library by Design*, September 18, 2013, http://lj.libraryjournal.com/2013/09/buildings/lbd/tomorrow-visualized-library-by-design/.
22. Ibid.
23. Freeman, "The Library as Place," 9.

Step Three

Retiring the Legacy Print Collection

> Academic libraries will face many choices in the coming years as they contin-
> ue to struggle with preserving and providing access to the cultural and scholar-
> ly records in an environment where the number and types of materials that
> they are expected to collect grow rapidly. As librarians grapple with these
> changes, it is important to recognize that the costs associated with a print-
> based world, often assumed to be small, are actually large.—Paul N. Courant
> and Matthew "Buzzy" Nielson [1]

Change is always hard, but this part of the change in library practice will be particularly difficult because is it will require changing the way we think about books, and books, especially for academics, are special. Libraries have, for as long as anyone can remember, measured excellence by counting how many books were in their collections. Going forward we will have to adjust our perspective and justify the space used to store books. Books will go from being the library's primary asset to being, in many cases, a liability. The space used to store books has an opportunity cost that has in the past rarely, if ever, been considered. Going forward, this will change.

There are several ways we can think about this opportunity cost. Paul N. Courant and Matthew "Buzzy" Nielson calculate the present value of the perpetual storage of a print book in open stacks to be $141.89 with an annual average (in 2009 USD) of $4.26. [2] Another way is to consider the space occupied by a book and the value it would create if it were withdrawn. A single-faced section of library shelving is generally assumed to hold 200 volumes and to occupy about 10 square feet of space. This means that with-drawing 20 volumes would create one square foot of space. If we assume that the space can be repurposed to create library or office space, the cost of this construction at a university is between $200 to $250 per square foot.[3] If we assume the lower figure, every book that is kept has an opportunity cost of $10. This is probably not quite fair as space freed by withdrawing books will require costs to repurpose, but even if we halve the cost (assuming the opportunity cost is $5), we can see that reducing the size of library collections can create significant value to the university. This is especially true because often library space is in the middle of campus and in most cases it is space that is open one hundred or more hours per week. Library space is prime real estate.

This becomes an especially important consideration because the circulation of print materials is declining across the board. The number of general and reserve circulations in academic libraries in the United States as reported by the National Centers for Education Statistics (NCES) declined by a third in the eighteen years between 1996 and 2014, from 231,503,477 circulations to 154,409,011.[4] This is a drop of more than 77 million circulations. An interesting analysis of these circulation figures was done by Will Kurt and reported in the *ACRL TechConnect Blog*. He asks not, "How many books are circulating?" but rather, "How many books are students checking out?" He does a simple linear regression on the Circulations per Users at PhD-granting institutions using National Center for Educational Statistics data. This analysis indicates that there will be little or no circulation in any academic libraries by 2020. Kurt admits the limits of this method, as there will certainly be some flattening of the curve, but still concludes, "The most important thing to take away is that, regardless of cause, user behavior has changed and by all data points is still changing. In the end, the greatest question is how will academic libraries adapt? It is clear that the answer is not as simple as a transition to a new media. To survive, librarians must find the answer before we have enough data to prove these predictions."[5]

From a strategic perspective, retiring the legacy print collection requires action on the national level that will enable action at the local level. At the national level, a collective print collection will need to be created from the many local collections and the preservation of this collection will need to be assured. Once this has been done, local collections can be crafted to meet local needs, which will increasingly be limited, and volumes that are unnecessary can be weeded out. This will create space that can be repurposed. Absent the national-level, coordinated action, individual institutions can, and probably will have to, act—but they will have to accept more risk in doing so and the case for action at the campus level will be less compelling.

So how big is the national collective collection? Brian F. Lavoie and Roger C. Schonfeld provide a good working number. They begin with a version of the WorldCat database from January 2005 that contains 55 million records and 950 million holdings. Of the 55 million records, 41 million are "monographic language-based materials" or books. They removed government documents; theses and dissertations; electronic, microfilm, and Braille items; and came up with a final number of 32 million printed books cataloged in WorldCat. Using OCLC's FRBR work set algorithm, they determined that the 32 million printed books represent 26 million distinct works. There were 450 languages represented, with 52% of the items being in English. Approximately half of the books were published after 1977 and only 18% before 1923. The holdings of the 32 million books is interesting: 9.5 million or about 36% were held by only one library; 2.4 million were held by more than 50 libraries.

Lavoie and Schonfeld considered earlier estimates of the worldwide book collection by Iwinski in 1911 and Merritt in 1940. If the Iwinski and Merritt estimates were accurate the WorldCat database represents 45% to 48% of the actual historical book collection. They also compared UNESCO estimates on current book production with what was in WorldCat and this analysis suggests that WorldCat is capturing about two-thirds of current world book production. So while library holdings do not by any means include everything ever published or even everything currently being published, Lavoie and Schonfeld give us the general sense of what is currently in library collections—that is, about 32 million books as of 2005. UNESCO estimates that about one million books are produced each year and Lavoie and Schonfeld estimate that about 70% of these are added to library collections.[6] Should this estimate hold, this would mean that in 2015 the total collective collection would be approximately 38 million books.

We know that when viewed from a national perspective, academic library collections are hugely redundant and large portions of most academic collections are not used. Over the past one hundred plus years this is how they were built. Collections were built "just in case." This made good sense given the importance of having items close at hand and the difficulty and expense of acquiring out-of-print titles. The fact that this collection strategy led to large numbers of books that had not and would not be used was well understood by those who paid attention to the research. In 1979 the Kent study at the University of Pittsburgh showed that about 40% of the books acquired in a given year had not circulated after six years and that since most use occurred in the years immediately following acquisition of the item, it was unlikely that many of the unused titles would ever be used in the future.[7] The Kent study established the 80/20 rule for library collections. It turns out that if a somewhat wider view is taken, the 80/20 rule misrepresents the portion of the collection that is heavily used. A 2011 study conducted by Julia Gammon and Edward T. O'Neill from OCLC of OhioLINK's 89 academic institutions found, as they put it, "The most fascinating result of the study was a test of the '80/20' rule. Librarians have long espoused the belief that 80% of a library's circulation is driven by approximately 20% of the collection. The analysis of a year's statewide circulation statistics would indicate that 80% of the circulation is driven by just 6% of the collection."[8]

The consulting firm Sustainable Collection Services, which specializes in collection analysis, in a recent study of 128 U.S. academic libraries with a total of 43 million holdings, found that in the average library nearly 43% of the titles had zero circulations, with a range for different libraries of 10% to 98%. More than 77% of the average library's titles were held in the exact edition by more than 100 other U.S. libraries, with the range being 27% to 95%. They also found that the average library had 1% of the titles that were held by fewer than five other U.S. libraries, with a range of 0% to 13%. For the average library, titles available in the HathiTrust were about 43% copyrighted and about 5% in the public domain.[9] If for the typical library half of the zero-uses titles were also available in more than 100 U.S. libraries, it seems reasonable to argue that these volumes could be withdrawn with little if any impact on the library's users and little risk to the national collective collection. This study's average library, which had a book collection of about 450,000 titles, could thus withdraw more than 90,000 titles. This would create 4,500 square feet of space in each of these libraries, which would provide these libraries with an average value of between $900,000 and $1,125,000.

Work laying the groundwork for a national collective print collection has been going on for some time, much of it research by Constance Malpas at OCLC. It began in 2009 with a study on the research library policies required to underpin the development of a shared print collection. The study found that, "in at least some areas, consensus is emerging around the core requirements for a policy framework governing inter-institutional management of library print resources. We learned that entering into a shared print agreement is not as difficult as we expected it would be, provided that the agreement covers a few basic elements."[10] These elements were as follows:

- An assurance that items contributed to a shared collection would be retained;
- An escape clause that allowed libraries to recall contributed items from the shared collection, and;
- A commitment to provide access to the shared collection so the shared collection could replace local holdings.

This is a cautious and in some ways not a particularly promising statement. It makes clear how difficult the paradigm shift will be. Research libraries were prepared to share collections, but only with clear guarantees and the ability to back out.

In 2011 Malpas looked at the HathiTrust and how its holdings overlapped research library print holdings. The results of this study made it clear that there was a solid basis on which to build alternative collection strategies. At the time of the study, the HathiTrust had digital versions of 30% of the collections of the ARL libraries and it was expected that this could rise to 60% by 2014. This would provide the opportunity for a typical research library to recoup 45,000 assignable square feet and could save $500,000 to $2 million per ARL library. As Malpas put it,

> Based on a year-long study of data from the HathiTrust, ReCAP, and World-Cat, we concluded that our central hypothesis was successfully confirmed: there is sufficient material in the mass-digitized library collection managed by the HathiTrust to duplicate a sizeable (and growing) portion of virtually any academic library in the United States, and there is adequate duplication between the shared digital repository and large-scale print storage facilities to enable a great number of academic libraries to reconsider their local print management operations.[11]

Malpas argues that one of the key missing pieces that would ease the transition to a different collection strategy is the lack of licensing models for copyrighted, digitized content. Unfortunately, given the ongoing animosity between publishers and authors and Google and the HathiTrust, the near-term likelihood of resolving the copyright/licensing problem seems small.

In their 2012 report, *Print Management at "Mega-Scale": A Regional Perspective on Print Book Collections in North America*, Brian Lavoie, Constance Malpas, and JD Shipengrover present a framework for thinking about collective print collections. They begin with a definition of print consolidation: "For the purposes of this report, *print consolidation* refers to any strategy undertaken by a group of institutions to achieve a mutual purpose by imposing some degree of integration across their local print collections."[12] They argue that the two dimensions of this definition "mutual purpose" and "degree of integration" are the "why" and "how" of building the collective print collection. They then argue that for each of the two dimensions there are two alternatives, though with variation within each.

Why have a collective print collection? The first answer is that the print collection is to serve as a shared back-up collection of print originals with digital surrogates providing access. Second, the collection is a consolidated collection of little-used items to serve the access needs of a multi-institution population. How to create a collective print collection? The first answer is a physically combined collection in a central repository. The second answer is a virtually consolidated collection where each institution maintains responsibility for some items and discovery and delivery systems allow for shared use.

This is a useful way to think about the problem, but for many academic libraries it is beside the point. The reality is that in the near term, say the next decade, the national library community will mostly want to share little-used items across institutions and that in a decade or so the main need will be to have a safe and secure, print back-up for the digital collection that will be the near universal means of access. I would also suspect that the ultimate national collective print collection will consist of a series of regional hubs, mostly the large ARL libraries or their collaborative shared print repositories like ReCAP. There will need to be some number of use copies and some number of dark copies with geographic distribution of both to make delivery of the use copies easier and to reduce the risk of loss by catastrophe. OCLC seem likely to be the discovery mechanism, or OCLC linked to HathiTrust and Google Books. FedEx, UPS, and the Postal Service will do just fine as the delivery mechanism.

One requirement for such a system is adequate capacity in print storage facilities. In a 2007 study, Lizanne Payne documented 68 high-density storage facilities in the United States and Canada with a capacity of 70 million volumes total. This is approximately 7% of the one billion volumes held by academic libraries in the two countries.[13] These facilities are secure and provide environmental conditions suitable for the long-term preservation of physical materials and in most cases have delivery services associated with them. Since Payne's study, additional high-density storage has been added both through the construction of additional, free-standing print-book repositories and by the popularity of robotic book storage systems that have many of the same characteristics of the facilities in the study. As we discussed in the previous chapter, a number of new libraries, for example the James B. Hunt Jr. Library at North Carolina State University and the Mary Idema Pew Library at Grand Valley State University, use such robotic book storage systems.

Is this enough capacity? Yes, it is, if we use Lavoie and Schonfeld's estimate and assume that we will want to keep all of the copies of all works with fewer than ten copies and that we want to keep ten copies of all of the remaining works in high-density secure repositories. This calculation gives us a desired collective print collection of about 180 million volumes. Similar data for English-language books as of January 2015 (provided by Lavoie) would lead to a somewhat higher number of about 250 million.[14] This is of course only books and not journals. Without any good figures and for the sake of argument, let's assume that journals will add an additional 50%. This gives us somewhere between 250 million and 400 million volumes. The capacity identified by Payne would accommodate between 18% and 25% of this collection.

Given that Lavoie and Schonfeld's estimate is for the world's collection and Payne's estimates North American storage, the situation is actually not that bad. In addition, it is likely that most of the items that have only one or two holdings in OCLC are likely already in special collections and already securely stored. We will certainly want a good representation of the world's books and journals, but it is not the responsibility of the United States and Canada alone. Of course nearly a decade has passed since Payne's storage capacity studies and more capacity undoubtedly exists. A significant effort will be required to coordinate the use of the storage capacity, but all things considered, it seems like a manageable problem.

There will be a lot of work to be done, but it is the kind of work that the library community understands and once the commitment to move forward is made it is the kind of work the library community is good at. In addition, the work will be done in general by 50 to 100 of the largest research libraries. They have the means and the motivation to take on this task. The rest of the academic library community can get a free ride on this effort. The free riders will likely, and appropriately, need to make some financial contribution to the collective print collection, either through some annual assessment or an item borrowing fee. This may take some getting used to as the traditional way of thinking of library resource sharing was that all libraries contributed, even if it was only in a small way. It was sharing.

In the near future what we will have is the 50 to 100 big libraries building and maintaining the collective collection and the rest of the library community tagging along. Each of the rest of the smaller free-riding libraries will have some very small number of unique items and how to get them into the system will take some sorting out, but this will be a sideshow to the main event. As Lorcan Dempsey and his colleagues put it in their 2013 report, *Understanding the Collective Collection: Towards a System-wide Perspective on Library Print Collections*, "However, many libraries may prefer to be consumers rather than providers of shared collections, and may wish to participate more selectively, on a fee or membership basis, relying on collaborative or third-party arrangements to manage print collections. Others again may feel no need to make such a contribution."[15]

Roger C. Schonfeld reviews the progress to date on efforts to build print collections for long-term preservation.[16] He notes that to date most of these efforts are regional and not national and that in most cases preservation commitments have been made only for limited time periods. He points out the potential gap between stated preferences and revealed preferences—that is, the gap between what we say and what we do. Schonfeld is appropriately concerned that when push comes to shove, libraries and their parent institutions will not make or continue to make the investments that are required. He documents a discomfort that seems to exist in the library community when regional cooperative efforts move to national scale and become distant and appear bureaucratic. Libraries begin to view the organizations managing these efforts as vendors rather than seeing then as shared resources to which we all need to contribute. Schonfeld concludes, "But as I have shown, our history here in the United States shows that we should be skeptical of our ability to sustain national-level efforts to preserve little-used print materials."[17]

I recognize the concerns Schonfeld raises, but I am more optimistic than he seems to be. In my view, the preservation of the legacy print collection is a task that academic libraries, at least in North America, are quite capable of accomplishing, though we will need to expand on current efforts. There are appropriate incentives and this task fits within our current ways of thinking about what we do. There is some complexity and some expense, but in the end it will happen and we, as a community, can count on it. The print books as a scholarly resource for the future will be safe.

There remains a question about the extent to which individual libraries will want to maintain print collections when they are not needed for the collective collection. David M. Durant and Tony Horava argue that print books have a distinct value because of the nature of reading in print. As they say, "By preserving print collections in concert with providing access to digital materials, libraries would be protecting not just a format, but also an entire way of thinking and doing research that is complementary to online uses of scholarly information."[18] Durant and Horava go on to argue for a hybrid collection containing both print and digital books. They go on to say, "Conceiving of the library as a place where ideas are formulated and dis-seminated requires the library to provide access to both print and digital forms of reading, because each format leads to a different way of thinking and doing research and thus produces different types of ideas. Only through supporting the full spectrum of reading cultures and styles of research can the library truly fulfill this vision of creating, combining, and sharing ideas old and new."[19]

I am less convinced than Durant and Horava of what seems to be an almost moral imperative to preserve print, but as a practical matter they are probably correct that libraries will have hybrid collections for some time. Once there is an established and stable collective collection, individual li-braries will reduce their local print collections to match their needs based on actual use or the perceived pedagogical value of a print book collection. One can imagine browsing collections of current popular books, print books as decoration in reading rooms to set a tone of quiet reflection, or a collection of print works that becomes part of an expanded special collection. In all likeli-hood most academic libraries will have printed books for all three purposes for some time.

As print collections become smaller, it is likely that we will need to think differently about book storage. As noted above we can expect a national collective collection to reside in a series of distributed print book repositories either based on the Harvard model or bookBots. Libraries will face a tension as the collections they hold locally decline. In most cases these collections will be books that are either used with relative frequency or are titles that are relatively rare. At least for titles in the second category the books are likely to need more protection than the current open-stack model provides. There will be concerns about environmental conditions and theft. Closed stacks, which all but vanished by the 1950s, could return as a solution for books that are too rare or valuable to leave on open stacks. For many libraries this change will be an architectural challenge.

NOTES

1. Paul N. Courant and Matthew "Buzzy" Nielson, "On the Cost of Keeping a Book," in *The Idea of Order: Transforming Research Collections for 21st Century Scholarship* (Washington, DC: Council on Library and Information Resources, June 2010), 102, http://www.clir.org/pubs/reports/pub147/pub147.pdf.

2. Ibid., 81–105.

3. See Chart 5: Profile of New Buildings Currently Underway in "2013 College Construction Report," *College Planning & Management* (February 2013): CR6, http://collegeplanning.epubxp.com/i/109241-feb-2013/23.

4. See National Center for Education Statistics (NCES): Library Statistics Program at http://nces.ed.gov/surveys/libraries/Academic.asp for various reports.

5. Will Kurt, "The End of Academic Library Circulation?," *ACRL TechConnect* (blog), February 1, 2012, http://acrl.ala.org/techconnect/?p=233.

6. Brian F. Lavoie and Roger C. Schonfeld, "Books without Boundaries: A Brief Tour of the System-Wide Print Book Collection," *JEP: The Journal of Electronic Publishing* 9 no. 2 (Summer 2006), doi: http://dx.doi.org/10.3998/3336451.0009.208.

7. Allen Kent, et. al., *Use of Library Materials: The University of Pittsburgh Study* (New York: Marcel Dekker, 1979).

8. OhioLINK Collection Building Task Force, Julia Gammon, and Edward T. O'Neill, *OhioLINK–OCLC Collection and Circulation Analysis Project 2011* (Dublin, OH: OCLC Research, September 2011), 31, http://www.oclc.org/research/publications/library/2011/2011-06r.html.

9. "SCS [Sustainable Collection Services] Monographs Index," OCLC, accessed July 6, 2015, https://www.oclc.org/sustainable-collections/resources.en.html.

10. Constance Malpas, *Shared Print Policy Review Report* (Dublin, OH: OCLC Research, January 2009), 5, http://www.oclc.org/content/dam/research/publications/library/2009/2009-03.pdf.

11. Constance Malpas, *Cloud-sourcing Research Collections: Managing Print in the Mass-digitized Library Environment* (Dublin, OH: OCLC Research, January 2011), 8–9, http://www.oclc.org/research/publications/library/2011/2011-01.pdf.

12. Brian Lavoie, Constance Malpas, and JD Shipengrover, *Print Management at "Mega-Scale": A Regional Perspective on Print Book Collections in North America* (Dublin, OH: OCLC Research, 2012), 10, http://www.oclc.org/content/dam/research/publications/library/2012/2012-05.pdf?urlm=163087.

13. Lizanne Payne, *Library Storage Facilities and the Future of Print Collections in North America* (Dublin, OH: OCLC Programs and Research, October 2007), www.oclc.org/programs/publications/reports/2007-01.pdf.

14. Brian Lavoie, e-mail message to author, March 10, 2015.

15. Lorcan Dempsey et al., *Understanding the Collective Collection: Towards a System-wide Perspective on Library Print Collections* (Dublin, OH: OCLC Research, December 2013), 4–5, http://www.oclc.org/content/dam/research/publications/library/2013/2013-09.pdf.

16. . Roger C. Schonfeld, *Issue Brief: Taking Stock: Sharing Responsibility for Print Preservation* (New York: Ithaka S+R, July 8, 2015), http://sr.ithaka.org/sites/default/files/files/SR_IssueBrief_Taking_Stock_070815.pdf.

17. Ibid., 11.

18. David M. Durant and Tony Horava, "The Future of Reading and Academic Libraries," *portal: Libraries and the Academy* 15 no. 1 (January 2015): 19, doi:10.1353/pla.2015.0013, http://muse.jhu.edu/journals/portal_libraries_and_the_academy/v015/15.1.durant.pdf.

19. Ibid.

Step Four

Preserving Digital Content

Any document that is not collected and preserved is likely to be lost, unavailable [to readers] both now and in the future. It is difficult to predict what might be of interest to someone in the future. When in doubt it is prudent to preserve nonrenewable resources.—Michael Buckland[1]

Libraries keep documents for the long haul. This has been a key component of their mission for as long as there have been libraries. For the university in the print era, the preservation of knowledge was linked to access. Universities needed to provide documents to students and faculty so they could do their academic work and research. In order to accomplish this, university libraries collected documents and these collections grew over time. Importantly, institutional status was gained as the result of building large collections—both general and special. Investment in these collections paid back to the university in terms of privileged access to these items for their faculty and students. The result was an increased status for the university because of the quality of the faculty and students they could attract. As Buckland notes, "The principal reason for most investment in collection development is not preservation but the need to provide convenient access to materials that people want to see *where* they want to see them. If someone asks to see a book, it is not entirely satisfactory to answer that a copy exists and is being carefully preserved in some foreign national library."[2] So while libraries in the paper world were most often explicitly most concerned with easy access to collections the fortunate byproduct was a robust, if generally uncoordinated, system of preservation. As Roger C. Schonfeld has put it, "Proliferation was a preservation strategy that involved the acquisition of many print copies of the same material at dozens or hundreds of libraries, many of which retained them over time. As a self-organizing strategy, preservation through proliferation is imperfect but at the same time achieved great things."[3]

Important to this system was the status that universities gained from it. Investments in special collections tend to attract good press, and because by definition they are "special," they bring notoriety. They also have a tendency to attract gifts of similar materials. The extreme case is the February 2015 donation of $300 million in rare books by musician, musicologist, bibliophile, and philanthropist William H. Scheide to Princeton University. According to the Princeton news release, the collection includes "the 1455 Gutenberg Bible, the earliest substantial European printed book; the original printing of the Declaration of Independence; Beethoven's autograph[ed] (in his own handwriting) music sketchbook for 1815–16, the only [one] outside Europe; Shakespeare's first, second, third and fourth folios; significant autograph[ed] music manuscripts of Bach, Mozart, Beethoven, Schubert and Wagner." The press release goes on to quote Princeton President Christopher L. Eisgruber as saying, "Through Bill Scheide's generosity, one of the greatest collections of rare books and manuscripts in the world today will have a permanent home here . . . . It will stand as a defining collection for Firestone Library and Princeton University. I cannot imagine a more marvelous collection to serve as the heart of our library."[4] Scheide had actually given this collection to Princeton as a loan in 1959 and the 2015 estate gift only formalized what had happened decades before.

This gift exemplifies two things. First, libraries, especially large research libraries, are one of the few places where items of the rarity and value of those in the Scheide collection can be reliably kept. Keeping them almost anywhere else creates risks of all sorts, from theft to environmental concerns to all sorts of other mishaps. Second, even though Princeton assumes the long-term obligation of safely keeping these materials, which is quite costly, it does so happily because of the prestige the collection brings.

But of more importance than special collections was the status that accrued to universities and their libraries from large general collections. The Association of Research Libraries (ARL) Index ranks research libraries on the basis of a formula that, though it has changed over the years, generally puts the institutions with the largest collections and the most ongoing investment in collections at the top of the heap. The ranking of institutions is and has been important to librarians, university presidents, and trustees. Bragging rights matter to universities and the pecking order of their libraries is one of the things they can brag about. It is easy to recognize this if you look at the websites of ARL libraries. Columbia University is "one of the top five."[5] Indiana University Bloomington makes sure you know they come in at number 27.[6] The University of Kansas lays claim to being "one of the top fifty."[7] The pecking order is useful as it helps create the incentives for these institutions to carry the load for the preservation of the national collective collection. Without these incentives the retirement of the legacy print collection described in the previous chapter would be much more difficult.

Importantly, the investments required to build strong general and special collections are relatively modest, at least when considered from the perspective of all of the other things these universities do. While large library collections are not inexpensive, especially when new buildings are required, the cost of the library as a proportion of an institution's academic budget is generally modest. The 2011/2012 total of expenditures for all public and private, nonprofit, degree-granting, postsecondary institutions was $465.4 billion, and the total of operating expenditures for degree-granting postsecondary institution libraries was $7.0 billion, or 1.5% of the total institutional expenditures.[8] ARL statistics paint a similar picture, with library expenditures as a percentage of university expenditures falling from more than 3.5% in the 1980s to between 1.5% and 2.0% in 2011.[9]

Libraries have been dealing with print and its preservation for a very long time and they know how to handle it. As James Hilton and his colleagues put it,

> At its most basic level, scholarship is an enduring public conversation among scholars. The particular form of that conversation, whether it is based in data, rhetoric, or creative expression, matters less than the fact that it is both public and enduring. In the analog world, we know how to make this happen. Faculty members and their students publish, libraries collect and preserve, and the works are thereby made accessible to current and future generations. The workflows that sustain this process have evolved over the last six centuries and are now so deeply ingrained that they are practically invisible—complicated, to be sure, but deeply understood and well practiced.[10]

In the print world preservation happens. It is not perfect as was exemplified by the recognition in the 1980s that much of the paper produced in between the 1850s and the 1970s was high acidic and was slowly but surely "burning"; many of these books would quickly become so brittle that they would be unusable. The response by the research library community led to changes in paper standards—the ANSI NISO Standard Z39.48-1984 *Permanence of Paper for Publications and Documents in Libraries* was issued in 1984. Beyond this, libraries pursued concerted efforts to microfilm endangered items and to develop mass de-acidification processes so that important materials could be preserved. This was difficult and important work, but outside the research library world it received little notice. Most of the scholarly work assumed libraries were taking care of business, and they were.

Lorcan Dempsey and his colleagues' characterization of preservation in the print era posits less intention. They argue that most university library collections were built because, following Ronald Coase, high transaction costs made bringing the document provision function inside the university a sensible decision. Having large collections close at hand was a good investment, providing good service to students and faculty and prestige. Then as they put it, "Preservation is a benign artifact of the print publishing model as materials are redundantly available across libraries."[11] They go on to make an important point about preservation as we move into the digital networked world: "It moves concerns about preservation of resources away from the institution and toward a system-wide perspective, where incentives may be weak."[12] As libraries move from print to digital technologies, moving to multi-institution scale and providing the incentives to make the required investments is a general problem across a number of domains, but for preservation it may be particularly problematic.

In his State of the University speech in October 2013, Indiana University President Michael A. McRobbie stated,

> For over 25 centuries, the great universities of the world have always had three fundamental missions:
>
> • the creation of knowledge (that is, research and innovation),
> • the dissemination of knowledge (that is, education and learning), and
> • the preservation of knowledge.
>
> We tend, these days, to mainly associate the first two of these missions with a university. . . . However, the advent of the digital age, with the development of the Internet and the World Wide Web, is giving renewed rapidly increasing focus to the importance of the third mission of a university—the preservation of knowledge—and is allowing us to think about it in completely new ways.[13]

McRobbie's words might be an indication that creating the incentives to invest in preservation might not be all that difficult, and following the speech, Indiana University made a significant investment in the preservation of fragile audio and video materials. But I am skeptical. I am not sure any university president is prepared to solicit a gift from a major donor for preservation rather than scholarships, endowed chairs, or an upgrade to the football training facility. There is a reason universities have focused on teaching and research (and football). These are the activities that pay the bills. Preservation of knowledge might bring small bits of prestige, but it is not often likely to directly generate cash. This is a big problem for libraries and for the academy generally and I am unsure how it will be solved. If collaborative action at a national scale is required for digital preservation, how are incentives created that encourage contribution and discourage free riding? Can this be done without bragging rights or a pecking order? Maybe it is as simple as building funding for digital preservation into the formula for the ARL Index. If so, my concerns might be unjustified.

Amy Kirchhoff, Sheila Morrissey, and Kate Wittenberg define three levels of preservation for digital content:

1. Near-term protection or backup,
2. Mid-term protection or byte replication, and
3. Long-term protection or managed digital preservation [14]

Competently managed libraries with collections of digital content will have the first of these levels covered and many should have the second level covered as well. But byte replication is not sufficient. As Kirchhoff, Morrissey, and Wittenberg point out, file formats become obsolete, there is no guarantee that the content will remain discoverable, and devices or environments for using the content may no longer exist. One can imagine that in the future we will have digital archeologists who will be able to uncover and decipher old files the way archeologists now decipher ancient texts, but this is hardly optimal. What is required is a structure and systems for managed digital preservation.

Managed preservation of digital content requires at least the first four of the following items; in the absence of the fourth, the last two are necessary and are probably a good thing in every case:

1. There needs to be a technical infrastructure that can robustly assure that bits can be saved over long periods of time and that they can be retrieved and used with the technologies available at the time of this reuse.
2. The items being preserved must be discoverable.
3. There needs to be a mechanism to assure the authenticity of the content and to document its provenance.
4. There needs to be a long-term institutional commitment to steward the content. This will require at a minimum a one-time financial investment, and in the better case, an ongoing investment to look over the content and to assist with its use.
5. There needs to be an economic model that can support the technical infrastructure so that there is an assurance that the bills will be paid for the foreseeable future even in the face of institutional failure.
6. There needs to be a rights structure so that the legal use of the content is understood. It would be best if the content could be used even if the original owning individual or institution is no longer in existence.

If we look at things that persist over long periods of time, two principles become clear: First, the more copies there are, the more likely at least one copy will survive. Second, things that get used get preserved. This goes for physical structures as well as texts. The Roman amphitheater in Nimes has persisted for two millenniums not because it was well constructed in 70 AD, but rather because it was consistently used and therefore repaired as needed over time. The city's commitment to the structure, driven by its regular use, means that it is still used for bullfights and other events today. The many repairs over time mean that the structure is not exactly what it was when it was built, but it is still with us. In a similar way the classic texts were preserved: they have been translated and the form of the text is different, but texts that have been consistently used over time garner the attention required to carry them forward from one generation to the next.

There are currently several approaches to long-term digital preservation. The LOCKSS project housed at Stanford University uses the "lots of copies keep stuff safe" strategy, thus the name. It began as a strategy for preserving electronic journals and has grown to encompass digital content generally. LOCKSS uses open-source software and works by having a network of libraries each with their own local LOCKSS Box where digital content acquired by the library is stored. The content is distributed across the network so that multiple copies exist. The system has the means to validate content and revert to the most authoritative version. The LOCKSS Box is integrated into the library's link resolver so that in the event of a failure of a publisher's website, the content remains available. LOCKSS has agreements with a wide range of publishers and is used by numerous libraries and library consortiums. Libraries can join the LOCKSS Alliance for between $2,300 and $11,500, depending on institutional size. The cost of hardware falls to the institution. An offshoot of LOCKSS is CLOCKSS. CLOCKSS (*controlled* LOCKSS) is, as its website says, "a not-for-profit joint venture between the world's leading academic publishers and research libraries whose mission is to build a sustainable, geographically distributed dark archive with which to ensure the long-term survival of Web-based scholarly publications for the benefit of the greater global research community." Annual contributions for a library to be a member range from $450 to $15,000, depending on the size of the library's acquisitions budget.[15]

A preservation service of Ithaka, Portico, like CLOCKSS, is a dark archive that aims to preserve published e-journals, e-books, and digital collections. More than 900 libraries worldwide use the Portico service. Its library support payments structure is based on the library's total materials expenditures and ranges from a few thousand dollars per year to over $20,000. Portico describes its preservations strategy as follows:

> Portico's approach to digital preservation is comprehensive—combining long-term content management and organizational commitment with a philosophical dedication to addressing the needs of tomorrow's scholars.
>
> Portico preserves content through a format-based migration strategy. The key points of this strategy are

- identifying key preservation metadata at the initial point of preservation
- practical preservation of content, such that content is only migrated at the point where it becomes necessary.

In the case of major natural disaster or business failure, the Portico archive could be moved to new stewardship with ease. And, while the archive is dark, publishers and libraries are provided with audit privileges that allow them to review the status of content.[16]

Both Portico and CLOCKSS are focused on published content and assuring access to it in the event of failure of the publisher. Such failure creates a "trigger" event and access to the content is provided from either Portico or CLOCKSS or both. Between these two systems there may be a reliable preservation strategy for the most heavily used published digital content—the 20% that provides 80% of the use. But it is far from clear if this is really the case and there is considerable doubt about content that is even a bit out of the mainstream. Oya Y. Rieger and Robert Wolven reported on a study that looked at the e-journal collections at Columbia and Cornell and concluded that "one of the practical outcomes was a comparative analysis of Portico and LOCKSS preservation coverage for Columbia and Cornell's serial holdings. A key finding was that only 15–20% of the e-journal titles in the libraries' collections are currently preserved by these two initiatives."[17]

Because of the agreements Portico and CLOCKSS have with major publishers, this content is probably safe for the long haul. In other cases, the situation is less clear in large part because libraries sometimes have trouble dealing with content producers. An example of this situation was reported in the *Chronicle of Higher Education*: "In March 2011, the University of Washington's library tried to get a copy of a new recording of the Los Angeles Philharmonic, conducted by Gustavo Dudamel, playing Berlioz's *Symphonie Fantastique* that the library could lend to students. But the recording was available only as a digital download, and Amazon and iTunes forbid renting out digital files." The library was later offered a two year license for 25% of the album for a licensing fee plus a $250 processing fee. The library turned down the deal.[18] In the near term it is unlikely that either Amazon or iTunes will lose this work, but whether it is saved for decades is less certain.

At this time the Digital Preservation Network (DPN) appears to be a promising solution for long-term preservation of large quantities of digital content managed by libraries. The DPN will use a network of nodes to preserve multiple copies of content. Each node will use different technical infrastructures and the nodes will be geographically dispersed. In time the hope would be to also have political diversity among the nodes, although today they are all in the United States. The content would be audited and fixity checked and there would be strategies for repair of damaged content. Succession rights will be accounted for. DPN has developed an economic model that appears to be robust; it is based on an upfront payment when content is deposited into the network. A large portion of this upfront payment is used against future costs and the interest on this portion of the deposit fee provides a margin to assure that future costs can be covered. The DPN financial strategy is at its core an endowment provided to maintain the integrity of the bits. The expectation of reduced future costs for storage and other technical infrastructure is also important in the economic model.

The interesting question is this: will institutions make the required financial commitment? It appears that DPN upfront cost will be in the neighborhood of $5,000 per terabyte for 20 years of preservation. Given that a terabyte hard drive can easily be purchased for well under $100, this might seem like a large sum, but it is actually quite reasonable given the redundancy and continued monitoring and management that will be provided. For digital versions of documents the DPN costs are not unreasonable, but for audio or video content, or for large image datasets, the costs could be prohibitive. It is likely that some triage will be required for many institutions. Factors that will need to be considered include value, uniqueness, and the cost of redigitizing versus the cost of preserving the bits.

Another issue will be managing the preservation process inside the university. Libraries might not have a difficult time managing the collections they hold and have clear responsibility for, but given the decentralized nature of the university, there will inevitably be collections of significance outside of the library that will be harder to manage—or even find. That the library has as an important part of its mission the collection and curation, including preservation, of the output of the campus is not necessarily understood or accepted. The slow acceptance and use of institutional repositories is a sign that this is the case. It will be important for libraries to assert this role on campus while at the same time developing the strategies and capacities to effectively fill the role.

Kirchhoff, Morrissey, and Wittenberg conclude their article on digital preservation by saying, "Ultimately, it is the responsibility of those who produce and care for valuable content to understand preservation options and take action to ensure that the scholarly record remains secure for future generations."[19] What this ultimately means is that there needs to be an institutional commitment to acquire and preserve content. The important questions are about what will motivate an institution to care and to make the required investments. Will real benefits to researchers and students or the bragging rights motivate universities? Will interest in the past or pride of place motivate commitments? Will governments at the federal, state, or local level consider digital preservation an appropriate infrastructure investment? Today the beginnings of the required infrastructure for long-term digital preservation are being created. Portico, CLOCKSS, and DPN are good beginnings. Many libraries are beginning to accept the responsibility of digital preservation of campus assets and content produced on campus, but few have the human or fiscal resources to do what is required. Developing this capacity will be important and difficult.

There are two other items to note concerning digital preservation. The first is that it may be the case that infrastructure for digital preservation will arise because everyone will need it. As Brewster Kahle has said, "Between digitizing the boxes in our basements, filling hard drives with photos, and uploading our videos and e-mail on cloud services, we are creating a bountiful and disorganized mess of our personal histories. Currently, we lack the tools and approaches to save our own histories, much less those of our families and other people we care about."[20]

The Library of Congress has a program addressing Personal Digital Archiving and has supported an annual conference on the subject since 2010. In 2013 the Library of Congress report on personal digital archiving notes that digital preservation "requires a good deal of careful planning and attention. Acting now, and continuing to act tomorrow, is essential if digital materials are to carry memories into the future." The report goes on to say, "The same is true for individuals and families who want to pass on their personal digital memories. One of the still unfolding impacts of the computer age is that everyone now must be their own digital archivist. Without some focused attention, any personal collection is at high risk of loss—and quick loss at that."[21] As individuals come to recognize the danger that their personal and family artifacts are in, it may be that companies will find a market in assisting and some of the problems will get easier. Donald T. Hawkins documented some pioneers working on this in a chapter in the 2013 book *Personal Archiving: Preserving Our Digital Heritage.*[22] At that time there were many interesting products tackling some of the issues, but few appear to have gotten much traction.

The second point concerning digital preservation is that despite the challenges, digital preservation has some distinct advantages, especially if you are concerned with unique items. If a unique physical item is lost or destroyed, it is gone forever. Making digital copies of unique physical items is a hedge against such catastrophic loss. As an example of the risks, on July 6, 2013 a freight train carrying crude oil derailed in Lac-Mégantic, Quebec. The explosion and fire that resulted killed more than 50 people and burned more than 30 buildings in the town's center. One of these buildings was the town's public library. The library, as *Library Journal* reported, "was perhaps best known for its unique archival collection. The library started gathering historical documents and personal effects from residents in 1996, and the collection had since grown to include everything from local social club records to the earliest known photos of the town to information about Donald Morrison, a Lac-Mégantic resident and notorious 19th century outlaw." *Library Journal* goes on to quote Quebec Public Library Association Executive Director Eve

Lagacé who said, "The library is completely destroyed, including of course the collection. There is nothing left." She added, "The library had only recently received many historical and personal archives; not everything had been cataloged."[23] As Schnapp and Battles note, "It is the local or regional forms of culture, memory, and knowledge that run the greatest risk of slipping off the grid."[24] In Lac-Mégantic this is what happened. Had this collection been digitized and backed up off-site, the originals would have been destroyed, but the loss would have been much less significant.

NOTES

1. Michael Buckland, *Redesigning Library Services: A Manifesto* (Chicago: American Library Association, 1992), 45, http://digitalassets.lib.berkeley.edu/sunsite/Redesigning%20Library%20Services_%20A%20Manifesto%20(HTML).pdf.

2. Ibid.

3. Roger C. Schonfeld, *Issue Brief: Taking Stock: Sharing Responsibility for Print Preservation* (New York: Ithaka S+R, July 8, 2015), 10, http://sr.ithaka.org/sites/default/files/files/SR_IssueBrief_Taking_Stock_070815.pdf.

4. Princeton University, "Scheide Donates Rare Books Library to Princeton; Collection Is Largest Gift in University's History," news release, February 16, 2015, http://www.princeton.edu/main/news/archive/S42/38/60E50/index.xml?section=newsreleases.

5. "About Columbia University Libraries/Information Services," Columbia University Libraries/Information Services, accessed May 20, 2015, http://library.columbia.edu/about.html.

6. "About IUB Libraries," Indiana University Libraries: Administration, accessed May 20, 2015, http://libraries.iub.edu/about/administration.

7. "At a Glance,"The University of Kansas: Libraries, accessed May 20, 2015, http://lib.ku.edu/about.

8. "Digest of Educational Statistics: 2012," Institute of Education Sciences: National Center for Educational Statistics, 2012, http://nces.ed.gov/programs/digest/d12/. See Table 334.10 "Expenditures of public degree-granting postsecondary institutions, by purpose of expenditure and level of institution: 2005–06 through 2011–12," Table 334.30 "Total expenditures of private nonprofit degree-granting postsecondary institutions, by purpose and level of institution: 1999–2000 through 2011–12," and Table 701.40 "Collections, staff, and operating expenditures of degree-granting postsecondary institution libraries: Selected years, 1981–82 through 2011–12."

9. "Library Expenditure as % of Total University Expenditure" (Association of Research Libraries, 2013), LibQUAL+, accessed May 21, 2015, http://www.libqual.org/documents/admin/EG_4.pdf.

10. James Hilton et al., "The Case for Building a Digital Preservation Network," *EDUCAUSE Review* 48 no. 4 (July/August 2013): 46–47, http://www.educause.edu/ero/article/case-building-digital-preservation-network.

11. Lorcan Dempsey, Constance Malpas, and Brian Lavoie, "Collection Directions: The Evolution of Library Collections and Collecting," *portal: Libraries and the Academy* 14, no. 3 (July 2014): 395.

12. Ibid., 397.

13. Michael A. McRobbie, "Looking to the Future: Preparing for Indiana University's Bicentenary" (State of the University speech, Indiana University Bloomington, Bloomington, IN, October 1, 2013), http://president.iu.edu/speeches/2013/20131001-01.shtml.

14. Amy Kirchhoff, Sheila Morrissey, and Kate Wittenberg, "Networked Information's Risky Future: The Promises and Challenges of Digital Preservation," *EDUCAUSE Review* 50, no. 2 (March/April 2015): 50–51, http://www.educause.edu/ero/article/networked-informations-risky-future-promises-and-challenges-digital-preservation.

15. CLOCKSS website, accessed May 21, 2005, https://www.clockss.org/clockss/Home.

16. Portico website, accessed May 21, 2005, http://www.portico.org/digital-preservation/services/preservation-approach.

17. Oya Y. Rieger and Robert Wolven, "Preservation Status of e-Resources: A Potential Crisis in Electronic Journal Preservation" (presentation, Project Briefing Coalition for Networked Information Fall 2011 Meeting, Arlington, VA, December 13, 2011), http://www.cni.org/topics/digital-preservation/preservation-status-of-eresources/.

18. Steve Kolowich, "How Streaming Media Could Threaten the Mission of Libraries," *Chronicle of Higher Education*, August 22, 2014, http://chronicle.com/blogs/wiredcampus/how-streaming-media-threaten-the-mission-of-libraries/54357.

19. Kirchhoff, Morrissey, and Wittenberg, "Networked Information's Risky Future," 51.

20. Brewster Kahle, "Foreword," in *Personal Archiving: Preserving Our Digital Heritage* (Medford, NJ : Information Today, 2013), ProQuest ebrary e-book, xiii.

21. National Digital Information Infrastructure and Preservation Program, *Perspectives on Personal Digital Archiving: National Digital Information Infrastructure and Preservation Program* (Washington, DC: Library of Congress, 2013), 3, http://www.digitalpreservation.gov/documents/ebookpdf_march18.pdf.

22. Donald T. Hawkins, "Software and Services for Personal Archiving," in *Personal Archiving: Preserving Our Digital Heritage* (Medford, NJ : Information Today, 2013), ProQuest ebrary e-book, 47–72.

23. Elizabeth Michaelson, "Fire Destroys Canadian Library, Archive." *Library Journal* July 29, 2013, http://lj.libraryjournal.com/2013/07/industry-news/fire-destroys-canadian-library-archive/#.

24. Jeffrey T. Schnapp and Matthew Battles, *The Library Beyond the Book* (Cambridge, MA: Harvard University Press, 2014), 103.

Step Five

Making the Money Work

The cause of this collective free fall—a broken system of scholarly publishing—is by now well known. What bears mentioning, however, is the potential liberation that comes from recognizing the impossibility of buying ourselves free—the freedom of despair, if you like. . . . Should we embrace despair as an unshackling force that frees us to try new things? Might despair provide the excuse we need to spend money on ventures that—however risky—are less certain to fail than the system that bedevils us now? Perhaps it is precisely because resources are diminishing that we must spend those diminished resources on new initiatives. Hopelessness provides the impetus we need to make impossible choices.—Bryn Geffert[1]

Scholarly publishing has been in a period of transformation for at least the past 40 years. For the first 20 years the change was driven more by economics than technology, and for the last 20 years economics and technology have been intertwined. None of this has been good for academic libraries. They have largely been forced into a reactive mode as they attempt to respond. In particular, they struggled to respond to the takeover of scientific, medical, and technical journal publishing by a small number of for-profit publishers who realized that scientific journals were monopoly goods, acquired the most important ones, and then exploited these monopolies at the expense of libraries. This process began when journals were still distributed in print, but has carried over to and been pressed even harder as the distribution became digital. The academic library response to being exploited was not forward looking or strategic. The truth is that there was little that libraries could do, aside from complaining—which they did loudly and often—because they had little or no bargaining power. The big for-profit publishers held all of the cards and they played their hand well.

But there has been a shift. I believe academic libraries can now alter what they do in a strategic way. They can look forward and chart the course they wish without the constraints that previously held them back. The new digital technologies allow for new business models and radically lower the costs of entry into publishing. As Clay Shirky bluntly puts it, "With the old economics destroyed, organizational forms perfected for industrial production have to be replaced with structures optimized for digital data. It makes increasingly less sense even to talk about a publishing industry, because the core problem publishing solves—the incredible difficulty, complexity, and expense of making something available to the public—has stopped being a problem."[2] Shirky may overstate his point, but it is valid nonetheless. The for-profit publisher's monopolies still exist, at least for now, but they are less compelling and are quickly being eroded around the edges. There is good reason to believe the balance of power is changing.

I believe that academic libraries have an opportunity to alter their economic position in ways that will make their operations more efficient and potentially cheaper. At the very least they should be able to provide better service without the need for significant new influxes of funding. Saying this may make some librarians uncomfortable, and maybe it should, for taking advantage of the changing landscape of scholarly publishing will require changing practice. The alternative of continuing on the path academic libraries have travelled for the past several decades—begging for new funding to continue in an exploitive relationship with publishers and trimming only as a last resort and only at the edges—will not be viable given the current state of higher education funding.

There are several changes in the landscape of scholarly publication that will make new strategies possible:

- The growth of open access as the business model for scholarly publishing.
- The unbundling of the article from the journal.
- The ability of purchase-on-demand as a means of avoiding unnecessary expenditures, particularly for books.
- The growth of high quality free content of all kinds and free discovery tools on the web.

Geffert's quote at the beginning of the chapter might imply that there is no clear way forward and that we need to look to "impossible choices." I don't think this is the case. Rather, I believe the changes we can observe today provide an alternative strategy that, if applied, will lead away from despair and toward a better service model. The simple version of the strategy is that we need to stop relying on a library collection as the means to providing documents and move to other ways of providing our users the documents they need.

The growth of "open access" in scholarly journal publishing is the most compelling example of a new publishing model that takes advantage of the web and creates new ways of publishing. It is too early to judge conclusively whether open access will become the dominant form of scholarly journal publishing, though I believe this will be the case.[3] Open access journals of course are given away to readers and libraries need not purchase them, so to the extent that they become the model for journal publishing, library acquisitions costs will be reduced. There may be author costs such as article processing fees that the library or the university may choose to support, but the bulk of the required author-side funding, especially in the sciences, will likely be covered by grants. Even if the library assumes some responsibility for author-side costs, open access journal publishing will reduce library expenditures in many if not all institutions. This is a very significant development because the increased cost of journals in the sciences has been the single most important driver of the cost increase that academic libraries have had to absorb over the past three or four decades and has been the driver of most library budgeting. This then is potentially the place where the largest savings are in the future.

To the extent that subscription journals continue, there are opportunities to purchase articles one at a time rather than to purchase full journals. In some cases, this will result in lower costs and service that is as, or nearly as, quick as the availability provided by subscriptions. Price points for individual articles from services like the Copyright Clearance Center's Get It Now service are about $25 and they guarantee delivery in several hours. Science Direct (Elsevier) charges between $15 and $40 per article or chapter and access is immediate.[4] It is easy to imagine that libraries could build systems that connect with their link resolvers and purchase articles in ways that would appear to the user to be no different from subscription access. As with any purchase-on-demand arrangement, the library accepts some financial risk in the event of heavier-than-expected use, nonetheless it seems hard to imagine that there are not some savings to be had. I also suspect that the ability of publishers to increase the prices of articles will be more constrained than pricing for subscriptions. Some significant portion of individual article sales are to individuals who are likely to be more price sensitive than libraries have been—especially if the purchase is done with the individual's money. Even when the library pays, there would seem to be a price point at which researchers would be appalled by the cost and look for alternative ways of getting a copy of the required article, like e-mailing the author or looking for a preprint in an institutional repository.

For many years it has been understood that libraries purchase large numbers of books that are never used. In the pre-Internet world this made sense.

Even for expert and experienced librarians, predicting which books would ultimately be used is an art at best and more often a guessing game. But given that many academic books went quickly out of print and the used book market was expensive and slow, it made good sense to pursue a just-in-case strategy. The Internet and the remarkable changes it has brought to both the new and used book markets, combined with print-on-demand publishing, mean that you now do not need to purchase just-in-case, even for print books. I have sometimes joked that my library should load the bibliographic records for all of the books Amazon sells into our catalog with a location code that says "remote storage facility, allow 48 hours for delivery." There would of course be no real remote storage facility, we would simply order the book if and when a request came, and in most cases we would be able to deliver the book within 48 hours. As an example of how this can be done, the Bucknell University library moved to an exclusively patron-driven purchase model for books and significantly decreased the amount of money spent, which between 2012 and 2014 declined from slightly less than $600,000 to just over $100,000, without any notable decline in circulations. The result was "a vibrant collection that receives significant use."[5]

Gail Herrera considered the feasibility of large-scale, patron-driven acquisitions from a different perspective. She looked at the titles that were used for the first time at the University of Mississippi Libraries (UML). As she reports, "Of the 8,020 unique titles used for the first time in 2012, 76% (6,130 titles) were available for purchase. Out of the 6,130 titles available for purchase, 3% (165 titles) were both available for purchase and freely available online." Of the remaining 1,682 titles, 94% could be obtained through ILL with partners in the regional consortia. If you consider only the 4,172 titles published since 2000, only 266, or 6.4%, were not available for purchase. Herrera concludes, "For libraries considering or employing a print PDA program at any scale, the findings of this study should be reassuring since the vast majority of print books needed by UML users were available for purchase."[6]

When a library should purchase a book is an interesting question. The answer will be different for different libraries, but in all cases many fewer books should be purchased in anticipation of use. There should be significant savings here both from the cost of the books (as was the case at Bucknell University) and from fewer acquisitions, reduced cataloging costs, and savings of librarians' time that is no longer dedicated to selection. The move to purchase-on-demand rather than just-in-case not only means fewer purchases, but also means purchasing in a very different way. Collections and the accompanying bibliographic apparatus will no longer be built one at a time, item by item, but rather will be built with large blocks of content with the batch loading of accompanying bibliographic data or automatic purchasing with automatic loading of bibliographic data. It has traditionally been the case that the cost of acquiring and processing a book would be roughly equal to the cost of the book itself with most of these costs in staff time. This should change and the processing cost should drop to a fraction of the book cost.

This change in purchasing strategy will also have an impact on scholarly book publishers who do not yet appear to appreciate that their sales to libraries might decrease as libraries stop buying books they do not yet need. As libraries become more efficient in the use of their book purchasing dollars, fewer books will be purchased. Scholarly publishers have long counted on the redundant purchasing by academic libraries. In the future, this redundant purchasing should be significantly reduced.

Finally, while it is the most difficult of the four areas to quantify, it is clearly the case that an increasing amount of quality content and good discovery tools are available for free on the web. *Wikipedia* and Google Scholar are the obvious examples. Data.gov and the Digital Public Library of America are portals to large and growing bodies of content. TED, NPR, the BBC, the World Bank, and many others host large stores of free quality content. Google Books and the HathiTrust have made millions of public domain books available. JSTOR makes its journal content, published prior to 1923 in the United States and prior to 1870 elsewhere, freely available. Government and international organization data, like that from the World Bank, are clear substitutes for purchased content. NPR and the BBC are sources most libraries did not, or could not, access in the past so they are not clear substitutes, but they might replace newspaper or other purchased news content. While it is hard to predict how libraries will be able to reduce purchased content as a result of this growing body of high-quality, web-based content, it is inevitable that opportunities will arise.

All of this should provide an opportunity to spend less on all aspects of collections while at the same time providing more access to content. A just-in-case collection strategy is by definition limited by the amount of content that the library can afford. The promise to the users in the past with the just-in-case strategy was that the library would spend the money it gets as wisely as it could and build the best collection it could to meet user's needs. In contrast, the promise of the just-in-time strategy is that the library will get whatever the user needs when they need it as quickly and as easily as possible given the limits of the resources that are provided. Libraries have of course always used a mix of these two strategies, but in general the mix has been tilted heavily toward just-in-case. Tilting heavily the other way—toward just-in-time—should be the way of doing business going forward. I believe that, with little or no real dollar increases in their materials expenditures, an assertive move to a just-in-time strategy for books, a shift to article purchases rather than subscriptions for journals in conjunction with a reasonable growth in the amount of open access content (particularly STEM journal content), and the growth of other quality, free, web-based content should make it possible for libraries to provide the documents their users need. I believe this to be the case even if prices for journal subscriptions continue to increase at 6% to 8% per year.

From the perspective of a library administrator, there is an interesting question in this change of strategy. It may seem silly, but I think there's a real dilemma. There are a number of ways of asking the question: should we tell anyone, especially the faculty, what we are now doing? Is it better to be frank and open and explain how the library is adapting to changing circumstances, or should we hope that increases in the quality of what we provide will be convincing? Will the fact that we can do more with less overcome the concerns that the library is no longer behaving in the way it always has?

One would think that openness and honestly would win the day, but as was reported in the *Inside Higher Ed* article, "Clash in the Stacks," a number of library directors have lost their jobs because of "clashes with faculty and administrators over how much—and how fast—the academic library should change."[7] My own view is that the best path is a continued conversation with the campus on the changing nature of scholarly communication and the more effective way of spending library resources, combined with ongoing development of the means of implementing new strategies that demonstrate their effectiveness. Unfortunately, as the cases documented by *Inside Higher Ed* demonstrate, some institutions are not ready for the conversation, let alone a change in strategy.

A second important question may be as difficult to discuss. If academic libraries change the strategies they use to provide their users with documents, how does this impact the broader ecosystem of scholarly publishing? As librarians, we need to be concerned with how what we do impacts others. There is a dilemma here. The whole ecosystem is in flux. The technological changes that are providing libraries with new opportunities are impacting all of the other players in scholarly communication. As Christensen would tell us to expect, the whole value chain is being disrupted. It is in the interest of the library to be part of a healthy ecosystem and we will need to play a part in shaping it. We need a different scholarly ecosystem, but in creating it we need to think about and act in ways, both individually and collectively, that lead to an ecosystem in which scholarship can prosper.

THE FUTURE OF ACADEMIC LIBRARY MATERIALS EXPENDITURES: A THOUGHT EXPERIMENT

In the argument made above I asserted that I believe it is possible to create a strategy, or set of strategies, that would make it possible for libraries to provide the documents their users need with little or no real dollar increases in their materials expenditures. I went as far as to assert that I believe this to be the case even if prices for journal subscriptions continue to increase at 6% to 8% per year. Simply asserting this is really not sufficient, so what follows is the example of how this might be done. We will do this by modeling a hypothetical library materials budget, making some assumptions about price increases and how purchasing strategies can change in light of the four trends. We will look at this over a ten-year time frame (2015 to 2024). The changes will involve four strategies:

1. Moving to a PDA model for book purchases
2. Purchasing individual articles as an alternative to journal subscriptions
3. Replacing subscriptions with open access
4. Replacing databases with free web content

THE HYPOTHETICAL MATERIALS BUDGET

Our hypothetical budget will begin as shown in the following table. We will assume that print and e-books are purchased from the same bucket of funds and will not concern ourselves with what will inevitably be an increase in the purchase of e-books and the purchase of fewer print books. For the purpose of our experiment we will assume costs for both formats behave in the same way. What is included in the databases category is somewhat nebulous, but will include reference tools; aggregations of content such as EBSCO, Pro-Quest, JSTOR or MUSE; statistical compilations; and so forth. Journals will include subscriptions directly from publishers, either individual titles or packages.

Materials Fund in 2015

	Expenditures	% of Total
Books (print and e-books)	$450,000	15.0%
Journals	$1,740,000	58.0%
Document delivery	$60,000	2.0%
Databases	$750,000	25.0%
Total costs	$3,000,000	100.0%

PRICE INCREASES

We will assume that price increases are as follows:

Books: 3% per year
Journals: 8% per year
Articles (purchased individually): 5% per year

Databases: 5% per year

Implementing Strategy 1: Moving to a PDA Model for Book Purchases

For the purposes of our experiment we will assume that by moving to a PDA model for book purchasing over three years, our hypothetical library can reduce the amount spent on books by 20% in each of these years. This is a notably less dramatic implementation than was done at Bucknell University. We will assume that the cost of an average book in 2015 is $50.00. The results of this change in the strategy for book purchasing are shown in the following table.

	2015	2018	2021	2024	10-year % change
Book costs	$450,000	$251,764	$275,110	$300,620	-33.2%
Cost per book	$50.00	$54.64	$59.70	$65.24	30.5%
Books purchased	9,000	4,608	4,608	4,608	-48.8%

Over the decade the expenditures drop by 33.2%, or about $150,000 even as book prices increase by 30.5%. After the initial change in purchasing strategy the number of books purchased per year remains the same—just a bit less than 50% of the number purchased before the change.

If we were to be more aggressive and reduce the amount spent on books by 25% in each of the first three years, which would be close to the Bucknell University experience, the results would be as shown in the next table.

	2015	2018	2021	2024	10-year % change
Book costs	$450,000	$207,447	$226,683	$247,703	-45.0%
Cost per book	$50.00	$54.64	$59.70	$65.24	30.5%
Books purchased	9,000	3,797	3,797	3,797	-57.8%

The expenditures on books at the end of the 10-year period would have declined by 45.0% and the number of books purchased would have declined by 57.8%. For our model we will assume the first implementation of this strategy.

Implementing Strategy 2: Purchasing Individual Articles as an Alternative to Journal Subscriptions

While there are clearly situations where the level of use of a particular journal title makes a subscription the most economical choice, there are also likely to be journals in many library collections where the required uses can be provided less expensively by purchasing individual articles. At the most basic level, establishing this is quite simple. If the number of uses multiplied by the cost to purchase individual articles is less than the subscription cost, then individual article purchase is the more economical means of providing users with the articles they need. So, for example, if a journal title is expected to have 100 uses per year and the cost of purchasing individual articles is $25 per article, then the total cost would be expected to be $2,500 annually. If the subscription to the title is $3,000, then $500 can be saved and the title should be cancelled and articles purchased separately. If, on the other hand, the subscription is $1,200, it should be kept.

There are two other considerations. The first is the uncertainty of use. It may be wise to err on the side of keeping a subscription if the use varies by year or if the breakeven is close to the subscription cost. The other consideration is that in most cases, a library is entitled to access to the back files of a title it has paid for as part of a subscription even if the subscription is cancelled. This means that the only articles that will need to be purchased will be those published after the cancellation goes into effect. Initially this will involve only a small number of issues. The gap will widen over time and more articles will need to be purchased, but this factor reduces the risk of this strategy in the short run.

To model the implementation of this strategy, we will assume that the number of journals subscribed to was reduced by 10% in 2016, 2018, and 2020 and that each time subscriptions were cut, the document delivery budget was increased by 30%. We are assuming the cost of a separately purchased article is $25 in 2015. The results are shown in the following table.

The journals costs increased 45.7% and the document delivery costs increased by 240.8%, with the total cost of providing journal articles increased $940,154 or 52.2%. The number of journal subscriptions declines by 27.1% and the number of articles purchased increases 119.7%.

This might not seem like it would be worth the effort, but despite the fact that costs are not contained to the extent we might hope, it does make a big difference. If this strategy were not implemented, the result over the decade would have been quite different. The total cost of providing articles would have risen to $3,571,348 or nearly double what it was at the beginning of the period. Thus implementing this strategy would mean the annual cost of articles would be $831,195 less and the total amount saved over the ten years would be $4,678,284. This is not chump change.

	2015	2018	2021	2024	10-year % change
Journal costs	$1,740,000	$1,775,438	$2,012,887	$2,535,657	45.7%
Cost per subscription	$1,000	$1,260	$1,587	$1,999	99.9%
Journal subscriptions	1,740	1,409	1,268	1,268	-27.1%
Document delivery costs	$60,000	$117,383	$176,651	$204,496	240.8%
Cost per article	$25.00	$28.94	$33.50	$38.78	55.1%
Articles purchased	2,400	4,056	5,273	5,273	119.7%
Total cost	$1,800,000	$1,892,821	$2,189,538	$2,740,153	52.2%

Implementing Strategy 3: Replacing Subscriptions with Open Access

It is unclear how a library will be able to build a strategy to reduce expenditures on journal subscriptions based on the growth of Gold OA, but it should be the case that some reduction is possible. There are two issues that need to be considered: The first is what rate of substitution can we expect. The second is how a library can reduce its collection of subscription journals based on the growth of Gold OA.

Let's look at the first issue. My recent prediction for the rate of substitution, based on the assumption that Gold OA is a disruptive innovation and that it follows substitution trends of other disruptive innovations, is shown in the first line of the table below. I have assumed that the Gold OA substitution stops at 90%. If we assume a 5% straight-line increase beginning with Gold OA having 20% penetration, we get the figures in the second line of the table below. For the purposes of our model, I will use an intermediate assumption. We will assume a penetration of Gold OA in 2015 of 20% and add an increasing percentage as follows to that base: 2.5% in 2016, 3.0% in 2017, 3.5% in 2018, etc. These different assumptions are shown in the following chart and graph.

	2015	2018	2021	2024
Lewis projection	22.8%	38.2%	63.8%	90.0%
5% increase per year	20.0%	26.6%	35.4%	47.2%
Model	20.0%	29.0%	42.5%	60.5%

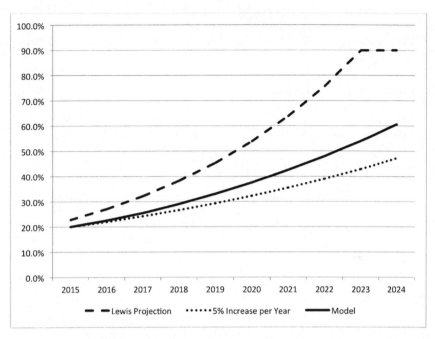

Rate of Gold OA Substitution.

The second issue that we need to resolve is how a library can take advantage of the increasing substitution of Gold OA for subscriptions. It might be argued that libraries will need to keep many of their existing subscriptions even as Gold OA expands because the new Gold OA titles are not really substitutes, but rather are new and different titles. Substitution may happen, as in the example of the *Lingua* and *Glossa*, where the editorial board quit one journal and started another, shows. It is unclear whether this is the beginning of a trend or a one-time event.[8] For the purposes of our model we will first assume that our hypothetical library will be able to capture half of the savings represented by the increase in Gold OA. The results are shown in the next table.

	2015	2018	2021	2024	10-year % change
Journal costs	$1,740,000	$2,066,187	$2,346,756	$2,465,054	41.7%
Cost per subscription	$1,000	$1,260	$1,587	$1,999	99.9%
Journal subscriptions	1,740	1,640	1,479	1,233	-29.1%

If half of the substitution of Gold OA for subscriptions can be captured, then journal costs rise 41.7% and the number of journals subscribed to decreases by 507, or 29.1%.

Combining Strategies 2 and 3

If both strategies for mitigating journal costs increase are employed, the results are shown in the next table. The combination of the two strategies means that journal costs increase only $57,025, or 3.3%, over the decade. The number of journals subscribed to decreases by 841, or 48.3%.

	2015	2018	2021	2024	10-year % change
Total cost	$1,740,000	$1,673,612	$1,710,785	$1,797,025	3.3%
Cost per subscription	$1,000	$1,260	$1,587	$1,999	99.9%
Journal subscriptions	1,740	1,329	1,078	899	-48.3%

Strategy 4: Replacing Databases with Free Web Content

As noted above it is difficult to anticipate how free content on the web will substitute for the variety of database content purchased by libraries. It is easy, however, to imagine that many libraries will soon find that the money they spend on some resources is no longer justified given the free alternatives. For the purpose of this exercise we will assume that the database portion of the budget can be reduced by 2% each year because of the substitution of free content for content that would previously have been purchased. The projected results would be as shown in the following table. Over the decade, costs of databases would increase by $220,062, or 29.3%.

	2015	2018	2021	2024	10-year % change
Database costs	$750,000	$817,161	$890,335	$970,062	29.3%

Overall Effect of Instituting these Four Strategies

The overall effect of implementing the four strategies laid out in this model is shown in the following table and graph.

	2015	2018	2021	2024	10-year % change
Book costs	450,000	207,447	226,683	247,703	-45.0%

Journal costs	1,740,000	1,673,612	1,710,785	1,797,025	3.3%
Document delivery costs	60,000	117,383	176,651	204,496	240.8%
Database costs	750,000	817,161	890,335	970,062	29.3%
Total costs	3,000,000	2,815,603	3,004,455	3,219,286	7.3%

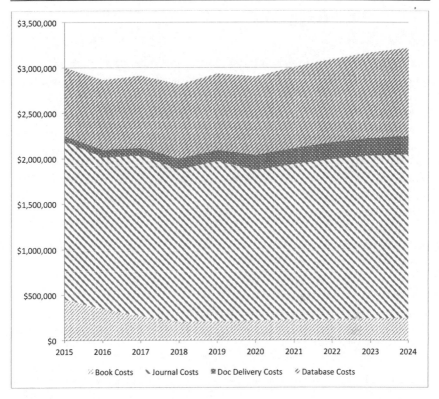

Total Expenditures from 2015 to 2024.

The overall result over the decade of the model would be a $219,286, or 7.3%, increase in the cost of materials for our hypothetical library. It is interesting to note that the cost of providing books and journals is $776 less at the end of the decade than it was at the beginning. For much of the decade the costs are below what they were at the beginning. In fact, the total expenditures over the decade are $29,918,156. If the library were able to maintain its beginning $3,000,000 budget and bank the savings from year to year, at the end of the decade the library would have had $81,845 left in the bank.

Two more aggressive variations on this strategy would allow our hypothetical library to have expenditures at the end of the decade that are about the same as they were at the beginning. If the library were able to reduce its databases by 5% per year—that is, keeping a constant dollar expenditure for databases throughout the decade—it would have a total expenditure of $2,982,516, or 0.6% below the initial $3,000,000. Alternatively, if the library were able to capture 70% of the substitution of Gold OA rather than only 50%, then it would end the decade with a materials expenditure of $2,980,771, or again 0.6% below where it began the decade.

CONCLUSION TO THE THOUGHT EXPERIMENT

For a long time, academic libraries have faced relentless price increases, especially for journals and more recently for databases. For a long time there was little that libraries could do besides belt tightening and begging their campuses for more money. Recent developments are driven by the digitization of content. These include the ability to purchase content only when there is an actual need, the development of open-access publishing, and the development of increasing quantities of quality, free content on the web of all types. These developments mean that strategies exist, or can be easily imagined, that will provide libraries with the opportunity to provide their users with the content they require without continued unreasonable increases in expenditures.

Welcome to a new world.

NOTES

1. Bryn Geffert, "A Librarian's Defense of Despair," *Chronicle of Higher Education: The Conversation* (blog), March 6, 2015, http://chronicle.com/blogs/conversation/2015/03/06/in-defense-of-librarians-despair/.

2. Clay Shirky, "Newspapers and Thinking the Unthinkable," *Clay Shirky* (blog), March 13, 2009, http://www.shirky.com/weblog/2009/03/newspapers-and-thinking-the-unthinkable/.

3. David W. Lewis, "The Inevitability of Open Access," *College & Research Libraries* 73, no. 5 (September 2012): 493–506, http://crl.acrl.org/content/73/5/493.full.pdf+html and http://hdl.handle.net/1805/2929; and David W. Lewis, "The Inevitability of Open Access: Update One," *ScholarWorks*, August 2013, https://scholarworks.iupui.edu/handle/1805/3471.

4. "Article Choice," Elsevier, accessed May 16, 2015, http://www.elsevier.com/online-tools/sciencedirect/articles#pay-per-view.

5. Param Bedi and Jason Snyder, "Making a Difference: Moving Your Organization from Transactional to Transformational," *EDUCAUSE Review*, March 16, 2015, http://www.educause.edu/ero/article/making-difference-moving-your-organization-transactional-transformational.

6. Gail Herrera, "Testing the Patron-Driven Model: Availability Analysis of First-Time Use Books," *Collection Management*, 40 no. 1 (January 2015): 7–8, doi:0.1080/01462679.2014.965863.

7. Carl Straumsheim, "Clash in the Stacks," *Inside Higher Ed*, December 10, 2014, https://www.insidehighered.com/news/2014/12/10/rethinking-library-proves-divisive-topic-many-liberal-arts-institutions.

8. See Scott Jaschik, "Language of Protest," *Inside Higher Education*, November 2, 2015, https://www.insidehighered.com/news/2015/11/02/editors-and-editorial-board-quit-top-linguistics-journal-protest-subscription-fees; and Ellen Wexler, "What a Mass Exodus at a Lin-

guistics Journal Means for Scholarly Publishing," *Chronicle of Higher Education*, November 5, 2015, http://chronicle.com/article/What-a-Mass-Exodus-at-a/234066.

Step Six

Working with the Smart Machine

In the context of networked information, librarianship looks less like a profession with perks and prescriptions, and more of a sensibility. In a sense, then, we're all librarians now.—Jeffrey T. Schnapp and Matthew Battles [1]

We're close to the point where the available knowledge at the hands of the individual, for questions that can be posed clearly and articulately, is not so far from the knowledge of the entire world. Whether it is through Siri, Google, or Wikipedia, there is now almost always a way to ask and—more importantly— a way to receive the answer in relatively digestible form.—Tyler Cowen [2]

On May 11, 1997, IBM's Deep Blue computer defeated Garry Kasparov, then the world's most accomplished human chess player. When asked about the defeat Kasparov was quoted by the *New York Times* as saying, "I'm a human being. When I see something that is well beyond my understanding, I'm afraid." [3] Fourteen years later in February 2011 another IBM machine, Watson, played *Jeopardy!* against Brad Rutter and Ken Jennings, two of the most successful *Jeopardy!* champions. Watson won going away. Jennings said later in a TED talk, "I felt like 'quiz show contestant' was now the first job that had become obsolete under this new regime of thinking computers." [4] In two of what had previously been assumed to be humanity's greatest intellectual arenas—chess and *Jeopardy!*—a computer had beaten the best human players. For Watson *Jeopardy!* was only the beginning. IBM working with the Memorial Sloan Kettering Cancer Center and the insurance company WellPoint is using Watson's capacities in absorbing huge quantities of data and interpreting human questions to diagnose and recommend treatments for cancer. Two years after the *Jeopardy!* victory, IBM was putting on a demonstration for potential customers and, according to the *New York Times*, had Watson design a breakfast pastry, a Spanish-inspired crescent whose ingredients include cocoa, saffron, black pepper, almonds, and honey.[5]

On March 13, 2004, DARPA, the Defense Advanced Research Projects Agency, held its first Grand Challenge competition to develop the technologies for an autonomous ground vehicle, in essence, a driverless car. They set out a 240-kilometer course in the Mojave Desert. The Sandstorm car developed by a team from Carnegie Mellon University won the competition by traveling further than any other vehicle, not quite 12 kilometers, before it got stuck on a rock. Ten years later in the spring of 2014 Google announced it was building a prototype fleet of 100 experimental, electric-powered, self-driving vehicles with only two controls, a start button and a red "e-stop" button for panic stops. As the *New York Times* put it, "The car would be summoned with a smartphone application. It would pick up a passenger and automatically drive to a destination selected on a smartphone app without any human intervention."[6]

Watson and Google's driverless car are but two examples of what is becoming increasingly common—the smart machine. The smart machine is not automation as we are used to thinking about it, rather the smart machine can, more quickly and accurately, accomplish functions that until very recently were thought to be the sole province of human intelligence. As Nicholas Carr puts it in *The Glass Cage: Automation and Us*,

> Google's car resets the boundary between human and computer, and it does so more dramatically, more decisively, than have earlier breakthroughs in programming. It tells us that our idea of the limits of automation has always been something of a fiction. We're not as special as we think we are. While the distinction between tacit and explicit knowledge remains a useful one in the realm of human psychology, it has lost much of its relevance to discussions of automation.[7]

It was long thought that machines could manage tasks, even very complicated ones, where only explicit knowledge is required. However, when the task requires tacit knowledge, the things we people can do without thinking, but cannot be easily described, machines will come up short. As Carr says, it seems this assumption was wrong. The smart machine will have consequences and will require a change in how we think about work and what it means to be a professional.

In the summer of 2014 the Pew Research Center canvassed nearly 1,900 technology experts and asked, "Will networked, automated, artificial intelligence (AI) applications and robotic devices have displaced more jobs than they have created by 2025?" The respondents split down the middle with 48% saying more jobs would be displaced and 52% saying more would be created. But there was general agreement that there were huge implications for a wide range of industries and for the first time many professionals will be replaced by automated systems. [8]

Tyler Cowen in his book on work with intelligent machines, *Average Is Over*, suggests that increasingly work will be like Freestyle chess. [9] Freestyle chess is played by people, often in teams, and any form of assistance is allowed. The usual assistance is provided by one or more chess-playing computer programs. It should not be a surprise that it turns out that the level of chess played by the combination of human and computer is much better than when the game is played by humans alone. As Cowen puts it, "The top games of Freestyle chess probably are the greatest heights chess has reached." Then he adds, "though who actually is to judge?" [10] What might be surprising is that the skills required to be an elite Freestyle chess player are very different from those possessed by human grandmasters of the past. An exceptionally deep knowledge of chess is not required. Most of the best Freestyle chess players are not grandmasters. What is required is knowledge of the strengths and weakness of the computer systems you are working with and an understanding of when and how to take the advice they offer. Importantly you need to understand your limits. Thinking that you are smarter than the machine is almost never a winning strategy. This form of human-computer teamwork, Cowen argues, will increasingly be a significant component in professional work and the results will be similar to chess where quality is enhanced. This is not particularly frightening, except that we need to recognize that the machines will continue to get smarter. Moore's Law is not going away. Smart machines will continue to absorb human expertise and over time the human component will become a less significant part of the team.

For librarians, especially reference librarians who have been around for a while, the predictions made by Cowen should sound familiar. It's what has happened to reference work over the past 40 years. In 1980 Brian Nielson published an article in *Online Review* titled "Online Bibliographic Searching and the Deprofessionalization of Librarianship." [11] At the time, computer-based bibliographic searching was a new service that had only been offered in most academic libraries for a couple of years. New skills were required of librarians, a full understanding of Boolean logic, and how to use subject vocabularies. Searches were expensive, sometimes costing $100 or more, and users were often charged in order to recover these costs. But librarians with the new computer tools could create complex custom bibliographies and save scholars and researchers days or even weeks of tedious work. Nielson had surveyed librarians concerning their attitudes toward online searching and found that their enthusiasm for it was based on the increased professional status the activity brought rather than an enthusiasm for the technology.

What Nielson understood that escaped other observers at the time was that this increased status would be short lived. Online search systems would quickly become designed for the end user and special skills that had been reserved for librarians would be available to everyone. Nielson was correct, and within a decade online catalogs and indexes—first on CD-ROM and then Internet-based—were not the exception but the rule. Yahoo briefly used librarians to organize the web, but this approach did not last long. Sophisticated algorithms and huge databases soon proved their superiority at organizing the web and they did so in ways that most people can't comprehend.

As the tools developed, the role of the reference librarian changed. In the print world, reference librarians assisted users with collections. They had a broad and often deep knowledge of reference books and the ways in which they could lead users to answers to their questions, and to articles and books in the library's general collection and in the world beyond it. With the first computer systems, reference librarians needed to master Boolean logic and understand the vocabularies of various databases and know when to use which databases. As systems became more broadly available and simpler to use, reference librarians stepped back and, rather than doing the searching, they were more likely to teach users how to do it for themselves. Today the focus is not library or bibliographic instruction, but rather information literacy. This reflects a change from teaching the use of tools, which now for many uses are quite simple and powerful, to teaching information evaluation.

This pattern in the evolution of professional roles is not unusual. Tyler Cowen argues that most professionals will work with smart machines and the evolution of roles will follow the same trajectory as the one experienced by reference librarians. As we look forward, it is clear that we are only at the beginning of the automation of knowledge work. What happened to basic reference work can be expected to happen in most other domains of professional library work.

The quote from Schnapp and Battle that begins this chapter speaks to the fact that as information moves to the network and powerful tools for managing information are developed at network scale, the library dissolves and becomes something that is everywhere—and everyone becomes their own librarian. As they say about reference work, "The library is everywhere and the reference oracle is a search box with algorithmically sorted results. . . . In the era of social media and networked communications, reference is self-reference: democratized, user driven, user centered." [12]

This is certainly true to a great extent, but Schnapp and Battle go on to claim an ongoing role for librarians: "The networks that deliver information . . . function best in the context of participation. Librarians foment and facilitate such participation, helping citizens to forge their own connections with the life of information. . . . Where librarians once acted as gatekeepers guarding limited resources, they now become lock-pickers and safecrackers." [13] It is hard for me to imagine exactly what this means except that there will be high levels of expertise that will on occasion need to be brought to bear and that people will turn to librarians for it. If this turns out to be the case, we need to be ready.

Most of the things professional librarians did when I began my career in the mid-1970s no longer matter much. In my graduate school cataloging class we learned how to punctuate a catalog card. We learned how many spaces to indent before beginning the call number. As a reference librarian early in my career, I knew which books were most likely to contain the answers to the questions students asked. I knew where the books were located and the color of their bindings. A few years later, tackling the latest technology and mastering Boolean logic, I learned how to do online searches. Before becoming an administrator, I bought books and built collections. None of the expertise I had then is of much use now. The only bit of expertise from my early career that that has survived is teaching, though what is taught, and in many cases how it is taught, is much different now from what it was then. So what can librarians do now, and what will they do in the future?

In trying to sort out how to respond to changes in technology and other aspects of our environment, it is interesting to look at the ACRL's 75th anniversary report, *New Roles for the Road Ahead*.[14] After cataloging the challenges of the current environment for libraries and higher education the report's three authors, Steven Bell, Lorcan Dempsey, and Barbara Fister, all thoughtful and prolific commentators, lay out the new roles as they see them. Fister calls for repositioning library space and for creating a common ground and catalysts for collaboration for the campus. Bell calls for engagement in the community beyond the campus as part of campus outreach. I agree that these are good things, but I'm not sure that there are, as Clayton Christensen would put it, jobs here that our campuses will hire us to do, or at least not big enough jobs to keep all of the current library labor force occupied.

Fortunately, the report does not stop here. There are two areas that at least potentially can create jobs that the people on our campuses will hire us to do. The first is supporting knowledge creation and the curation and preservation of local content. This results from the shift in collecting strategies from what Dempsey describes as "outside-in" to "inside-out." The second is a role in student learning. As Joan K. Lippincott says in an *American Libraries* article in a special issue on forecasting the future of libraries, "I believe that the greatest opportunities for librarians lie in deeper connections to the curriculum, adapting to new modes of pedagogy, linking technology-rich and collaborative spaces in libraries to learning, and ensuring that individuals who enrich the library's role in teaching and learning are on staff. Overall, the trajectory is for the increasing integration of librarians and libraries into the teaching and learning program of the college or university."[15] Let's look at each of these in turn.

Fister makes the general case for the library as the campus hub for knowl-edge creation: "Conceptually, the library as an organization, a physical and digital location, and a well-recognized cultural institution, is a natural setting for supporting the creation of new knowledge. Libraries are perhaps uniquely positioned as a campus crossroads where all of the disciplines come together, where students socialize, study, and snooze, where the mission and the dis-tinguishing characteristics of the institution intersect with the wider world of knowledge, past and present."[16]

Dempsey notes that the campus mission and the extent to which it is engaged in research will determine the extent that there will be local content that will have a notable external audience. When it is the case that a campus creates a significant amount of content with an external audience, there are a number of potential jobs to be done. These might include people working with various kinds of tools—for example, geographic information systems, statistical programs, or various digital humanities tools. It could also include people working on data management at all stages from grant applications to its creation, to archiving and preservation, as well as work with institutional repositories, publishing initiatives, and providing advice on copyright and the management and use of intellectual property. The upside here is that there is much interesting and important work here and while some of it might be subject to being usurped by smart machines, much of it looks like it might be with us for a while. Most of these jobs are best done in person and human relationships are a critical component of success in accomplishing them. The downside is that none of these jobs need to be done in the library. Other units on campus could easily claim responsibility for any of them. A corollary is that none of these jobs require a library degree and arguably expertise at the level required would be more likely to be found in individuals with creden-tials other than an MLS. Jim Neal's case for "feral" librarians could be attractive.

Library engagement in student learning has a long history in academic libraries. Frances L. Hopkins traces the roots of instruction in libraries to the second half of the nineteenth century. She cites the examples of Azariah Root at Oberlin College and Edwin Woodruff at Cornell, who taught courses on library organization and bibliographic resources in the last decades of the 19th century and the early years of the 20th. Hopkins concluded her article, published in 1982 and using the then current term "bibliographic instruc-tion," or BI for short, by saying,

> BI librarians are therefore justified in claiming a central role for bibliographic
> instruction both within librarianship and within the larger academic enterprise.
> Their predecessors once saw the teaching of research methods as a basic
> function of academic libraries; the present generation may see the realization
> of their vision. This generation of instruction librarians knows more about the

structures of disciplines and the ways of learning than did previous generations. And in the increasingly specialized and divided groves of academe, the
need for an integrative role for BI is even greater.[17]

In 2014 the Lumina Foundation published The *Degree Qualifications Profile*. The publication was motivated by the need to move beyond credentials
to measuring knowledge and skills. Jamie P. Merisotis, President and CEO of
the Lumina Foundation, wrote,

> You see, students don't need just credentials. What they need—and what our
> global economy and democratic society increasingly demand—is the learning
> those credentials signify, the highly developed knowledge and skills that post-
> secondary education provides. That's why, in the drive to increase college
> attainment, it's not enough to simply count credentials; the credentials them-
> selves must count. This document, the Degree Qualifications Profile, is de-
> signed to ensure that they do.[18]

The report lists six intellectual skills "that transcend the boundaries of particular fields of study. They overlap, interact with and enable the other major
areas of learning." One of these skills is the Use of Information Resources.
As the report states, "There is no learning without information, and students
must learn how to find, organize, and evaluate information in order to work
with it and perhaps contribute to it."[19] Most librarians engaged in instructional activities would agree. The Lumina report, because of the authority it
conveys, should position librarians to make a more significant contribution to
the curriculum.

Unfortunately, this might not be as easy a sell as we might hope. The
Ithaka S+R US Faculty Survey 2012 asked faculty about their students'
research abilities and whose responsibility it was to develop these abilities.
Librarians were given credit by 45% of the faculty respondents for helping to
develop students' research skills and slightly more than 50% were given
credit for contributing significantly to students' learning by helping them
find and use resources.[20] While not overly discouraging, this is hardly a
ringing endorsement of librarians' contributions. Sadly, it gets worse. It is
worth quoting the report at length:

> Overall, nearly half of respondents feel their undergraduate students have
> "poor skills related to locating and evaluating scholarly information," and an
> especially large share of faculty in the humanities reported significant concern
> regarding these skills. And our questionnaire did not elicit a clear answer as to
> how students should develop these skills from respondents. About 40% agreed
> strongly that "developing the research skills of my undergraduate students
> related to locating and evaluating scholarly information is principally my re-
> sponsibility." Despite a substantial focus in the library community on estab-
> lishing a library role in developing information literacy, only about 20% of

faculty member respondents agreed that "developing the research skills of my undergraduate students related to locating and evaluating scholarly information is principally my academic library's responsibility." This raises significant questions about faculty members' engagement with library-led information literacy programs.[21]

That 20% of faculty think there is a job here that librarians should do might be seen as reasonable market penetration, or it might be viewed as an opportunity to grow the job from a low base. My own inclination is to view the glass as half full. There seems to me to be opportunities both to increase the number of faculty who view librarians as partners in teaching research skills and in working with faculty to develop tools to help them fulfill the role in teaching research skill that they see as theirs. An Association of Research Libraries report on the liaison role for librarians states,

> In many research libraries, programmatic efforts with information literacy have been too narrowly defined. It is not unusual for libraries to focus on freshman writing programs and a series of "one-shot" or invited guest lectures in individual courses. While many librarians have become excellent teachers, traditional one-shot, in-person instructional sessions can vary in quality depending on the training librarians have received in this arena; and they neither scale well nor do they necessarily address broader curricular goals. Librarians at many institutions are now focusing on collaborating with faculty to develop thoughtful assignments and provide online instructional materials that are built into key courses within a curriculum and provide scaffolding to help students develop library research skills over the course of their academic careers.[22]

In either case one of the keys will be to demonstrate that research skills have a clear positive impact on student academic success. Connecting all of the dots required to make this case is not easy and to date it has not been made convincingly, but good work is being done in this area and I suspect the case will be built.

Both of the prospective jobs to be done—the first, supporting knowledge creation and its curation and preservation, and the second, embedding information literacy and research skills in the curriculum—require liaison librarians to have deep knowledge of the work of faculty and to work closely with them in this work. There was a time when close connections were not required. In the past, librarians could learn much of what they needed to know about what was happening in the classroom by answering questions at the reference desk. They could learn much about faculty research by the books and the journals they requested that the library purchase. These passive information sources are largely gone. Some liaison librarians have good working relations with some of their faculty, but it is rare that librarians comprehensively stay abreast of the research of their faculty by actively monitoring scholarly output or have a comprehensive knowledge of departmental and school curriculums of the sort that is acquired through curriculum mapping. Actually, librarians are not alone in not having this comprehensive view of the work in their institutions. In most cases the institutions themselves don't know. This is changing though, and tools such as VIVO and Academic Analytics, which provide the means of comprehensively tracking the work of faculty, are being implemented at many institutions. Librarians should monitor the development of these systems and position themselves to take advantage of the information they collect.

Librarians both need to use comprehensive means for monitoring the research and instructional activities and need to promote what they can do to support faculty in these areas. That is, faculty need to come to understand that there is a job to be done and that librarians can help them do that job. For librarians this will require defining the liaison role somewhat differently from what has been the case in the past. General reference and general collection building will be much less important. A librarian alone could do the tasks that are going away, though engagement with faculty was useful. In the new roles, close collaboration with faculty is essential.

It will also likely be the case that the library will have to think more programmatically about the services it is offering. This is likely to constrain the autonomy of librarians and require more consistency in approaches than has been common practice. In her 2010 *College & Research Libraries* article, Kara J. Malenfant looks at how liaison work was shifted at the University of Minnesota to include a focus on scholarly communication. Her work is a case study of a single institution, but it captures the changes that I believe will be required in all academic libraries. Malenfant quotes Karen Williams, the first Associate University Librarian for Academic Programs, who was responsible for making the change: "My take on our profession is that we've done fairly well for ourselves. Prior to the last decade we had it pretty easy. We were independent, could decide how we wanted to spend our time and what we wanted to do. Some people think that's how it should be on a day-to-day basis still, and I respectfully disagree." Williams then goes on to say, "We've changed, and it's not about collections anymore; we have to work together to provide services. It can't be that a library, a department, or a campus receives the service that a particular librarian feels like providing. Going forward it's very dysfunctional for librarians to think they get to choose what they get to do."[23]

I think Williams is exactly right. A culture change in the library will be required. Librarians will need to begin to think of themselves as part of a team, not as individual and isolated contributors. The ARL liaison report makes the same point in a less confrontational way: "Everyone interviewed recognized the need for collaboration as new library roles and models emerge. As previously noted, the hybrid model of liaisons and functional specialists requires a team approach as well as a strong referral system. And, of course, the very use of the term 'liaison,' which refers to a librarian's connection with academic departments, suggests collaboration and partnership with faculty."[24] As Malenfant puts it, "Librarians and librarianship must change dramatically to remain viable. Individuals cannot be autonomous in setting their own priorities or remain isolated in the library any longer. They must talk to faculty regularly and be an active part of the academic life of the campus."[25] Malenfant goes on to provide a clear statement of the difficulty of the change librarians are going to have to make:

> So liaisons are asked to loosen their ties to the activities that traditionally defined them as librarians. This puts them at a crossroads of competing values. They wonder, "What happens if I turn my back on the collection, the reference desk, my departmental library? Who am I anymore?" This is a major shift in mental models about what it means to be a librarian in the twenty-first century. It requires one to come to terms with the changes, let go, and reorient oneself. Understandably, some fear the loss of competence.[26]

Malenfant is correct in identifying the loss of competence and the fear surrounding this loss, but this situation is neither new to librarians, who have been suffering from similar losses for several decades, nor will it be unique to librarians. The advent of the smart machine will force similar change and similar loss on many professionals both within and outside the academy.

In reviewing Malenfant's article, Anne R. Kenney takes an optimistic view of the role liaisons can play. She asks, "Can library liaisons play a key role in revitalizing human-to-human interactions by engaging individuals collectively in problem solving, creativity, and the production of new knowledge and awareness? Can the library become the center for engagement on campus, with liaisons providing critical human support and analysis that cuts across technology, disciplines, hierarchies, social norms, and institutional and cultural contexts?" She answers by saying, "By focusing on the process rather than the role, appreciating the unevenness of change, bridging the last mile, measuring impact and success, and moving upstream and outward, liaisons will reconfirm that not only is the library the place to go when you don't know, it's also the place to reengage with each other."[27] I hope Kenney is correct as I think there is much interesting and important work for librarians to do. The trick will be to work with and not against the smart machine and to deepen relationships—particularly with faculty at the job of making teaching, learning, and research more effective.

NOTES

1. Jeffrey T. Schnapp and Matthew Battles, *The Library Beyond the Book* (Cambridge, MA: Harvard University Press, 2014), 49.

2. Tyler Cowen, *Average Is Over: Powering America Beyond the Age of the Great Stagnation* (New York: Dutton, 2013), 7.

3. Bruce Weber, "IBM Chess Machine Beats Humanity's Champ," *New York Times*, May 12, 1997, A1.

4. Ken Jennings, "Watson, Jeopardy and Me, the Obsolete Know-It-All," filmed February 2013, TEDxSeattle, video, 17:52, http://www.ted.com/talks/ken_jennings_watson_jeopardy_and_me_the_obsolete_know_it_all/transcript?language=en.

5. Steve Lohr, "And Now, from I.B.M., Chef Watson," *New York Times*, February 27, 2013, http://www.nytimes.com/2013/02/28/technology/ibm-exploring-new-feats-for-watson.html.

6. John Markoff, "Google's Next Phase in Driverless Cars: No Steering Wheel or Brake Pedals," *New York Times*, May 27, 2014, http://www.nytimes.com/2014/05/28/technology/googles-next-phase-in-driverless-cars-no-brakes-or-steering-wheel.html.

7. Nicholas Carr, *The Glass Cage: Automation and Us* (New York: W. W. Norton & Company, 2014), 10–11.

8. See Key Findings in Aaron Smith and Janna Anderson, "AI, Robotics, and the Future of Jobs," Pew Research Center, August 2014, 4–6, http://www.pewinternet.org/2014/08/06/future-of-jobs/.

9. See chapter 5, "Our Freestyle Future," in Cowen, *Average Is Over.*

10. Cowen, *Average Is Over*, 81.

11. Brian Nielsen, "Online Bibliographic Searching and the Deprofessionalization of Librarianship," *Online Review* 4, no. 3 (September 1980): 213–23.

12. Schnapp and Battles, *The Library Beyond the Book*, 53.

13. Ibid., 49.

14. Steven Bell, Lorcan Dempsey, and Barbara Fister, *New Roles for the Road Ahead: Essays Commissioned for ACRL's 75th Anniversary*, ed. Nancy Allen (Chicago: Association of College & Research Libraries, 2014). CommentPress version at http://acrl.ala.org/newroles/; PDF of December 5, 2014 draft at: http://acrl.ala.org/newroles/wp-content/uploads/2014/11/New-Roles-for-the-Road-Ahead-COMMENT-DRAFT.pdf.

15. Joan K. Lippincott, "The Future for Teaching and Learning: Librarians' Deepening Involvement in Pedagogy and Curriculum," *American Libraries* 46, no. 3/4 (March/April 2015): 34, http://americanlibrariesmagazine.org/2015/02/26/the-future-for-teaching-and-learning/.

16. Barbara Fister, "Librarians Supporting the Creation of New Knowledge," in *New Roles for the Road Ahead: Essays Commissioned for ACRL's 75th Anniversary*, by Steven Bell, Lorcan Dempsey, and Barbara Fister, ed. Nancy Allen (Chicago: Association of College & Research Libraries, December 5, 2014), 94, http://acrl.ala.org/newroles/wp-content/uploads/2014/11/New-Roles-for-the-Road-Ahead-COMMENT-DRAFT.pdf.

17. Frances L. Hopkins, "A Century of Bibliographic Instruction: The Historical Claim to Professional and Academic Legitimacy," *College & Research Libraries* 43, no. 3 (May 1982), 43, doi:10.5860/crl_43_03_192, http://crl.acrl.org/content/43/3/192.full.pdf+html.

18. Jamie P. Merisotis, "Foreword: It's Time to Define Quality—For Students' Sake," in *The Degree Qualifications Profile: A Learning-Centered Framework for What College Graduates Should Know and Be Able to Do to Earn the Associate, Bachelor's or Master's Degree*, by Cliff Adelman et al. (Indianapolis, IN: Lumina Foundation, 2014), 2, http://www.luminafoundation.org/resources/dqp.

19. Cliff Adelman et al., *The Degree Qualifications Profile: A Learning-Centered Framework for What College Graduates Should Know and Be Able to Do to Earn the Associate, Bachelor's or Master's Degree* (Indianapolis, IN: Lumina Foundation, 2014), 16, http://www.luminafoundation.org/resources/dqp.

20. Ross Housewright, Roger C. Schonfeld, and Kate Wulfson, *Ithaka S+R US Faculty Survey 2012* (New York: Ithaka S+R, April 8, 2013), 53, http://www.sr.ithaka.org/sites/default/files/reports/Ithaka_SR_US_Faculty_Survey_2012_FINAL.pdf.

21. Ibid.

22. Janice M. Jaguszewski and Karen Williams, *New Roles for New Times: Transforming Liaison Roles in Research Libraries* (Washington, DC: Association of Research Libraries,

August 2013), 6, http://www.arl.org/storage/documents/publications/nrnt-liaison-roles-revised.pdf.

23. Kara J. Malenfant, "Leading Change in the System of Scholarly Communication: A Case Study of Engaging Liaison Librarians for Outreach to Faculty," *College & Research Libraries* 71, no. 1 (January 2010): 72, doi:10.5860/crl.71.1.63, http://crl.acrl.org/content/71/1/63.full.pdf+html.

24. Jaguszewski and Williams, *New Roles for New Times*, 13.

25. Malenfant, "Leading Change in the System of Scholarly Communication."

26. Ibid.

27. Anne R. Kenney, "From Engaging Liaison Librarians to Engaging Communities," *College & Research Libraries* 76, no. 3 March 2015): 390, doi:10.5860/crl.76.3.386, http://crl.acrl.org/content/76/3/386.full.pdf+html.

Conclusion

Ten Things to Do Now

In thinking about what needs to happen to next, let's begin by going back to where we started. I began with the assertion that libraries have always done the following:

- They have kept documents for the long haul.
- They have provided the knowledge and information that the communities and institutions that fund them need.
- They have assisted individuals in finding and using information.

They have done so, I argued, to assure that communities and individuals are productive and so that civilizations are long-lasting. The particulars have changed hugely over time, most especially in the transition from paper to the digital world, but the three things remain important and, I concluded, libraries will continue to do them.

In the past, in the era of paper, libraries accomplished these goals, these jobs that needed doing, by building local collections and staffing them with people who organized and knew how to find documents and facts in them. With the industrialization of printing in the late 19th century a package of collection and service strategies came together that defined how libraries operated until about 25 years ago. In this package, documents that were published around the world were collected and preserved for local use and much of the professional expertise was focused on the complexities of organizing these large paper collections and assisting in their use. As we have seen, when documents become digital, the package of services and collection that will do the jobs that students and faculty need to have done changed.

Going forward the documents to be kept for the long haul will be mostly locally produced or will be special or unique in some way. They will be largely digital and the responsibility will be to preserve them so that they can be made available to the world. Expertise will be focused less on finding and using information, for there will be powerful network-scale tools that will provide this service. Rather, expertise will be primarily focused on helping faculty and students create content so that it is accessible and preserved. Organization of this content will remain important, but the emphasis will be on the discovery of locally held documents in network-scale tools.

As we look 10 or 15 years into the future then, what might we expect academic libraries to look like? If our reimagining is anywhere near correct, what will academic libraries look like and what will academic librarians do? I do not have a crystal ball, but as I said at the outset, I think there are some trends that we can expect to play out.

We can expect that there will still be buildings on college and university campuses called "libraries." They will be centrally located and well furnished and will be the primary nonclassroom academic space on campus. They will be heavily used. There will be a variety of space for individual and group study, some quiet and some not. There will be a café and the hours will be long. There will be some books, but not large collections of them, and the space freed up by reducing the size of book collections will now be filled with a mix of campus units that support student academic success and units to assist faculty and students in managing, preserving, and providing access to research and many of the outputs of research, including publishing programs. There will be technical expertise and infrastructure to support these activities, though some of it likely will be outsourced to national organizations. The library will continue to have a credible claim to be the heart of the university.

There will be people who support these activities and some may be called librarians, though it is likely that the MLS will not be the only academic credential possessed by the professionals working in the library. The boundaries that exist today between the library organization and other units that support student academic success and faculty and student research will have blurred and, following the trend in many small colleges, many will have merged to create a new hybrid organization. There will be a small part of the organization that will purchase academic content, nearly always digital, using subscriptions when they are cost effective and using purchase-on-demand when this is the cheaper alternative. Special collections of both paper and digital content will be more dominant than they are today.

So how do we get to there? In ending I want to be concrete and practical. What follows is my advice for those who will have to lead academic libraries through the next 10 or 20 years. What matters most is that we not dally. We need to move with purpose and we need to move now. There are large opportunity costs if we delay and there is the risk that if the library does not move assertively, others, either on campus or off, will do the jobs our students and faculty need to have done and the library will become increasingly less relevant. These are the steps I believe will lead to achieving the reimagined academic library.

1. Retire the Legacy Print Collection Now. This is the first step because until it is made, resources cannot be redirected. And these resources will be needed to do the other things that need doing. This is going to take a while, so you need to begin today. As we have discussed, most libraries will be able to rely on the large ARL libraries to carry the largest load here. But it will be important for individual libraries to have a clear strategy that outlines what they will keep and why. In my view collaboration with state or regional peers will make creating such a strategy easier. It will also make it easier to implement, as it will decrease the political pressure on the campus to maintain the status quo. Collection studies that document how little use large parts of the collection get and show that other copies of these works are available are probably worth their cost. When done with a state or regional group, it may also lay the groundwork for forward-looking collection coordination.

2. Develop a Space Plan. Space is one of the three key assets the library has. The other two are its people and its collection budget. As collections and the space they require are reduced, space becomes available. Some of this space is likely to go to other campus purposes and some will want to be repurposed for study space and for new library services. Absent a large infusion of cash, which will not happen in most places, this transition could take a decade or more. Having a clear plan will be important to assure that steps cumulate to a good whole. Involving design talent early will be a good investment—first because it will help define in a clear program what the library wants to become with some idea of the costs. Second, it will help build a campus consensus on the plan. Both will be critical for success. It will also be important to impress on campus leadership the value of library space so that they do not fritter it away inappropriately.

3. Have a Materials Budget Strategy to Manage the Transition from Traditional Publishing Models to Open Access. Open Access will displace the traditional business model for much academic publishing over the next 20 years, but it will do so in uneven ways across different disciplines. A budget strategy that accounts for this and assures that change can be made will be politically difficult and will need to be clearly articulated and advocated for. Transitionary or bridging strategies, especially purchase-on-demand for books and journal articles, will be required. Giving up buying books just-in-case is critical. It will be difficult to actually do, but this is one of the key places money can be saved. It will also be necessary to limit subscription expenditures for expensive science and technology journals. The trick will be to limit expenditures in a way that clearly demonstrates the unreasonableness of the current scholarly publishing economics, while not unduly disadvantaging the researchers on your campus. In my view, any strategy that does not include a clear limit to the dollars going to the large for-profit journal publishers is inadequate. The strategy also needs to include funding for open access initiatives. Without this you are eating your seed corn. In all likelihood this is close to a zero-sum game. This means that developing alternative strategies for providing documents and generating savings from decreased investments in print collections will be required.

4. Support the Creation of, Access to, and Preservation of the Scholarly Content Created on Your Campus. This is the flip side of the budget plan. It is the critical pivot the library needs to make. It will require developing technical infrastructure and staff expertise. Repository and publishing platforms will be necessary as will a preservation system to assure that digital documents last for the long haul. New positions such as scholarly communications or data librarians will need to be developed and the role of liaison librarians will need to be expanded to include work in these areas. Funds to pay article processing fees need to be developed, hopefully with support from the research office and academic units. Early successes need to be celebrated and these stories told. Many libraries have done pieces of this work well and best practices are being established. Going forward every academic library will need to put the full suite of services into practice. Current funder policies will make this easier, especially on research-oriented campuses as compliance with funder mandates will force adoption in ways that would otherwise be difficult.

5. Commit to the Special Collections Your Library Will Support and Make the Required Investments. Twenty years from now the content your library holds that is unique and special will be what distinguishes it. You should decide now what these areas will be—where your library can make a distinctive contribution to the national or worldwide collective collection. This will inevitably be driven by a special campus expertise or focus, or in some cases it will be driven by the opportunities for philanthropic support. In many cases the items in these collections will be digital, but they will certainly include paper documents as well. Support for these collections will require staffing and funds for acquisitions. Where items are digital, there should be a firm commitment to makes the items openly accessible to the fullest extent possible. One way to think about this is that these special collections are the portion of the scholarly record that your library is committing to curate and preserve. The politics of redirecting funds from general to special collections might be difficult, but this shift needs to be made.

6. Infuse the Curriculum with the Skills Necessary to Create and Consume Information Productively. This is a bit fuzzy I know, but that is because I am not at all certain what university instruction is going to look like five or ten years from now. It will certainly be in some significant way online. I would expect there to be more service and experiential learning, a continued focus on group work in many contexts, and an increased focus on undergraduate research. It will be important for librarians to be flexible about where the best place to provide instruction is and what the best mechanism to provide it is. I suspect it will increasingly not be with in-person classroom instruction, but rather will be with digital tools. Assessment to demonstrate value, which has begun, is important, as is working with faculty on innovative ways of assuring that students have the information skills they need to be successful as students and as graduates.

7. Understand the Demographics of Your Organization and Have a Plan to Hire or Develop the Expertise the Library Will Need. There are two truths about the people now working in your libraries that need to be recognized. The first is that the people you have are the people who will need to make the change, and you cannot wait to get an ideal staff together to begin doing the work. The second truth is that the skills the current people have will not be sufficient for what will be required five to ten years from now. Getting from where you are now to where you need to be will require developing new skills in current staff and hiring people with skills you do not now possess. Accomplishing this will require a concerted effort and a clear understanding of when and where opportunities exist so that they are not lost. Different approaches will work in different libraries, but as an example, my library made a choice some years ago to promote from within when leadership positions became available and fill vacancies with entry-level professionals. This provided a career path for existing staff and allowed the library to attract individuals with skills we needed. Had we hired leadership positions in full national searches we would have lost both opportunities.

8. Get the Culture Right. The changes that are coming require an organization that has a culture that embraces change and the challenges it brings. It needs to be prepared to experiment and to tolerate failure while rewarding success. It needs to be prepared to recognize new forms of contribution while maintaining an expectation of excellence. As Christensen would tell us, an organization's culture does not change easily. It will be better if your library's culture change is proactive rather than reactive, for if it is reactive it is likely to be reacting to some significant failure or severe financial distress. Changing culture will require investing in organizational development both with time and money. This needs to be a regular, continued investment. The IUPUI University Library has for more than 20 years conducted two "organization weeks" each year, one in January and one in May. They are typically three to four days each with a "state of the library" talk from the dean, various workshops or planning activities, and a community lunch as the conclusion. All library staff are involved; sometimes we use internal library or campus resources and sometimes external consultants are brought in. This

level of investment in organizational development needs to be the norm—
not, as I expect it is now, the exception.

9. Support the Development and Sustainability of Network-Level Tools and Services. The academic library community needs SPARC, the Coalition for Networked Information, the Digital Library Federation, DSpace, Fedora, the Open Journal System, OLE, the HathiTrust, the Digital Preservation Network, LOCKSS, Portico, and many other pieces of the technical and organizational infrastructure. We all need all of this to make our local libraries work. Today most of these tools and services exist on their own or they are part of small organizations like DuraSpace or the Open Knowledge Project. Each funds itself through start-up grants and/or regular (usually annual) membership solicitations. This hodgepodge approach is understandable given the history, but it is inefficient and makes it difficult for many libraries, especially smaller and poorer ones, to contribute. A better structure is required going forward. In my view, we need something like the United Way. Under this model all libraries could contribute and a trusted organization could make resource allocations to common good projects. Figuring out how to establish such a system should be a priority for national library leaders.

10. Sell the Change. The reimagined library is different from its predecessor in many ways. The story that needs to be told is complex with many interlocking pieces. Many of the people who need to be convinced of the need for change, especially faculty, are often quite fond of libraries the way they used to be. Campus administrators need to be convinced that new investments are required, even as some traditional expenditures are reduced. For some of the library staff, the basis for their professional status will be diminished and in some cases jobs will be at risk. The role of academic library leaders will be to sell the change to all of the library's constituencies. Telling a consistent and compelling story over and over again at budget hearings, donor events, staff meetings, and everywhere else there is an opportunity should be the first priority of academic library leaders. If this is not done, everything else will be very difficult.

There is much to do and in many libraries good beginnings have been made, but now is the time for everyone to put it all together and to create the complete reimagined academic library. It is essential and, I believe, exciting work. Now we need to just do it.

Bibliography

This bibliography includes a selected list of the materials that have most contributed to my thinking. I have also included the works that provide important evidence for my arguments. I have left out news reports, articles in reference, and statistical sources. Only the most important blog posts and similar items have been included.

Acharya, Anurag, Alex Verstak, Helder Suzuki, Sean Henderson, Mikhail Iakhiaev, Cliff Chiung Yu Lin, and Namit Shetty. "Rise of the Rest: The Growing Impact of Non-Elite Journals." *Google Scholar Blog.* October 9, 2014. http://arxiv.org/pdf/1410.2217.pdf.

Adelman, Cliff, Peter Ewell, Paul Gaston, and Carol Geary Schneider. *The Degree Qualifications Profile: A Learning-Centered Framework for What College Graduates Should Know and Be Able to Do to Earn the Associate, Bachelor's, or Master's Degree.* Indianapolis, IN: Lumina Foundation, 2014. https://www.luminafoundation.org/files/resources/dqp.pdf.

Adema, Janneke. "The Monograph Crisis Revisited." *Open Reflections* (blog). January 29, 2015. https://openreflections.wordpress.com/2015/01/29/the-monograph-crisis-revisited/.

Anderson, Rick. "My Name Is Ozymandias, King of Kings." *The Scholarly Kitchen* (blog). January 7, 2015. http://scholarlykitchen.sspnet.org/2015/01/07/my-name-is-ozymandias-king-of-kings.

Angevaare, Inge. "On-line Scholarly Communications: vd Sompel and Treloar Sketch the Future Playing Field of Digital Archives." *KB Research* (blog), January 22, 2014, http://blog.kbresearch.nl/2014/01/22/on-line-scholarly-communications-and-the-role-of-digital-archives/.

Atkinson, Ross. "Text Mutability and Collection Administration." *Library Acquisitions: Practice & Theory* 14, no. 4 (1990): 355–58. doi:10.1016/0364-6408(90)90006-G.

Baker, Nicholson. "The Author vs. the Library." *New Yorker* 72, no. 31 (October 14, 1996): 50–62.

Baron, Naomi S. *Words Onscreen: The Fate of Reading in a Digital World.* New York: Oxford University Press, 2015.

Bedi, Param, and Jason Snyder. "Making a Difference: Moving Your Organization from Transactional to Transformational." *EDUCAUSE Review.* March 16, 2015. http://www.educause.edu/ero/article/making-difference-moving-your-organization-transactional-transformational.

Bell, David A. "The Bookless Future," *New Republic,* May 2, 2005, http://www.newrepublic.com/article/books-and-arts/the-bookless-future.

Bell, Steven, Lorcan Dempsey, and Barbara Fister. *New Roles for the Road Ahead: Essays Commissioned for ACRL's 75th Anniversary—Draft for Comments.* Edited by Nancy Allen. Chicago: Association of College & Research Libraries, 2014. http://acrl.ala.org/newroles/wp-content/uploads/2014/11/New-Roles-for-the-Road-Ahead-COMMENT-DRAFT.pdf (pdf of December 5, 2014 draft).

Benkler, Yochai. *The New Open-Source Economics.* Filmed July 2005. TEDGlobal. Video, 17:52. http://www.ted.com/talks/yochai_benkler_on_the_new_open_source_economics.html.

———. *The Wealth of Networks: How Social Production Transforms Markets and Freedom.* New Haven, CT: Yale University Press, 2006. http://cyber.law.harvard.edu/wealth_of_networks/Main_Page.

Bennett, Scott. "Learning Behaviors and Learning Spaces," *portal: Libraries and the Academy* 11, no. 3 (July 2011): 765–89. doi:10.1353/pla.2011.0033, http://muse.jhu.edu/journals/portal_libraries_and_the_academy/v011/11.3.bennett.pdf.

Blumenstyk, Goldie. *American Higher Education in Crisis? What Everyone Needs to Know.* New York: Oxford University Press, 2014.

Borghuis, Martyn. *TULIP: Final Report.* New York: Elsevier Science, 1996.

Bostrom, Nick. *Superintelligence: Paths, Dangers, Strategies.* Oxford: Oxford University Press, 2014.

Bricklin, Dan. "The Cornucopia of the Commons: How to Get Volunteer Labor." *Dan Bricklin. Writings* (blog). August 7, 2000. http://www.bricklin.com/cornucopia.htm.

Brynjolfsson, Erik, and Andrew McAfee. *The Second Machine Age: Work, Progress, and Prosperity in a Time of Brilliant Technologies.* New York: W. W. Norton & Company, 2014.

Buckland, Michael. *Redesigning Library Services: A Manifesto.* Chicago: American Library Association, 1992. http://digitalassets.lib.berkeley.edu/sunsite/Redesigning%20Library%20Services_%20A%20Manifesto%20(HTML).pdf.

Carr, Nicholas. *The Glass Cage: Automation and Us.* New York: W. W. Norton & Company, 2014.

Chavan, Vishwas, and Lyubomir Penev. "The Data Paper: A Mechanism to Incentivize Data Publishing in Biodiversity Science." *BMC Bioinformatics* 12, no. S15 (2011): S2. doi:10.1186/1471-2105-12-S15-S2. http://www.biomedcentral.com/1471-2105/12/S15/S2.

Chesapeake Digital Preservation Group. "'Link Rot' and Legal Resources on the Web: A 2013 Analysis by the Chesapeake Digital Preservation Group." Chesapeake Digital Preservation Group. Accessed January 26, 2016. http://cdm16064.contentdm.oclc.org/cdm/linkrot2013.

Christensen, Clayton M. *Innovator's Dilemma: When New Technologies Cause Great Firms to Fail.* Boston: Harvard Business School Press, 1997.

———. *The Innovator's Prescription: A Disruptive Solution to the Healthcare Crisis.* Cambridge, MA: MIT Video, May 13, 2008. Video, 1:27:38. http://video.mit.edu/watch/the-innovators-prescription-a-disruptive-solution-to-the-healthcare-crisis-9380/.

———. "SC10 Keynote with Clayton Christensen." Portland, OR: Inside HPC, December 4, 2010. Video, 1:00:28. http://insidehpc.com/2010/12/video-sc10-keynote-with-clayton-christensen/.

Christensen, Clayton M., Scott Cook, and Taddy Hall. "Marketing Malpractice: The Cause and the Cure." *Harvard Business Review* 83, no. 12 (December 2005): 74–83.

Christensen, Clayton M., Jerome H. Grossman, and Jason Hwang. *The Innovator's Prescription: A Disruptive Solution for Health Care.* New York: McGraw-Hill, 2009.

Christensen, Clayton M., Michael B. Horn, and Curtis W. Johnson. *Disrupting Class: How Disruptive Innovation Will Change the Way the World Learns.* New York: McGraw-Hill, 2008.

Christensen, Clayton M., Michael B. Horn, Louis Soares, and Louis Caldera. *Disrupting College: How Disruptive Innovation Can Deliver Quality and Affordability to Postsecondary Education.* Washington, DC: Center for American Progress, February 8, 2011. http://www.americanprogress.org/issues/labor/report/2011/02/08/9034/disrupting-college/.

Christensen, Clayton M., Michael E. Raynor, and Rory McDonald. "What Is Disruptive Innovation?" *Harvard Business Review* 93 (December 2015): 44–53. https://hbr.org/2015/12/what-is-disruptive-innovation.

Coase, Ronald Harry. "The Nature of the Firm." *Economica* 4, no. 16 (1937): 386–405.

Coates, Heather L. "Building Data Services from the Ground Up: Strategies and Resources." *Journal of eScience Librarianship* 3, no. 1 (December 2014): 52–59. http://escholarship.umassmed.edu/jeslib/vol3/iss1/5/.

Courant, Paul N., and Matthew "Buzzy" Nielsen. "On the Cost of Keeping a Book." In *The Idea of Order: Transforming Research Collections for 21st Century Scholarship*, 81–105. Washington, DC: Council on Library and Information Resources, June 2010. http://www.clir.org/pubs/reports/pub147/pub147.pdf.

Cowen, Tyler. *Average Is Over: Powering America Beyond the Age of the Great Stagnation.* New York: Dutton, 2013.

Crossick, Geoffrey. *Monographs and Open Access: A report to HEFCE.* London: HEFCE, January 2015. http://www.hefce.ac.uk/pubs/rereports/year/2015/monographs/.

Darnton, Robert. "The Library: Three Jeremiads." *New York Review of Books,* December 23, 2010. http://www.nybooks.com/articles/archives/2010/dec/23/library-three-jeremiads/.

Davidson, Cathy. "Gutenberg-E Publishing Goes Open Access: Is It a Success?" *HASTAC: Humanities, Arts, Science and Technology Alliance and Collaboratory* (blog), February 26, 2008. https://www.hastac.org/blogs/cathy-davidson/2008/02/26/gutenberg-e-publishing-goes-open-access-it-success.

Davis, Denise M. "Library Retirements: What We Can Expect." *American Libraries* 36, no. 8 (September 2005): 16.

Deloitte. "Mind the Gaps: The 2015 Deloitte Millennial Survey: Executive Summary." Deloitte. Accessed January 26, 2016. http://www2.deloitte.com/content/dam/Deloitte/global/Documents/About-Deloitte/gx-wef-2015-millennial-survey-executivesummary.pdf.

Dempsey, Lorcan. "Thirteen Ways of Looking at Libraries, Discovery, and the Catalog: Scale, Workflow, Attention." *EDUCAUSE Review,* December 10, 2012. http://www.educause.edu/ero/article/thirteen-ways-looking-libraries-discovery-and-catalog-scale-workflow-attention.

Dempsey, Lorcan, Brian Lavoie, Constance Malpas, Lynn Silipigni Connaway, Roger C. Schonfeld, J. D. Shipengrover, and Günter Waibel. *Understanding the Collective Collection: Towards a System-wide Perspective on Library Print Collections.* Dublin, OH: OCLC Research, December 2013. http://www.oclc.org/content/dam/research/publications/library/2013/2013-09.pdf.

Dempsey, Lorcan, Constance Malpas, and Brian Lavoie. "Collection Directions: The Evolution of Library Collections and Collecting." *portal: Libraries and the Academy* 14, no. 3 (July 2014): 393–423.

Dimitrova, Daniela V., and Michael Bugela. "The Half-Life of Internet References Cited in Communication Journals." *New Media & Society* 9, no. 5 (October 2007): 811–26. doi:10.1177/1461444807081226.

Doctorow, Cory. *Information Doesn't Want to Be Free: Laws for the Internet Age.* San Francisco: McSweeney's, 2014.

Duke, Lynda M., and Andrew D. Asher, eds. *College Libraries and Student Culture: What We Now Know.* Chicago: American Library Association, 2012.

Durant, David M., and Tony Horava. "The Future of Reading and Academic Libraries." *portal: Libraries and the Academy* 15, no. 1 (January 2015): 5–27. doi:10.1353/pla.2015.0013. http://muse.jhu.edu/journals/portal_libraries_and_the_academy/v015/15.1.durant.pdf.

Edington, Mark D. W. "The Commons of Scholarly Communication: Beyond the Firm." *EDUCAUSE Review* 50, no. 1 (January/February 2015): 54–55. http://www.educause.edu/ero/article/commons-scholarly-communication-beyond-firm.

Foster, Nancy Fried, and Susan Gibbons, eds. *Studying Students: The Undergraduate Research Project at the University of Rochester.* Chicago: Association of College & Research Libraries, 2007.

Frazier, Kenneth. "The Librarians' Dilemma: Contemplating the Costs of the 'Big Deal.'" *D-Lib Magazine* 7, no. 3 (March 2001). http://www.dlib.org/dlib/march01/frazier/03frazier.html.

Freeman, Geoffrey T. "The Library as Place: Changes in Learning Patterns, Collections, Technology, and Use." In *Library as Place: Rethinking Roles, Rethinking Space*, 1–9. Washington, DC: Council on Library and Information Resources, February 2005. http://www.clir.org/pubs/reports/pub129/pub129.pdf.

Frischmann, Brett M. *Infrastructure: The Social Value of Shared Resources*. New York: Oxford University Press, 2012.

"From Papyrus to Pixels. The Digital Transformation Has Only Just Begun." *The Economist Essay* (London: The Economist, 2015). http://www.economist.com/news/essays/21623373-which-something-old-and-powerful-encountered-vault.

Gantz, Paula. "Digital Licenses Replace Print Prices as Accurate Reflection of Real Journal Costs." *Professional/Scholarly Publishing Bulletin* 11, no. 3 (Summer/Fall 2012): 1–5. http://publishers.org/sites/default/files/uploads/PSP/summer-fall_2012.pdf.

Geffert, Bryn. "A Librarian's Defense of Despair." *Chronicle of Higher Education: The Conversation* (blog), March 6, 2015. http://chronicle.com/blogs/conversation/2015/03/06/in-defense-of-librarians-despair/.

Goh, Dion Hoe-Lian, and Peng Kin Ng. "Link Decay in Leading Information Science Journals." *Journal of the American Society for Information Science and Technology* 58, no. 1 (January 2007): 15–24. doi:10.1002/asi.20513.

Goldstein, Evan. "The Undoing of Disruption." *Chronicle of Higher Education: The Chronicle Review*, September 15, 2015. http://chronicle.com/article/The-Undoing-of-Disruption/233101/.

Guédon, Jean-Claude. *In Oldenburg's Long Shadow: Librarians, Research Scientists, Publishers, and the Control of Scientific Publishing*. Washington, DC: Association of Research Libraries, 2001. http://www.arl.org/storage/documents/publications/in-oldenburgs-long-shadow.pdf.

Hawkins, Donald T., ed. *Personal Archiving: Preserving Our Digital Heritage*. Medford, NJ: Information Today, 2013, ProQuest ebrary e-book.

Herrera, Gail. "Testing the Patron-Driven Model: Availability Analysis of First-Time Use Books." *Collection Management* 40, no. 1 (January 2015): 3–16. doi:10.1080/01462679.2014.965863.

Hilton, James L., Tom Cramer, Sebastien Korner, and David Minor. "The Case for Building a Digital Preservation Network." *EDUCAUSE Review* 48, no. 4 (July/August 2013): 37–47. http://www.educause.edu/ero/article/case-building-digital-preservation-network.

Hopkins, Frances L. "A Century of Bibliographic Instruction: The Historical Claim to Professional and Academic Legitimacy." *College & Research Libraries* 43, no. 3 (May 1982): 192–98. doi:10.5860/crl_43_03_192. http://crl.acrl.org/content/43/3/192.full.pdf+html.

Ingwersen, Peter, and Vishwas Chavan. "Indicators for the Data Usage Index (DUI): An Incentive for Publishing Primary Biodiversity Data through Global Information Infrastructure." *BMC Bioinformatics* 12, no. S15 (2011): S3. doi:10.1186/1471-2105-12-S15-S3. http://www.biomedcentral.com/1471-2105/12/S15/S3.

Jabr, Ferris. "The Reading Brain in the Digital Age: Why the Brain Prefers Paper." *Scientific American* 309, no. 5 (November 2013): 48–53. doi:10.1038/scientificamerican1113-48.

Jackson, Heather Lea, and Trudi Bellardo Hahn. "Serving Higher Education's Highest Goals: Assessment of the Academic Library as Place." *College & Research Libraries* 72, no. 5 (September 2011): 428–42. http://crl.acrl.org/content/72/5/428.full.pdf+html.

Jaguszewski, Janice M., and Karen Williams. *New Roles for New Times: Transforming Liaison Roles in Research Libraries*. Washington, DC: Association of Research Libraries, August 2013. http://www.arl.org/storage/documents/publications/nrnt-liaison-roles-revised.pdf.

Jemielniak, Dariusz. "Wikipedia, a Professor's Best Friend." *Chronicle of Higher Education: Commentary*, October 13, 2014. http://chronicle.com/article/Wikipedia-a-Professors-Best/149337.

Johnson, L., S. Adams Becker, V. Estrada, and A. Freeman. *NMC Horizon Report: 2014 Library Edition*. Austin, TX: The New Media Consortium, 2014. http://www.nmc.org/publications/2014-horizon-report-library.

Johnson, Steven. *How We Got to Now: Six Innovations That Made the Modern World*. New York: Riverhead Books, 2014.

Jones, Elisabeth A., and Paul N. Courant. "Monographic Purchasing Trends in Academic Libraries: Did the 'Serials Crisis' Really Destroy the University Press?" *Journal of Scholarly Publishing* 46, no. 1 (October 2014): 43–70. doi:10.1353/scp.2014.0033. https://muse.jhu.edu/login?auth=0&type=summary&url=/journals/journal_of_scholarly_publishing/v046/46.1.jones.pdf.

Jurski, Danielle. "2013 Study of Subscription Prices for Scholarly Society Journals: Society Journal Pricing Trends and Industry Overview." *Allen Press*, 2013. http://allenpress.com/system/files/pdfs/library/2013_AP_JPS.pdf.

Kenney, Anne R. "From Engaging Liaison Librarians to Engaging Communities." *College & Research Libraries* 76, no. 3 (March 2015): 386–91. doi:10.5860/crl.76.3.386. http://crl.acrl.org/content/76/3/386.full.pdf+html.

Kent, Allen, Jacob Cohen, K. Leon Montgomery, James G. Williams, Stephen Bulick, Roger R. Flynn, William N. Sabor, and Una Mansfield. *Use of Library Materials: The University of Pittsburgh Study*. New York: Marcel Dekker, 1979.

King, Andrew A., and Baljir Baatartogtokh. "How Useful Is the Theory of Disruptive Innovation?" *MIT Sloan Management Review* 57, no. 1 (Fall 2015): 77–90.

Kirchhoff, Amy, Sheila Morrissey, and Kate Wittenberg. "Networked Information's Risky Future: The Promises and Challenges of Digital Preservation." *EDUCAUSE Review* 50, no. 2 (March/April 2015): 50–51. http://www.educause.edu/ero/article/networked-informations-risky-future-promises-and-challenges-digital-preservation.

Klein, Martin, Herbert Van de Sompel, Robert Sanderson, Harihar Shankar, Lyudmila Balakireva, Ke Zhou, and Richard Tobin. "Scholarly Context Not Found: One in Five Articles Suffers from Reference Rot." *PLOS ONE* 9, no. 12 (December 26, 2014): e115253. doi:10.1371/journal.pone.0115253. http://journals.plos.org/plosone/article?id=10.1371/journal.pone.0115253.

Kurzweil, Ray. *The Singularity Is Near: When Humans Transcend Biology*. New York: Viking Penguin, 2005.

Lambert, Craig. "The 'Wild West' of Academic Publishing: The Troubled Present and Promising Future of Scholarly Communication." *Harvard Magazine* 117, no. 3 (January–February 2015): 56–60. http://harvardmagazine.com/2015/01/the-wild-west-of-academic-publishing.

Larivière, Vincent, Stefanie Haustein, and Philippe Mongeon. "The Oligopoly of Academic Publishers in the Digital Era," *PLOS ONE* 10, no. 6 (June 10, 2015): e0127502. doi:10.1371/journal.pone.0127502. http://journals.plos.org/plosone/article?id=10.1371/journal.pone.0127502.

Larivière, Vincent, George A. Lozano, and Yves Gingras. "Are Elite Journals Declining?" *Journal of the Association for Information Science and Technology* 65, no. 4 (2014): 649–55. doi:10.1002/asi.23005.

Lavoie, Brian, Eric Childress, Ricky Erway, Ixchel Faniel, Constance Malpas, Jennifer Schaffner, and Titia van der Werf. *The Evolving Scholarly Record*. Dublin, OH: OCLC Research, June 2014. http://oclc.org/content/dam/research/publications/library/2014/oclcresearch-evolving-scholarly-record-2014-5-a4.pdf.

Lavoie, Brian, and Constance Malpas. *Stewardship of the Evolving Scholarly Record: From the Invisible Hand to Conscious Coordination*. Dublin, Ohio: OCLC Research, 2015. http://www.oclc.org/content/dam/research/publications/2015/oclcresearch-esr-stewardship-2015.pdf.

Lavoie, Brian, Constance Malpas, and JD Shipengrover. *Print Management at "Mega-Scale": A Regional Perspective on Print Book Collections in North America*. Dublin, OH: OCLC Research, 2012. http://www.oclc.org/content/dam/research/publications/library/2012/2012-05.pdf?urlm=163087.

Lavoie, Brian F., and Roger C. Schonfeld. "Books without Boundaries: A Brief Tour of the System-Wide Print Book Collection." *JEP: The Journal of Electronic Publishing* 9, no. 2 (Summer 2006). http://dx.doi.org/10.3998/3336451.0009.208.

Lepore, Jill. "Cobweb: Can the Internet Be Archived?," *New Yorker*, January 26, 2015. http://www.newyorker.com/magazine/2015/01/26/cobweb.

———. "The Disruption Machine: What the Gospel of Innovation Gets Wrong." *New Yorker*, June 23, 2015. http://www.newyorker.com/magazine/2014/06/23/the-disruption-machine.

———. "The New Economy of Letters." *Chronicle of Higher Education: The Chronicle Review*, September 3, 2013. http://chronicle.com/article/The-New-Economy-of-Letters/141291/.

Lewis, David W. "Academic Library Staffing a Decade from Now." In *The Expert Library: Staffing, Sustaining, and Advancing the Academic Library in the 21st Century,* edited by Scott Walter and Karen Williams, 1–29. Chicago: Association of College & Research Libraries, 2010.

———. "From Stacks to the Web: the Transformation of Academic Library Collecting." *College & Research Libraries* 74, no. 2 (March 2013): 159–76. http://crl.acrl.org/content/74/2/159.full.pdf+html.

———. "The Inevitability of Open Access." *College & Research Libraries* 73, no. 5 (September 2012): 493–506. http://crl.acrl.org/content/73/5/493.full.pdf+html and and http://hdl.handle.net/1805/2929.

———. "The Inevitability of Open Access: Update One." *ScholarWorks*, August 2013. https://scholarworks.iupui.edu/handle/1805/3471.

———. "*The Innovator's Dilemma*: Disruptive Change and Academic Libraries." *Library Administration & Management* 18, no. 2 (Spring 2004): 68–74. https://scholarworks.iupui.edu/handle/1805/173.

———. "A Strategy for Academic Libraries in the First Quarter of the 21st Century." *College & Research Libraries* 68, no. 5 (September 2007): 418–34. http://crl.acrl.org/content/68/5/418.full.pdf+html.

Lippincott, Joan K. "The Future for Teaching and Learning: Librarians' Deepening Involvement in Pedagogy and Curriculum." *American Libraries* 46, no. 3/4 (March/April 2015): 34–37. http://americanlibrariesmagazine.org/2015/02/26/the-future-for-teaching-and-learning/.

Lozano, George A., Vincent Larivière, and Yves Gingras. "The Weakening Relationship between the Impact Factor and Papers' Citations in the Digital Age." *Journal of the American Society for Information Science and Technology* 63, no. 11 (November 2012): 2140–45. doi:10.1002/asi.22731.

Lynch, Clifford A. "The TULIP Project: Context, History, and Perspective." *Library Hi Tech* 13, no. 4 (1995): 8–24.

Malenfant, Kara J. "Leading Change in the System of Scholarly Communication: A Case Study of Engaging Liaison Librarians for Outreach to Faculty." *College & Research Libraries* 71, no. 1 (January 2010): 63–76. doi:10.5860/crl.71.1.63. http://crl.acrl.org/content/71/1/63.full.pdf+html.

Malpas, Constance. *Cloud-sourcing Research Collections: Managing Print in the Mass-digitized Library Environment.* Dublin, OH: OCLC Research, January 2011. http://www.oclc.org/research/publications/library/2011/2011-01.pdf.

———. *Shared Print Policy Review Report.* Dublin, OH: OCLC Research, January 2009. http://www.oclc.org/content/dam/research/publications/library/2009/2009-03.pdf.

Marcum, Deanna. *Educating the Research Librarian: Are We Falling Short?* New York: Ithaka S+R, May 7, 2015. http://www.sr.ithaka.org/wp-content/mig/files/SR_Issue_Brief_Educating_the_Research_Librarian050715.pdf.

———. *Talent Management for Academic Libraries.* Issue brief. New York: Ithaka S+R, September 1, 2015. http://www.sr.ithaka.org/publications/talent-management-for-academic-libraries/.

———. "Technology to the Rescue: Can Technology-Enhanced Education Help Public Flagship Universities Meet Their Challenges?" Briefing paper. New York: Ithaka S+R, 2014. http://www.sr.ithaka.org/sites/default/files/files/SR_BriefingPaper_Marcum_20140421.pdf.

Mathews, Brian. "Librarian as Futurist: Changing the Way Libraries Think about the Future." *portal: Libraries and the Academy* 14, no. 3 (July 2014): 453–62.

McRobbie, Michael A. "Looking to the Future: Preparing for Indiana University's Bicentenary." State of the University speech, Indiana University Bloomington, Bloomington, IN, October 1, 2013. http://president.iu.edu/speeches/2013/20131001-01.shtml.

Morris, Shaneka, and Martha Kyrillidou. "Minority Representation in US ARL University Libraries as of 2012–2013: Taking a Closer Look at the Evidence." Association of Research

Libraries: *ARL News*, September 10, 2014. http://libraryassessment.org/bm~doc/24morris-poster.pdf.

Mullins, James L. "Are MLS Graduates Being Prepared for the Changing and Emerging Roles That Librarians Must Now Assume within Research Libraries?" *Journal of Library Administration* 52, no. 1 (2012). doi:10.1080/01930826.2011.629966.

National Digital Information Infrastructure and Preservation Program. *Perspectives on Personal Digital Archiving: National Digital Information Infrastructure and Preservation Program*. Washington, DC: Library of Congress, 2013. http://www.digitalpreservation.gov/documents/ebookpdf_march18.pdf.

Neal, James G. "A New Age of Reason for Academic Libraries." *College and Research Libraries* 75, no. 5 (2014): 612–15. doi:10.5860/crl.75.5.612. http://crl.acrl.org/content/75/5/612.full.pdf+html.

———. "Raised by Wolves: Integrating the New Generation of Feral Professionals into the Academic Library." *Library Journal* 131, no. 3 (February 15, 2006): 42–44. http://lj.libraryjournal.com/2006/02/academic-libraries/raised-by-wolves/.

Nielsen, Brian. "Online Bibliographic Searching and the Deprofessionalization of Librarianship." *Online Review* 4, no. 3 (September 1980): 215–24.

Oakleaf, Megan. *Value of Academic Libraries: A Comprehensive Research Review and Report*. Chicago: Association of College & Research Libraries, September 2010. http://www.ala.org/acrl/sites/ala.org.acrl/files/content/issues/value/val_report.pdf.

OCLC. *At a Tipping Point: Education, Learning and Libraries*. Dublin, OH: OCLC, 2014. http://www.oclc.org/reports/tipping-point.en.html.

Oldenburg, Ray. *The Great Good Place: Cafés, Coffee Shops, Community Centers, Beauty Parlors, General Stores, Bars, Hangouts, and How They Get You through the Day*. New York: Paragon House, 1989.

O'Neill, Edward T., and OhioLINK Collection Building Task Force. "OhioLINK Collection and Circulation Analysis." *OCLC Research*. Last modified August 11, 2015. http://oclc.org/research/activities/ohiolink.html.

Payne, Lizanne. "Library Storage Facilities and the Future of Print Collections in North America." Dublin, OH: OCLC Programs and Research, October 2007. www.oclc.org/programs/publications/reports/2007-01.pdf.

Roosendaall, Hans E., and Peter A. Th. M. Geurts. "Forces and Functions in Scientific Communication: An Analysis of Their Interplay." Paper used for The First International Workshop: Cooperative Research Information Systems in Physics, Oldenburg, Germany, August 31–September 4, 1997. http://www.physik.uni-oldenburg.de/conferences/crisp97/roosendaal.html.

Schmid, Oona. "Faster and Cheaper: Can a Digital-Centric Workflow Transform the Book Review?" *Ithaka S+R.: Scholarly Communication* (blog), August 27, 2014. http://www.sr.ithaka.org/blog/faster-and-cheaper-can-a-digital-centric-workflow-transform-the-book-review/.

Schmidt, Jason. "Academic Journals: The Most Profitable Obsolete Technology in History." *Huffington Post:HuffPost Education: The Blog*, December 23, 2014, http://www.huffingtonpost.com/jason-schmitt/academic-journals-the-mos_1_b_6368204.html.

Schnapp, Jeffrey T., and Matthew Battles. *The Library Beyond the Book*. Cambridge, MA: Harvard University Press, 2014.

Schonfeld, Roger C. *Does Discovery Still Happen in the Library? Roles and Strategies for a Shifting Reality*. New York: Ithaka S+R, 2014. http://www.sr.ithaka.org/sites/default/files/files/SR_Briefing_Discovery_20140924_0.pdf.

———. *Issue Brief: Taking Stock: Sharing Responsibility for Print Preservation*. New York: Ithaka S+R, July 8, 2015. http://sr.ithaka.org/sites/default/files/files/SR_IssueBrief_Taking_Stock_070815.pdf.

Schuessler, Jennifer. "A Tribute to the Printer Aldus Manutius, and the Roots of the Paperback." *New York Times*, February 26, 2015. http://www.nytimes.com/2015/02/27/arts/design/a-grolier-club-tribute-to-the-printer-aldus-manutius.html?_r=0.

Shapiro, Carl, and Hal R. Varian. *Information Rules: A Strategic Guide to the Network Economy*. Boston: Harvard Business School Press, 1998.

Shirky, Clay. "The End of Higher Education's Golden Age." *Clay Shirky* (blog), January 29, 2014. http://www.shirky.com/weblog/2014/01/there-isnt-enough-money-to-keep-educating-adults-the-way-were-doing-it/.

———. *Here Comes Everybody: The Power of Organizing without Organizations*. New York: Penguin Press, 2008.

———. "How Social Media Can Make History." Filmed June 2009. TED video, 15:48. http://www.ted.com/talks/clay_shirky_how_cellphones_twitter_facebook_can_make_history.html.

———. "Newspapers and Thinking the Unthinkable." *Clay Shirky* (blog), March 13, 2009. http://www.shirky.com/weblog/2009/03/newspapers-and-thinking-the-unthinkable/.

Smith, Aaron, and Janna Anderson. "AI, Robotics, and the Future of Jobs." Pew Research Center: Internet, Science, and Tech, August 6, 2014. http://www.pewinternet.org/2014/08/06/future-of-jobs/.

Suber, Peter. *Open Access*. Cambridge, MA: MIT Press, 2012. http://cyber.law.harvard.edu/hoap/Open_Access_%28the_book%29#About_the_book.

Tenopir, Carol, Suzie Allard, Kimberly Douglass, Arsev Umur Aydinoglu, Lei Wu, Eleanor Read, Maribeth Manoff, and Mike Frame. "Data Sharing by Scientists: Practices and Perceptions." *PLOS ONE* 6, no. 6 (June 29, 2011): e21101. doi:10.1371/journal.pone.0021101. http://www.plosone.org/article/info%3Adoi%2F10.1371%2Fjournal.pone.0021101.

Tenopir, Carol, Donald W. King, Lisa Christian, and Rachel Volentine. "Scholarly Article Seeking, Reading, and Use: A Continuing Evolution from Print to Electronic in the Sciences and Social Sciences." *Learned Publishing* 28, no. 2 (April 2015): 93–105.

Tillery, Kodi. "2012 Study of Subscription Prices for Scholarly Society Journals: Society Journal Pricing Trends and Industry Overview." *Allen Press*, 2012. http://allenpress.com/system/files/pdfs/library/2012_AP_JPS.pdf.

Tran, Millie. "Revisiting Disruption: 8 Good Questions with Clayton Christensen," *American Press Institute* (blog), January 23, 2014, http://www.americanpressinstitute.org/publications/good-questions/revisiting-disruption-8-good-questions-clayton-christensen/.

University Leadership Council. *Redefining the Academic Library: Managing the Migration to Digital Information Services*. Washington, DC: Advisory Board Company, 2011. http://www.uab.edu/2015compliancecertification/IMAGES/SOURCE82E1.PDF?id=5a6caa2c-4a1e-e411-99c8-86539cf2d30e#page=8.

Van de Sompel, Herbert, Sandy Payette, John Erickson, Carl Lagoze, and Simeon Warner. "Rethinking Scholarly Communication." *D-Lib Magazine* 10, no. 9 (September 2004). http://www.dlib.org/dlib/september04/vandesompel/09vandesompel.html#Roosendaal.

Verstak, Alex, Anurag Acharya, Helder Suzuki, Sean Henderson, Mikhail Iakhiaev, Cliff Chiung Yu Lin, and Namit Shetty. "On the Shoulders of Giants: The Growing Impact of Older Articles." *The Scholarly Kitchen* (blog), November 4, 2014. http://arxiv.org/pdf/1411.0275v1.pdf.

Wilder, Stanley. "The Academic Library Workforce in Transition: New Results from the 2010 ARL Demographic Data." Presentation at the Association of Research Libraries-ACRL Human Resources Symposium, Washington, DC, November 16, 2012. http://www.arl.org/focus-areas/copyright-ip/fair-use/code-of-best-practices/1071-the-academic-library-workforce-in-transition-new-results-from-the-2010-arl-demographic-data#.VAhwNkvj_74.

———. *The Age Demographics of Academic Librarians: A Profession Apart: A Report Based on Data from the ARL Annual Salary Survey*. Washington, DC: Association of Research Libraries, 1995.

———. *Demographic Change in Academic Librarianship*. Washington, DC: Association of Research Libraries, 2003.

Wittenberg, Kate. "The Gutenberg-e Project: Opportunities in Publishing Born-Digital Monographs." *Learned Publishing* 22, no. 1 (January 2009): 36–41. doi:10.1087/095315108X378767.

Yakoboski, Paul J. "Understanding the Faculty Retirement (Non)Decision: Results from the Faculty Career and Retirement Survey." TIAA-CREF Institute: Trends and Issues, June 2015. https://www.tiaa-crefinstitute.org/public/pdf/understanding-the-faculty-retirement-nondecision.pdf.

Index

Adema, Janneke, 26
Advisory Board Company, xii
Amazon, 24
Askey, Dale, 87
ASRS. *See* boolBots
Association of American Publishers, 58
American Chemical Society, 49
Anderson, Rick, xi
arXiv, 39
article-on-demand purchasing, 53
Atlas, James, 24
Association of College & Research
    Libraries (ACRL), xv, 90
Association of Research Libraries, 51, 54,
    55, 64, 114
Atkinson, Ross, 31
audiobooks, 24
Automated Storage and Retrieval Systems.
    See bookBots

Baby Boom Generation, 64, 65, 66, 67
Baker, Nicholson, xix
Baron, Naomi S., 22
Battles, Matthew, 141
Bell, Steven, 145
Bellardo Hahn, Trudi, 94
Benkler, Yochai, 78, 79
Bennett, Scott, 95
Berra, Yogi, vii
"Big Deal," 8, 53, 54, 58
Blumenstyk, Goldie, xii

bookBots, 99, 100, 110
Bostrom, Nick, vii
Bradford, Samuel C., 47
Bradford's Law of Scattering, 47, 49, 53
Bricklin, Dan, 78
BRS, xix
Brynjolfsson, Erik, xi
Buckland, Michael, xi, xv, xvii, xviii, xx,
    85, 89, 113
Bugela, Michael, 38

Carlson, Scott, 93
Carr, Nicholas, 142
Chavan, Vishwas, 36
Chesapeake Digital Preservation Group, 38
Christensen, Clayton, viii, xvii, 3, 9, 27,
    77, 85
Christian, Lisa, 49
Clemons, G. Scott, 23
clerical staff, 62, 70, 72
CLOCKSS, 118, 119, 120
Coase, Ronald, 85, 115
Coates, Heather, 36
codex, 21
collection analysis, 106
Consumer Price Index, 54, 57
content drift, 39, 40
copyright, 77
Courant, Paul N., 57, 103
Cowen, Tyler, 141, 143, 144
Creative Commons, 78

Crossick, Geoffrey, 26

Darnton, Robert, 21, 22, 45, 51, 56
Davidson, Cathy, 27
data sets, 34, 37
data sharing, 36
Deep Blue, 141
Dempsey, Lorcan, xv, 86, 109, 115, 145, 146
DIALOG, xix
digital books, 23, 24
digital documents, 13; easily changed, 16, 33; incorporates different media, 16; marginal cost, 17; new marketplace for, 17; preservation, 16
digital preservation, 117, 118, 119, 121
Digital Preservation Network (DPN), 119, 120
Dimitrova, Daniela V., 38
disruptive innovations, 5, 6, 7, 9, 11
Doctorow, Cory, 21, 75
Dougherty, Richard, 51
Dryad, 35
Durant, David M., 110

EBSCO, 58
Edington, Mark D. W., 80
80/20 rule, 53, 105
Elsevier, 36, 39, 49, 50, 51, 53

Facebook, 37
first copy cost, 17, 27
first sale doctrine, 17
Fister, Barbara, 95, 98, 145, 146
Frazier, Kenneth, 53
Freeman, Geoffrey T., 93, 94, 100
Frischmann, Brett M., 89

Gale, 58
Gantz, Paula, 58
Garfield, Eugene, 49
Geffert, Bryn, 125
Generation X, 64, 65, 66, 67
Get It Now, 127
Geurts, Peter A. Th. M., 37
GI Generation, 64, 65
Gingras, Yves, 14, 15
Gladwell, Malcolm, xii
goods, rival or nonrival, 76, 77

Google, xix, 14, 15, 87, 88
Google Scholar, 129
Gorman, Michael, 18
Greenfield, Jeremy, 25
Guédon, Jean-Claude, 47
Gutenberg-e Project, 26, 27

HathiTrust, 106
Haustein, Stefanie, 49, 50
Hawkins, Donald T., 121
Herrera, Gail, 128
Hilton, James, 115
Hoe-Lian Goh, Dion, 38
Hopkins, Frances L., 146
Horava, Tony, 22, 23, 110
Huffington Post, 50
Hunt Library. *See* James B. Hunt Jr. Library

impact factor, 49
information literacy, 147, 148, 156
InfoTrac, xix, xx
interlibrary borrowing, 55, 57
internet, 13; half-life of references, 38; persistence of references, 38
Ithaka, 118
Ithaka S+R, xiv, 18, 87

Jackson, Heather Lea, 94
James B. Hunt Jr. Library, 99, 100
Jemielniak, Dariusz, 18, 19
John Wiley & Sons, 50
Johnson, Steven, xiv, xvi
Jones, Elisabeth A., 57
journal citation study, 14
journal prices, 49, 54, 58
journal subscriptions, personal, 49
JSTOR, 58, 129

Kahle, Brewster, 121
Kenney, Anne R., 150
Kin Ng, Peng, 38
King, Donald W., 49
Klein, Martin, 39
Kirchhoff, Amy, 117, 120
Kurzweil, Ray, vii

Larivière, Vincent, 14, 15, 49, 50, 53

Lavoie, Brian, 31, 32, 34, 41, 104, 105, 107, 108
Law of Scattering. *See* Bradford's Law of Scattering
Lepore, Jill, 47, 48
LexisNexis, xix, xx
librarians, 31, 70; feral, 70, 71; aging of, 64; faculty status, 63, 71; diversity, 68, 69, 70
library budgets, 54, 55, 56
Library Company of Philadelphia, 89
library workforce, 61, 62, 63
library, role of, 32
Library of Congress, xix, 121
Lippincott, Joan K., 145
link rot, 38, 39, 40
Lockheed, xix
LOCKSS, 118
Lozano, George A., 14, 15
Lumina Foundation, xiv, 147
Lynch, Clifford A., 53

Maker Spaces, 100
Malenfant, Kara J., 149, 150
Malpas, Constance, 31, 32, 41, 106, 107
Manutius, Aldus, 23
MARC, xix
Marcum, Deanna, xiv, 61, 67
Mary Idema Pew Library, 99, 100
Master of Library Science degree. *See* MLS
Mathews, Brian, vii, 94
McAfee, Andrew, xi
McRobbie, Michael A., 116
MEDLARS, xix
Merisotis, Jamie P., 147
MethodsX, 36
Millennium Generation, 64, 65, 66, 67
MLS, 64, 67, 68, 70, 71, 72, 146, 154
Mongeon, Philippe, 49, 50
Morrissey, Sheila, 117, 120
Mullins, James L., 67
MUSE, 58

National Center for Education Statistics (NCES), 56, 61, 104
national collective print collection, 106, 107, 110, 155
National Institutes of Health, 34

National Library of Medicine, xix
National Science Foundation, 33, 34
Nature Group, 35
Neal, James G., xiii, 70
New Media Consortium, xiii
Nielson, Brian, 143
Nielson, Matthew "Buzzy," 103
non-rival goods. *See* good, rival or non-rival
Nutter, Susan, 99

Oakleaf, Meagan, 91
OCLC, xii, xv, xix, 88
Oldenburg, Ray, 96, 97, 98
open access, 18, 77, 126, 127, 134, 138, 155; gold, 134, 135; publications, 49
opportunity cost, 103

paper to the digital transition, xi
patron-driven acquisitions, 127, 131, 132
Payne, Lizanne, 108
Penev, Lyubomir, 36
Personal Digital Archiving, 121
Pittsburgh study, 105
Portico, 118, 119, 120
preservation, 16
Princeton University, 114
print to digital transition, 57, 58, 63
printing, xvi
ProQuest, 58
public good, 89
publishing industry, 45, 46, 47, 49, 50; profit margins, 50
PubMed Central, 39

reading studies, 22
ReCAP, 107
Reed-Elsevier. *See* Elsevier
remote storage facilities, 93
Research Library Group (RLG), xix
rival goods. *See* goods, rival or
Roosendaall, Hans E., 37
Rushdie, Salman, 13

Sage, 49
scholarly communication, 24, 37, 38
Scholarly Communication cycle, 45, 46; money flow in, 46, 47, 48, 50, 52

scholarly journals, 14; move from paper to
    digital, 14, 15
scholarly monograph, 28
scholarly record, 32, 33, 34, 39, 41, 42;
    custodial responsibility, 33
Science Citation Index (SCI), 49
Science Direct, 127
Scientific Data, 35
Schnapp, Jeffrey T., 141
scholarly societies, 50
Schonfeld, Roger C., 87, 104, 105, 108,
    109, 113
Schwartz, Meredith, 99
self-publishing, 25
Shapiro, Carl, 76
Shipengrover, JD, 107
Shirky, Clay, xi, xiii, xvii, 75, 79, 126
Silent Generation, 64, 65
SlideShare, 37
social production, 78, 79, 80
Springer, 49
Sputnik, 47
student workers, 62, 70
sustaining innovations, 4

Taylor & Francis, 49, 50

Tenopir, Carol, 36, 49
third place, 96, 97, 98
Treloar, Andrew, 39
Tillery, Kodi, 54
TULIP (The University Licensing Project),
    51, 53
Twitter, 37

university presses, 57

Value of Academic Libraries, 90
Van der Sompel, Herbert, 37, 38, 39
Varian, Hal, 76
Volentine, Rachel, 49

Wales, Jimmy, 19
Watson, 141
Wikipedia, xix, 17, 18, 19, 129
Wilder, Stanley J., 64, 68
Wiley-Blackwell, 49
Wittenberg, Kate, 117, 120
WorldCat, 104, 105, 107

YouTube, 37

zero marginal cost, 76